PENGUIN BOO

Champagne Football

'Part thriller, part warning from history, part social diary, *Champagne Football* is a forensic and often tragicomic investigation into the biggest story in Irish sport. It's a fantastic read' Malachy Clerkin, *Irish Times*, Sports Books of the Year 2020

'A jaw-dropping tale of power and ego going unchecked' *The Times*, Best Sports Books of the Year 2020

'A cracking read . . . [An] incredible amount of jaw-dropping detail' Matt Cooper

'A superb piece of investigative journalism, in which a tale of tawdry venality is told with wit, verve and just the right amount of disbelief' Fintan O'Toole, *Irish Times*, Best Books of 2020

'An astonishing story of how a man rose by understanding how Ireland operates and, more precisely, how Ireland can be operated . . . If you wanted to change Ireland, you would need to read this book' **Dion Fanning, *Currency***

'At last, the truth of his ruinous reign has been rigorously and painstakingly exposed' *Irish Daily Mail*

'Side-splittingly hilarious . . . Our intrepid duo left no stone unturned in revealing mismanagement and incompetence on a truly epic scale' *Guardian*

'Utterly COMPELLING, this book. I can't decide if Delaney is a Machiavellian mastermind or a lucky chancer' Marian Keyes

'Revelation after revelation of Delaney's incredible reign in an often hilarious, frequently dispiriting and consistently astonishing account' *Business Post*

'I read it in one sitting, it's a superb book' Eamon Dunphy, *The Stand*

ABOUT THE AUTHORS

Originally from Donegal, Mark Tighe is the legal correspondent of the *Sunday Times* in Ireland. As well as covering legal affairs, he specializes in investigative reporting. He was Irish Newspaper News Reporter of the Year in 2018 and 2019. In 2019 he also won the Journalist of the Year Award for his reporting on the FAI.

Born and raised in Dublin, Paul Rowan is the Irish football correspondent for the *Sunday Times*, and the author of *The Team That Jack Built* and *Making Ryan's Daughter*. In 2019 he was joint winner of the NewsBrands Campaigning Journalism and Investigative Journalism Awards (alongside Mark Tighe and Colin Coyle) for his work on the FAI.

Champagne Football

John Delaney and the betrayal of
Irish football: the inside story

MARK TIGHE AND
PAUL ROWAN

PENGUIN BOOKS

PENGUIN BOOKS

UK | USA | Canada | Ireland | Australia
India | New Zealand | South Africa

Penguin Books is part of the Penguin Random House group of companies
whose addresses can be found at global.penguinrandomhouse.com.

First published by Sandycove 2020
Published in Penguin Books 2021

002

Typeset in Bembo Book MT Std by Jouve (UK), Milton Keynes
Printed and bound in Great Britain by Clays Ltd, Elcograf S.p.A.

The authorized representative in the EEA is Penguin Random House Ireland,
Morrison Chambers, 32 Nassau Street, Dublin D02 YH68

A CIP catalogue record for this book is available from the British Library

ISBN: 978–0–241–99006–3

For Cara, Finn, Lyla and Rory Tighe
and
To the players, staff and supporters of Archibald Albion FC

Contents

Prologue: The Name is Delaney, John Delaney

21 October 2017

Eamon Dunphy and his wife, the film and television producer Jane Gogan, sat in the back of a chauffeur-driven car. They were being taken to rural Kilkenny. It was a Saturday night. They wondered why they were bothering to make the trip.

Dunphy had accepted an invitation to attend John Delaney's fiftieth birthday party in the Mount Juliet golf club after being persuaded by one of his best friends, John Giles. The two had worked side by side for over twenty years as the wise old men of RTÉ television's football coverage, having played for Ireland together as young men: Giles one of the finest players of his generation, Dunphy a journeyman.

Over the years Giles had grown close to Delaney, the Chief Executive of the Football Association of Ireland. The two would travel around the country dispensing cheques to amateur football clubs from a fundraising foundation bearing Giles's name that was run through the FAI.

Although Dunphy had been publicly supportive of Delaney as the FAI's boss, he did not regard Delaney as a friend. He was travelling down to Kilkenny out of a sense of duty to Giles, but also with half a mind on the ten Manchester United season tickets that Delaney had access to and occasionally allowed Dunphy to use. The pundit would always pay Delaney for the tickets, which were for a Man United-mad friend. The payments went through Delaney's personal assistant in the FAI.

Dunphy recalls being taken for dinner by Delaney at a time when Giovanni Trapattoni was the Ireland manager and Dunphy was 'on his case'. The FAI CEO had 'tried it on with me', Dunphy says, asking the pundit to lay off on his criticism of the Irish team. Dunphy recalls that while he joked with Delaney that he could buy a short amnesty from criticism with each supply of Man United tickets, he then made it clear that he would not hold back in criticizing the team when he felt it was justified.

The party at Mount Juliet was a lavish affair, according to a number of people who attended. Bursts of flames from a pyrotechnic display greeted guests clutching gifts as they entered the old manor house, smiling as a professional photographer captured their arrivals.

Delaney's fiancée, Emma English, a former model turned event planner, had organized a James Bond-themed party. English, a striking blonde, had been a firm favourite of newspaper photographers and their editors since she began publicly accompanying Delaney to matches and other work events in 2014.

After their first joint TV appearance, on *The Saturday Night Show*, presented by Brendan O'Connor, in 2014, English and Delaney had dined with fellow guest Jane Seymour, the actress who played Bond-girl Solitaire in *Live and Let Die*. That encounter, and Delaney's love for James Bond movies, had inspired the party theme. (A previous birthday party English had thrown for Delaney had had a teddy-bear theme, because, as she had told the nation on that TV chat show, Delaney was her 'teddy bear'.)

The centrepiece of the drinks reception was a huge ice sculpture of a Walther PPK pistol, Bond's weapon of choice. The ice sculpture was surrounded by the spy's favourite martini cocktail glasses. Nods to Delaney's football career came in the shape of several life-sized cardboard cut-outs of a footballer with Delaney's head superimposed, wearing a white Ireland jersey emblazoned with the number 50 and a captain's armband with the initials 'JD'.

A huge birthday cake had been styled to look like the Aviva Stadium, which the FAI had part-owned since it was built on the site of the old Lansdowne Road ground in 2010. Delaney had repeatedly claimed the stadium was his finest achievement, despite poor ticket sales and persistent media questions about whether the stadium debt was too great for the association to repay.

The baked version of the stadium came with working floodlights and a miniature crowd holding 'Happy birthday, John' banners. There was stadium advertising from Three, the Ireland team's main sponsor. Among the guests on the night was Davy Keogh, the well-known Ireland supporter. A 'Davy Keogh says hello' flag – a fixture at nearly every Irish away game – was visible on the cake.

When the guests moved from the old manor house towards a large marquee, they were greeted by waiters in skeleton costumes with face masks and top hats like the villains from *Live and Let Die*. The Bond baddies served drinks to each table. Around the large marquee, banners depicted a silhouette of a tuxedoed Bond holding his pistol. A sign over the posters read 'Happy birthday John Delaney'. The iconic Bond 007 logo, incorporating a pistol, had been modified to 'John Delaney 0050'.

For the many football people in the crowd, the extravagance of the party – which was being run by Franc, a well-known wedding planner who had his own TV show – made them laugh in bemusement. Some assumed Delaney, with his €360,000 salary, must be picking up the tab. Others weren't sure. Many of the guests had received their invites directly from an FAI official using an FAI email address, and FAI events staff had worked on organizing the party.

The invitees sat around nineteen tables that had tall white centrepieces filled with large ostrich feathers. 'If my wedding is half as big as this I'd be lucky,' mused one FAI staff member working on the event.

Amongst the guests was Aleksander Čeferin, the President of UEFA, the European governing body for football. Delaney had just been elected to the UEFA Executive Committee in April. Having led the FAI since 2004, Delaney was now one of the most powerful men in European football. A number of other senior UEFA officials, including Noel Mooney, a former FAI executive, were also in attendance. The FAI had considered booking helicopters to fly the dignitaries to Kilkenny, but were deterred by high winds in the aftermath of Hurricane Ophelia.

The other guests included Martin O'Neill, the Ireland manager, and Alan Kelly, a former government minister and TD from Tipperary, where Delaney has strong family connections. Sports journalists John Duggan and Paul Collins, who worked for Newstalk and Today FM, were also present. Their radio stations were owned by Denis

O'Brien, the billionaire who had pumped some €12 million into the FAI over the past decade to help it pay the salaries of Trapattoni, O'Neill and O'Neill's assistant, Roy Keane.

Delaney, wearing an open-necked shirt and suit, and English, in a blue evening gown, entered the marquee together as the invited guests stood and rhythmically clapped to the sound of 'Put 'Em Under Pressure', the Ireland team's anthem from the 1990 World Cup. Delaney shook hands and backslapped guests to the chorus of 'Olé, Olé, Olé, Olé' on his way to his seat at the top of the room.

Brendan O'Carroll, the creator and star of *Mrs Brown's Boys*, delivered a mild roast of Delaney from the stage. O'Carroll, a party guest along with his wife, Jennifer Gibney, was performing for free. The MC on the night was Aidan Power, a TV presenter who specializes in sports. The paid musical act was the High Kings, a popular Irish folk band.

Dunphy remembers being bowled over by the overt affection that Delaney and English showed for each other.

'I thought she was an incredible-looking woman,' he says of English, a separated mother of four. 'You know, you see people in photographs, but seeing her up close, she was beautiful. She was tugging out of him like, "He's my man." I just couldn't get my head around it. Like, he isn't God's gift, at all. There is nothing suave about John Delaney. He's fucking gauche and awful.'

There are times you just have to suspend your disbelief, Dunphy says, and this was 'one coupling that I had to just suspend my disbelief about'.

While Delaney loves to sing but has little talent, English has a fine voice. She took to the stage with the High Kings for an acoustic version of 'Mercy', a song by the Welsh singer Duffy about a woman driven mad over her lust for a man. Delaney danced and clapped in front of the stage. He would later sing 'Daisy a Day', a 1970s song by Jud Strunk about a man's undying love for a woman.

A lengthy video, professionally shot and edited, included tributes to Delaney from people who could not travel for the occasion. The highlight was a message from Sir Alex Ferguson, the former Manchester United manager. When Delaney took to the stage, which was dressed to look as though it was surrounded by ice, he read out a letter to himself, this one from Michael D. Higgins, the President of Ireland and a keen football fan. The letter noted that landmark birthdays 'are special moments in life' and the President passed on his 'best wishes'.

Delaney then made sure to thank 'my own staff' for their brilliant work at the party. To nervous laughter from the crowd, he joked that it wasn't a part of the normal jobs of 'his' FAI staff to organize birthday parties.

'They won't be doing it again for a while, trust me,' he laughed.

Amongst those looking on were senior directors of the FAI board and some of their wives. Tony Fitzgerald, the FAI President, and Michael Cody, its Honorary Secretary, both wearing green ties, took to the stage to make a presentation of a silver plate to their Chief Executive.

Delaney then paid a tearful tribute to Emma English. 'He started slobbering about their love,' says Dunphy. 'It was cringe city.'

Dunphy hadn't seen much of his good friend Giles, who spent much of the night up at a bar with Dr Alan Byrne, the Irish team doctor, having a sing-song. To make things worse, Dunphy had been seated at the same table as Michael Ring, the Fine Gael government minister for rural development, whom he strongly disliked. As Delaney dissolved into tears on stage while professing his love for his fiancée, Dunphy was getting kicks under the table from Jane Gogan. The couple decided to make their excuses and leave early.

They missed the High Kings belting out their final song, the Clancy Brothers' 'The Parting Glass'. As the guests drank their teas and coffees, Delaney and English slowly danced alone between tables, singing the lyrics to each other and kissing.

Despite the absence of Dunphy, a renowned party animal in his day, the celebrations went on until 5 a.m. back in the Mount Juliet manor house. A DJ accompanied by a saxophonist and a drummer kept the dance floor busy. The revelry was bolstered by the late arrival of several players from the Kilkenny senior hurling team.

On the following Monday morning Mario Rosenstock, Today FM's resident mimic, aired a well-informed skit about the party. The

FAI CEO was a big fan of Rosenstock's 'Gift Grub' segments on the *Ian Dempsey Breakfast Show* and loved when he was the subject, even if his leadership of the FAI inevitably came in for mockery.

On this particular morning, Dempsey interviewed Rosenstock's 'John Delaney', who explained that the birthday party was still going on despite a mistake made by the 'FAI catering committee' which meant the celebrations did not start in a brewery as initially planned. The FAI's inability to organize a piss-up in a brewery had been a running gag of Rosenstock's for years.

This skit also included 'Roy Keane' incredulously reading out a scripted tribute to Delaney that praised his 'generosity, razor-sharp intelligence, general competence and utter professionalism'.

At the end of the sketch, a laughing 'Delaney' was presented with the bill for the party. The clacking sound of the till printing out the final receipt seemed never-ending.

Rosenstock's gag about the bill that Delaney had racked up was more on the mark than anyone knew at the time. Mazars accountants would later establish that the FAI ended up spending over €80,000 on the party. This included €26,293 to Mount Juliet, €25,000 to Franc, €7,595 for the chauffeurs and €3,609 for the helicopters that never got off the ground.

When Delaney made a payment to the FAI to cover the cost of his own birthday party, it was for a nice round number: €50,000. The €30,000-plus difference was carried by the organization that ran the sport of football in Ireland – everything from the senior national team down to the amateur clubs, run by volunteers, that provide the game's lifeblood.

The association was already in a catastrophic financial position. Delaney had run it into the ground. But it would be a year and a half before he was exposed.

1. Sins of the Father

Joe Delaney, Honorary Treasurer of the Football Association of Ireland, was rarely without a twinkle in his eye. But on the evening of 8 March 1996, beset by damaging newspaper reports that had led him to offer his resignation, he arrived at the Westbury hotel, off Grafton Street, looking dishevelled, his eyes puffy and red. Sessions of the FAI Council were, for Joe Delaney, normally cheerful gatherings. This one was more like a court martial.

Joe Delaney did not arrive at the Westbury alone. By his side was his eldest son, John, a gangly figure with a long face and cowlick haircut. John Delaney was twenty-eight years old.

*

Two years earlier, in happier times, Joe Delaney had travelled to the 1994 World Cup in the United States. Who could forget the buzz and bonhomie around the lobby of the Orlando North Hilton in Florida? Memorable also was Joe Delaney's ticketing operation on the seventh floor of the hotel, in a room covered with match tickets and cash in multiple currencies worth tens of thousands of dollars.

Ireland had their training camp in Orlando, and played two games there – both of which they lost badly. Still, there was no stopping the legendary *craic*. Bishop Eamonn Casey, exiled to Ecuador after a sex scandal, slipped in and out of the hotel quietly to get his match tickets. The Dublin comedian Brendan O'Carroll was happy to entertain the fans. U2's Larry Mullen was amongst the throng as O'Carroll led the revellers in a bastardized version of the Smokie hit 'Alice', which included the chant 'Alice? Who the fuck is Alice?'

Eamon Dunphy arrived in Joe Delaney's room on a mission to help an acquaintance get four tickets.

'Joe was sitting on the bed,' Dunphy recalls. 'On the floor was the biggest suitcase I'd ever seen anywhere. I looked in the suitcase and all that was in it was dollar bills and tickets.'

Dunphy expected Joe to tell him to 'fuck off' when he asked for four, but was told it was 'no problem'.

Delaney dipped into his suitcase. 'They're four good ones.'

'How much do I owe you?'

'Nothing, tell him I gave them to you.'

'That,' says Dunphy, 'was the Irish way.'

It wasn't the right way for Brendan Menton, son of the former FAI President Brendan Menton Snr and himself a former FAI Council member. Menton was in Florida on a sporting holiday, away from his job as chief economist at AIB and amongst some old friends, when he hopped in the hotel elevator and arrived at Joe Delaney's nerve centre to buy tickets for the last-sixteen game against Holland. Menton looked at the bundles of tickets and cash strewn around the floor. He asked Joe if he would like him to assist in acquiring a credit-card machine to make payment more efficient.

Delaney politely declined the offer and told him it was 'cash only'.

Menton shrugged, paid for his tickets and left. He didn't think much more of it.

Joe Delaney moved his ticket operation to the environs of Mulvaney's pub in Church Street, where the Orlando cops intervened to restore order as Ireland fans jostled for tickets. Delaney was asked by the *Orlando Sentinel* how many tickets the FAI would have for sale on match day. He replied: 'How long is a piece of string?'

*

Qualification for the 1996 European Championship was beyond an ageing Ireland team, and it was clear that the magic of Euro '88, Italia '90 and the win over Italy in the World Cup opener in '94 had gone. The Jack Charlton era had run its course. Young blood was clearly needed on the pitch and in the dugout.

The FAI was coming under scrutiny for the way it handled its affairs. While Ireland had qualified for three major tournaments in ten years and beaten some of the biggest nations in world football, the association had made a loss from the two World Cups. Its financial records were kept in an old-fashioned ledger, and when the book-keeper, Maureen Lynch, left in the summer of 1994, the system broke down altogether. A new computer system for the association was lying in the basement, yet to be installed.

Peter Buckley, an accountant who arrived in the finance department in January 1995 after being recommended to Joe Delaney, found the place in a mess. One of his first jobs was to go through cheque stubs and work out who had been paid for what. That was particularly difficult when there was nothing written on the cheque stubs.

In February 1996, Sean Connolly, who held the title of FAI General Secretary, resigned after five years in the job. The association released a terse statement with no explanation given. Connolly told RTÉ's *Prime Time* that he had taken a 'loan' of £6,000 from the FAI, and that he had repaid it, but that the loan had been used as a pretext to get rid of him.

Two days after the announcement of Connolly's departure, Veronica Guerin reported in the *Sunday Independent* that, at the 1994 World Cup, senior FAI personnel had given tickets to a London-based ticket tout to sell on, that the tout had ripped the FAI off on a vast scale and that an unidentified FAI official had later personally made up the FAI's shortfall. The tout reportedly operated under the name of George the Greek, but his real identity remained a mystery.

One of those who read the story was Brendan Menton, who couldn't resist a wry chuckle as he recalled his encounter with Joe Delaney in Orlando. The day after Guerin's story broke, Menton was waiting at Dublin airport to pick up a friend when he was approached by the burly figure of Des Casey, a wily former trade union official who was then Honorary Secretary of the FAI. Casey was probably the biggest of the FAI beasts, as he also sat on the Executive Committee of UEFA, the first Irishman to rise to such an elevated position. Casey, who was now acting General Secretary in the wake of Connolly's departure, had his own daytime job as an arbitrator. He needed to get somebody in to run things and reckoned that Menton was the man.

Having just left AIB, Menton decided to take the job on an interim basis, even though he knew one previous incumbent who said the job was like 'being crawled over by snakes'.

In the days before Menton started in his new job, the FAI held a press conference to address Connolly's resignation and the *Sunday Independent* story about the ticket fiasco. The association's President, Louis Kilcoyne, acknowledged that the FAI had dealt with a tout, but said it did so for the sole purpose of gaining extra tickets for Ireland fans. Casey said he had received assurances from Joe Delaney that all funds had been accounted for. He referred to minutes of a meeting of the FAI Finance Committee in November 1994, and a statement attributed to the association's chief accountant, Michael Morris: 'No monies were owed by any officers of the association. No serious amounts of money were outstanding that caused them any concern or worry.' Delaney, sitting at the top table, said nothing.

The FAI's version of events did not hold up for very long. Two days later, Joe Delaney issued a statement admitting that he had made a personal payment to the FAI of Stg£110,000 to cover the losses arising from the FAI's dealings with a ticket tout. Casey had been made to look like an idiot, at best; at worst, it looked like he was involved in some kind of cover-up.

In the next edition of the *Sunday Independent*, Veronica Guerin reported that Delaney had made two electronic payments to the association, in November and December 1994, to values of Stg£140,000 and Stg£70,000, for a total value of Stg£210,000 – nearly twice the £110,000 Delaney had admitted to covering.

Menton started work at the FAI the following day, Monday, 26 February 1996. As he wrote in his book *Beyond the Green Door: Six Years Inside the FAI*, his wife Linda drove him from their home in Meath, and he arrived at the FAI's headquarters in Merrion Square at 9 a.m. Menton rang on the brass doorbell for ten minutes, but there was no response. Finally, he gained admittance – he didn't know about the back entrance, or the fact that work didn't start till 9.30 a.m. – and the first person he met was Joe Delaney. The Honorary Treasurer showed Menton into his new office. Before Menton had a chance to adjust his chair, Delaney offered a convoluted explanation about the ticketing payments. 'Was Joe Delaney telling me that the money from the FAI's World Cup tickets went through a personal account rather than the FAI's account?' Menton wrote. 'He seemed to be.'

Meanwhile, the FAI's accountant, Michael Morris, left the association. On 1 March, Morris issued a statement: 'I object to the timing of my resignation, a date fixed by Joe Delaney, and the circumstances with which it coincided.' Morris also said that he had queried the World Cup ticket situation in 1994, but had been told by Delaney that there was no reason for concern. Morris wasn't prepared to be the fall guy. 'During my time in office I was also periodically instructed by officers to edit the lists of ticket debtors, prior to advising the Finance Committee/Senior Council, and this editing would have included officers' names. I was never happy about this,' Morris said.

As part of an Irish footballing dynasty, Menton had heard any number of FAI horror stories before, but even he was shocked by what was emerging. His first act as General Secretary was to commission Bastow Charleton to produce a report on the FAI's World Cup ticketing. The 8 March meeting of the FAI Council in the Westbury would demand answers, and heads, if the explanations weren't satisfactory.

Further damaging revelations continued to spill out. It emerged in the press that Louis Kilcoyne had been arrested during Italia '90 for trying to sell a batch of tickets outside the last-sixteen game between Brazil and Argentina in Turin. The FAI had purchased the tickets because there was a chance that Ireland could have played in Turin that day had the group stage of the tournament worked out differently. Opponents had been waiting in the long grass for Kilcoyne ever since his family had sold Shamrock Rovers' Milltown ground to property developers, and now they were starting to emerge.

The FAI's somewhat Byzantine management structure and Ruritanian job titles had their roots in amateur football's culture of volunteerism. The General Secretary, sometimes also known as the Chief Executive, was not really a chief executive, but more the head of day-to-day administration at Merrion Square. The real power was held by the so-called 'five officers', a kind of executive board. The officers were unpaid volunteers (though they enjoyed a generous expenses regime and free travel). At the time the ticketing scandal broke, three of the five – Delaney, the Honorary Treasurer; Casey, the Honorary Secretary; and League of Ireland chairman Michael

Hyland – were the most powerful figures in the association. Their positions could be held indefinitely, whereas the President and Vice-President had shorter terms and thus tended to accumulate less influence. The fifty-two-member Council was effectively Irish football's parliament, reflecting the traditional view of the association as an amateur body run by committed volunteers. The Council elected the officers, who headed up an Executive Committee that consisted of between twenty and twenty-three members, also chosen from the voluntary ranks.

'The FAI was like Afghanistan; it was run by feudal lords, with no central authority,' says Bill Attley, an FAI Council member at the time. 'If I was here for the rest of the day to tell you how the Council carried on you wouldn't believe it. Approving the minutes used to take nearly an hour. Then there would be a row about what was said – "I spoke about this and it is not in the minutes." "I didn't get tickets for the international." "There were people in the VIP lounge who shouldn't have been there." That type of stuff.'

Joe Delaney had been chairman of Waterford FC in the 1970s, and this led to his becoming a member of the FAI Council. At some point in the 1980s, the role of Assistant Honorary Treasurer had been created for him, so that he could handle match-ticket distribution – a perennially contentious area. When Charlie Walsh stepped down in 1994, Delaney finally got his promotion to Honorary Treasurer.

In the run-up to the 8 March Council meeting, Casey reminded people that he knew nothing of the ticket dealings at the two previous World Cups, and he called on Delaney and Kilcoyne to resign. When they didn't, he tendered his own resignation. Pat Quigley, the Vice-President, quickly followed suit, as did Hyland. Finally, Delaney offered his resignation. Amongst the five officers, only Kilcoyne, the President, clung to office as the meeting began.

As members of the Council milled around the Westbury's Kildare Suite, where the meeting was to take place, they were handed copies of Bastow Charleton's draft report. Most of the Council members leafed through the draft as they sat in their seats waiting for the meeting to start. The accountants' report found that at USA '94 the FAI had purchased tickets for knockout fixtures that Ireland might or might not be involved in. Joe Delaney, it said, was responsible for this trove of tickets. Delaney told Bastow Charleton that after Ireland were knocked out, he handed over IR£296,000 worth of tickets to an unfamiliar agent without any security, other than a third-party cheque for $30,000.

Invited to address the Council, Delaney read from a lengthy statement in which he condemned a 'smear campaign' which 'has at its roots the belief that, as the person in charge with the responsibility of satisfying the huge ticket demands of Irish fans, I enriched myself in the process'. He said that the FAI had purchased tickets to various World Cup knockout matches with the intention of 'trading' them in order 'to secure as many tickets for Irish fans as possible'. He explained the discrepancy between Veronica Guerin's report that he'd paid the FAI Stg£210,000 to cover a ticket shortfall, and his own admission of having paid Stg£110,000, by explaining that he had managed to collect a total of Stg£100,000 from the ticket tout, and had topped this up with Stg£110,000 of his own money. He apologized to his fellow officers for not telling them what had happened. 'I have paid the ultimate price,' he said, 'for a foolish decision made for the best of reasons in the euphoria of the World Cup.'

As Delaney walked out of the meeting and into the Westbury's lobby, the media were waiting. He ignored questions from Veronica Guerin, but agreed to do an interview with RTÉ's Gabriel Egan.

'He was very upset and he found it difficult to find the words,' Egan recalls. 'He didn't want to do the interview and I kind of persuaded him. He knew me over the years so he trusted me. He was shattered.'

John Delaney, at his father's side, also spoke to the reporter.

'He was upset as well, and he was annoyed about what had happened to his father, there is no question about that,' Egan says. 'He said he was going to carry on and he was going to be part of the new set-up.'

Tony O'Donoghue, another RTÉ reporter who spoke with John Delaney that night, felt the scene was 'kind of Shakespearean'. In the years that followed, O'Donoghue 'would often think so much of [John's] motivation was to restore the reputation of Joe'.

The Council meeting continued without Joe Delaney into the early hours of Saturday morning. Kilcoyne lost a vote of confidence, but delegates voted not to accept the resignations of the other three senior officers of the association. One of them, Pat Quigley, was not only reinstated but immediately made President now that Kilcoyne was out. Most delegates insist that Joe Delaney also lost a vote of no confidence, though Bernard O'Byrne, who was president of the Leinster Football Association at the time, has a different recollection: he says there was no vote on Delaney, and that had he stood his ground he might just have scraped back in. Hyland and Casey were also reinstated, after they addressed the Council.

'I told them I felt humiliated and injured and victimized because of the fact that I'd gone in front of the press and the fact that we told lies,' Casey says. He had seen the back of Joe, but the Delaneys weren't going away. 'He [John] wanted to get revenge for the father. He felt the father had been unfairly dealt with.'

*

Joe Delaney's downfall caused John Delaney's life to take an irrevocable turn. He accepted his father had made mistakes, but claimed that he had been targeted because he had ambitious reforms of the FAI in mind. Imbued with a sense of injustice over the way many in the 'football family' had turned on his father, John Delaney proceeded on his own rapid ascent through Irish football.

As a boy, John looked up to the former Manchester United and Ireland player Shay Brennan. The European Cup winner had fallen on hard times after finishing his playing career with Waterford United, where Joe was chairman. Brennan came to live with the Delaney family for a number of years. He introduced the Delaneys to the likes of Sir Matt Busby, Bobby Charlton and Nobby Stiles at Old Trafford, where Joe attended about fifteen games a year. Joe ran a bakery and Brennan drove one of the family bread vans, with young John as his assistant.

After attending school in Tipperary town, John enrolled in an accountancy course at Waterford Institute of Technology. He also carved out a reputation for himself on the soccer field for his rugged approach playing for St Michaels in the Tipperary Southern League. He was also keen on Gaelic games, but soccer was his number one. His father was away a lot on football business, and John often tagged along. When Joe became the FAI's Head of Security – a job he held alongside his role as Assistant Honorary Treasurer – John was eventually seconded to work behind the scenes. Cruelly, one or two players gave him the name Yorkie, on the grounds that he was rich, thick and chunky, but it wasn't a particularly accurate description.

The younger Delaney's duties were hardly onerous. At the 1988 European Championship in West Germany, he provided an impromptu commentary of the Ireland–England game for Philip Green, the retired RTÉ commentator, who was too nervous to watch the closing stages of the match and had his head in his hands. Afterwards the FAI's young security man rubbed shoulders with the FA chairman and UEFA grandee Bert Millichip, and revelled in the shocked expression on his face as Ireland's 1–0 victory registered.

Later, John Delaney was involved in a number of business ventures around the country. There was a furniture shop in Athlone. There was a bakery in Tralee, Cameo Cakes, which his family had a stake in but which was in financial trouble. The business owed IR£100,000 in back taxes, and a health inspector had earmarked it for closure. Delaney warned off the health officials by asking if they wanted to be responsible for the loss of dozens of jobs. He then wrote ten post-dated cheques of £10,000 each to the Revenue sheriff. He got the business back on its feet and the cheques cleared. It had been a 'ballsy' move, he later boasted in an interview with the journalist Barry Egan.

By 1998, Irish football was in a state of flux. Participation levels had trebled after Jack Charlton's teams qualified for three tournaments between 1988 and 1994, but the feel-good factor failed to seep into the depressed League of Ireland. Wannabe Irish stars still had little alternative to the hit-and-miss approach of trying to break into the English league system.

A year after Joe's dramatic departure from the association, John was elected as Waterford United's representative on the FAI Council. This was an important step, even though the powers of the Council were under threat in the aftermath of the ticketing scandal. Menton had commissioned a report from the consultant Ray Cass on the structures and administration of the FAI. This found the Council 'unwieldy' and complained that there was a 'lack of clarity as to the purpose, responsibility and accountability of the Honorary Officer positions, encouraging an inappropriate and potentially dangerous concentration of power'.

Cass advised that more power should be vested in the Executive Committee, or Board of Management, as he wanted to call it. This should consist of a maximum of twelve members who could sit on it for no more than four years. The FAI did create a Board of Management, but this was little more than a name change for the Executive Committee. It still had more than twenty members, there were no term limits, and the informal 'five officers' power centre remained very much intact.

Nevertheless, a place on the Board of Management was the natural ambition for any tyro trying to ascend the FAI's greasy pole, and Delaney very much fitted that description. The story of his ascent to the board was tinged with tragedy for Irish football.

Dr Tony O'Neill, commonly known as 'The Doc', was one of the FAI's most respected administrators. O'Neill had come to prominence as the driving force behind UCD's establishment of a League of Ireland team in 1979. He rose through the FAI voluntary ranks as far as Honorary Treasurer, while also doing the bucket-and-sponge work at matches when treating injured players. When Charlton had a problem in the early days, he turned to The Doc rather than the General Secretary at the time, Peadar 'Big Dinner' O'Driscoll, who was rarely in the office. O'Neill himself then became General Secretary in 1988, but couldn't handle being pulled this way and that by the honorary officers. Taking a step back from the FAI after Italia '90, he returned to UCD as Director of Sport.

UCD's model involved relying on promising young players, many of whom were given scholarships. That meant offloading established players when they had been at the club for five or more years. The Doc also acted as a mentor to a young solicitor and UCD law graduate making his first forays into football administration after an enthusiastic amateur career as a goalkeeper. Brendan Dillon, aged thirty-three, was given responsibility in 1998 for handling UCD's transfers.

The Doc rang Dillon one day that summer and told him that Waterford United were interested in buying Robbie Griffin, a left-sided UCD midfielder originally from Waterford.

'Robbie had given us some great years, but we were happy enough to let him go,' Dillon recalls. 'Doc said, "If you got five grand for Robert it would be great." He was kind of struggling that year. So, he says, "John Delaney is going to give you a ring." '

Like Dillon himself, Delaney at thirty was regarded as a coming force in Irish football. He had impressed many with his straight talking and ability to grasp a brief. And there was plenty of sympathy in FAI ranks towards his father.

Waterford United had been struggling, but the club made national headlines when it reregistered as a public limited company with a plan to raise £1 million through a share issue after it was promoted back to the first division. John Delaney was one of three directors in the Waterford United PLC who together purchased 60,000 £1 shares. The club had ambitions to once more be a big player in the League of Ireland and a war chest was made available for signing new players.

Dillon knew Joe Delaney but had never spoken with John. He says he 'would have been guarded with anything to do with the Delaney name'.

Expecting Delaney to drive a hard bargain for the midfielder, Dillon opened with a bit of flattery: 'John, that's great money you raised in Waterford.' Maybe it worked, because the negotiation was easy.

'I put out an outrageous figure, it might have been twenty-five grand, thinking he wouldn't go anywhere near it,' Dillon recalls. 'I was expecting if we got £10,000 it would be absolutely fantastic.'

Delaney agreed to pay £18,000. 'It was so easy,' Dillon says. 'I was thinking, this guy's the emperor with no clothes.'

Dillon rang O'Neill afterwards and said, 'Fuck me, Doc. We just got £18,000 for Robert Griffin.' O'Neill was incredulous. Dillon wondered why John Delaney was getting such hype in football circles for his business acumen.

O'Neill continued to be an influence in Irish football as a member of the FAI Council and Board of Management until his sudden death in October 1999, at the age of fifty-three. The *Irish Times* lamented the passing of 'probably the most universally respected figure on a scene plagued by internal dogfighting and factionalism'.

After some typically arcane FAI trade-offs, Delaney was elected unopposed to replace O'Neill on the Board of Management.

*

John Delaney joined the FAI's top table as the association was grappling with the biggest and most ambitious project it had ever undertaken: the building of a dedicated football stadium in west Dublin. This became widely known as the Eircom Park project after a big-name sponsor was quickly found.

The driving force behind the stadium was Bernard O'Byrne, who had succeeded Joe Delaney as Honorary Treasurer. O'Byrne then became General Secretary on a full-time basis later in 1996.

Like Menton, O'Byrne came from a financial background. He had been a treasury manager at Cement Roadstone Holdings, and he got the FAI General Secretary post even though as a volunteer he had been the association's Head of Security – succeeding Joe Delaney – for the notorious 1995 Ireland–England friendly that was abandoned after twenty-seven minutes because of rioting by visiting fans.

O'Byrne was a combative figure. The Lansdowne Road riot had crystallized his desire for Irish football to find its own home away from the antiquated headquarters of the Irish Rugby Football Union (IRFU), where the FAI had been tenants since the early 1970s. O'Byrne settled on a site at Saggart for a 45,000-seater stadium. For the first time, the FAI would be masters of their own destiny and in control of their own revenue streams. The dream looked set to become a reality when the announcement was made in July 1999, with O'Byrne and manager Mick McCarthy photographed beside an impressive model of the new stadium at a glitzy launch in the Burlington hotel.

With sponsors pledging support and the FAI Board of Management unanimously supporting the project at first, all the momentum was with O'Byrne; but slowly his master plan started to unwind.

Having failed to get the job of General Secretary on a full-time basis, Menton had been appointed Honorary Treasurer. Charged with the association's purse strings, he had severe reservations about loosening them for Eircom Park. He complained that O'Byrne had only given him a day's notice for the Burlington launch, and that he was stonewalled when he asked for documents setting out estimated costs for the project.

When he finally got a chance to study the financial projections closely in December 1999 – he says they arrived in a huge bundle at his house on Christmas Eve – Menton became alarmed at the plethora of expensive consultants on board and the way the costs were racking up. The projections included a £300,000 bonus for O'Byrne should the stadium be completed.

Many of Menton's concerns were legitimate, but O'Byrne is convinced that his opposition was personal, arising from a lingering resentment about missing the General Secretary position. 'Brendan was very angry when he didn't get the job, very angry,' says O'Byrne. 'He was even more angry when it was me who got it. That wasn't a good start. Brendan had no inclination to work with me. I remember we went out to lunch, at my invitation, to try to work it through and see if we could move it forward, but that just convinced me that we weren't going to be able to. He was Treasurer and I was Chief Executive and the relationship was just crap.'

Had the opposition been restricted to Menton alone, O'Byrne probably would have won the day, but soon there were other forces working against him. Chief amongst them was the Taoiseach, Bertie Ahern, a sports nut who had once played football on the same Home Farm team as Menton. With the Irish economy booming, Ahern decided it was time to build a national stadium. Just as O'Byrne thought he was getting his project off the ground, the so-called Bertie Bowl project was announced, an 80,000-seater home for the big three sports – GAA, rugby and football – in Abbotstown in northwest Dublin. O'Byrne was deeply sceptical of the government's costings and Ahern's ability to deliver the project. While the FAI didn't dismiss the Bertie Bowl, there was no let-up in the preparations for Eircom Park. However, with planning applications for the

Saggart site dragging because of objections from the Air Corps and others – the stadium was to be near Ireland's military airbase in Baldonnel – construction costs began to escalate sharply.

Another member of the Board of Management, John Byrne – 'a stand up, card-carrying member of Fianna Fáil' as he described himself – then came out in support of Ahern's project. And Delaney, after joining the Board of Management in October 1999, wasted no time in placing himself firmly in the anti-Eircom Park camp. The fight over two stadiums that would never be built was about to get very dirty.

'A regular thing that happened eight or nine times was that if a board meeting was starting at 2 p.m., at 1.30 p.m. a letter would come over from the Taoiseach's office which would be handed in to the President, Pat Quigley,' says O'Byrne. 'He didn't have the option not to consider it at the meeting, even though he had only just received it, because they [Byrne and Delaney] would know that the letter had been delivered and they would ask: "Has there been any correspond-ence from the Taoiseach?" This type of thing. On one occasion the envelope was actually opened at the meeting. There was all this kind of stuff. Some of it was offers, some of it threats to try to bring down Eircom Park. They were successful tactics in the end.'

O'Byrne became very suspicious about a VAT query from the Revenue Commissioners and unsettling questions from government departments about adherence to tendering rules. The anti-Eircom Park faction also threatened legal action to get information about the stadium that was being withheld from them. When the first criti-cisms of the Eircom Park project emerged, the public relations firm employed by the association, Gallagher and Kelly, briefed a number of journalists against some of those within the FAI who were oppon-ents of the scheme. 'We were just doing what had been done to us,' O'Byrne says.

Still, O'Byrne found that you can't fight City Hall.

'I had a meeting one-on-one with Bertie in St Luke's, his base in Drumcondra,' he says. 'I was explaining to him why this would be good for football, and in the middle of our conversation he said to me, "If we build Abbotstown, we are going to need a CEO, Bernard." I said, "Bertie, I wish you hadn't said that," and that was the end of it. We were never going to have another one-on-one discussion or whatever. It wasn't a bribe, but it was kind of put in a way like, "Think about the bigger picture. Maybe the FAI is not the place to be for the rest of your career." '

O'Byrne found his stadium project firmly blocked by his own association. 'I remember one particular board meeting which was a turning point and John Delaney said, "Do you guys realize if this goes arse-over-tit people will come after your houses?" He was looking around at the members of the board and people's faces were whitening. I could see I was losing four or five of them here straight away because none of them could cope with this type of thing. It wasn't accurate. The FAI was a limited company but it didn't endanger board members. The late Charlie Cahill [an FAI Executive member at the time] worked on the buses. A nice man, but he wasn't made for that type of situation.'

Pat Quigley, a pharmaceuticals salesman in his day job, struggled as FAI President to impose even a semblance of unity on the Board of Management.

'Everything had just imploded at that stage,' O'Byrne says. 'You had Pat giving speeches at the end of board meetings for ten or fifteen minutes about the confidentiality of board meetings, and then you would turn on the radio half an hour later in the car going home and there would be interviews with board members. They didn't give a damn. They had momentum and they knew that no action would be taken against them. The whole thing had just fallen asunder.'

Who was giving the interviews?

'It was mostly John Delaney.'

O'Byrne felt Menton had genuine reservations about the stadium, but he believed Delaney was motivated at least in part by a desire to avenge what had happened to his father back in March 1996.

Delaney found himself defending his motives in an article in December 2000 for the Irish edition of the *Sunday Times*, a newspaper that was broadly supportive of his fledgling steps in football administration. The Eircom Park project was in its death throes at that point, but Delaney was in no mood to go easy on O'Byrne. Delaney focused on inflated stadium revenue predictions and the international sports management consultants IMG, whom O'Byrne had drafted in at enormous cost, before going on to defend his own behaviour in the conflict. He also made an impassioned call for financial transparency from the association. It was an elegant dismantling of his rival:

> The disclosure that IMG have sold £10 million less in corporate box and premium seat sales than was previously claimed has vindicated those of us who took a stand against Eircom Park. On one major issue our determination to ask questions has been justified. I don't believe that we would have secured this vital information if we hadn't threatened legal action.
>
> Bernard O'Byrne now has serious questions to answer. How long has he been aware of this information? Why wasn't it made available to us six months ago when promised? Why were we told we had sold thirty-three more boxes and 1,700 more premium seats than we actually had?
>
> If we've been misled on one issue, where do we stand on all the others, particularly the stadium cost, the land deal and Deutsche Bank's commitment to underwrite the project?

Delaney then turned to his own motives:

> It's also regrettable that, perhaps in order to pigeon-hole me, people have sought to drag my father, Joe, into the equation. Joe, you might recall, was FAI treasurer in 1996 and was one of those who resigned when a shortfall in ticket revenue was discovered. I fail to see how this has any relevance to Eircom Park.
>
> I've no problem saying that I still feel my dad was harshly treated. Perhaps I'm biased but, even though he sinned, the FAI didn't lose a single penny and others, who committed far more serious crimes, escaped with more lenient penalties.
>
> But to suggest that what happened to my father has coloured my stance on Eircom Park is a gross distortion. There are football people who were not kind to him in 1996 whom I get on well with now. Likewise, there are people who I was friendly with then whom I hardly speak to now. It's just not relevant to the current issue.

Delaney went on to decry O'Byrne's completion bonus of £300,000, complaining that 'too many people stand to gain financially if this stadium goes ahead'. At that stage Delaney did not know about O'Byrne's misuse of an FAI credit card to withdraw cash and make personal purchases. That emerged weeks later, in March 2001, just as the FAI board voted to go with the government stadium project rather than O'Byrne's. The Eircom Park dream was dead, but worse was to come for O'Byrne.

Brendan Menton and the new Head of Finance, Peter Buckley, raised the alarm over his FAI credit card, which involved about £20,000 worth of personal spending.

'Every penny spent by me,' O'Byrne said in a statement the day after the story appeared in the *Sunday Tribune*, 'was spent within an authorized system and settled in full by me over a four-year period. When some inadvertent misallocations were brought to my attention, they were rectified immediately.'

Nonetheless, O'Byrne was damaged. The following month he went into 'voluntary retirement' with a severance package of £250,000: only slightly less than the bonus he would have received had Eircom Park been completed.

O'Byrne went on to rebuild his career as Chief Executive of Basketball Ireland, but he would not be the last to learn that you crossed John Delaney at your peril.

2.   'What have we done?'

With O'Byrne's departure as General Secretary, Brendan Menton again applied for the job, and this time he got it. The contrast with O'Byrne's bludgeoning style could hardly have been more marked.

Menton's move meant the important post of Honorary Treasurer was now vacant again.

In his early thirties and about to start a family with his wife, Emer, a teacher, John Delaney insisted that he was too young to be Honorary Treasurer – but he seemed prepared to allow his arm to be twisted. Even FAI veterans now recognized that there was a need for fresh blood in the association. Some were wary of another Delaney rising to control the FAI's purse strings so soon after Joe's downfall, but many influential figures in the association saw John's elevation as a way of doing right by his father after his humiliating departure.

John Byrne, the FAI's Mr Fixit with the government, was seen as the man mentoring the promising young figure of Irish football administration. The pair became known as the Two Johns – John One (Byrne) was short and bald, John Two (Delaney) was lanky with a flop of dark brown hair.

A Galway United stalwart, Byrne had a warm and benign view of Delaney at the time. 'John gravitated towards me,' Byrne says. 'We stayed out in the Montrose [Hotel], and if we were stuck we shared the same room, and he would come to Galway for weekends and we would go down to his for weekends. Our two wives were very close and they used to ring one another, giving out about us being away all the time.'

Delaney's performance over Eircom Park had earned him Byrne's respect, and the older man had been pushing him to deepen his involvement with the association even before the Treasurer post opened up. 'If you are good enough you are old enough,' Byrne told Delaney, a sentiment with which John O'Brien in the *Sunday Times* clearly agreed in May 2001 when he wrote about the state of the association and a potential leader in waiting:

> [Bernard] O'Byrne may be gone but the FAI remains an organisation deep in spiritual if not financial crisis. The likely appointment of Menton exposes its most fundamental flaw – the dearth of available talent within its ranks. The FAI is so legislatively impaired that it makes its rival sporting organisations, dull and grey-suited as they are, seem visionary in comparison.
>
> Just study the picture. The next officer board will consist of Casey and Hyland, who are both in their seventies, as well as the middle-aged Milo Corcoran, who will probably be the least deserving president the FAI has ever had and, after Pat Quigley, that is saying something.
>
> Meanwhile the talent ebbs away or does not put itself forward. John Delaney, O'Byrne's most fearless and eloquent critic, would make a fine treasurer and a much better chief executive than Menton. But Delaney, a successful businessman and only thirty-three years old, is currently considering his future on the Board of Management, wondering whether the struggle to move this languid beast of a movement forward is worth the hassle.

When Delaney continued to demur, Byrne pledged his support to the only candidate to put his cards on the table, Bill Attley, who had been persuaded to run for office by Casey. Shortly after, Delaney called Byrne to tell him that he would run for the Treasurer position. Byrne was surprised, believing Delaney had told Attley he would support him as well.

'John said he had been approached by lots of people,' says Byrne. 'We were so friendly at the time that I rang Billy and told him I was supporting John. Billy understood, but I don't know whether he ever forgave me.'

Attley was the top union official in the country, and it was said of him that he never had a vote that he didn't know the result of. But Attley, a former referee, had far less power in footballing circles. He knew he was fighting a losing battle and withdrew his candidacy, leaving Delaney as the lone runner in the field. The venue for Delaney's coronation was the Rochestown Park hotel in Cork, where the FAI's 2001 AGM was held. Delaney wore a white suit like the man from Del Monte, and threw a champagne reception on the night of his unopposed election. He made a victory speech, pledging to be an Honorary Treasurer for all, and became emotional when talking about his father and his family.

*

Delaney was proud to be the youngest ever Honorary Treasurer, but he was hardly an FAI novice. He knew that the job derived its power from access to money and tickets. With the 2002 World Cup just around the corner, he quickly started flexing his muscles. At his first board meeting as Treasurer, Delaney announced some swingeing cuts, with business-class travel off the agenda.

Relations with Menton were poor from the start, despite their shared opposition to Eircom Park. 'Brendan challenged Delaney on lots of things, particularly on the financial side,' says John Byrne. 'Brendan wasn't an accountant, but he was an economist and he knew what he was talking about. I did accountancy up to the Leaving Cert. I wasn't going to be challenging Delaney on balance sheets, but Brendan could pick one up and have it analysed in two minutes.'

Delaney announced a sponsorship deal with Lucozade. This resulted in acrimonious exchanges at a board meeting with one of Menton's senior staff, the Commercial Manager Eddie Cox, who said the deal cut across the existing arrangement with 7-Up. Delaney got his way. Because of the spat, Menton was told by the officers that his executive staff were not welcome at future board meetings.

It wasn't just Menton and Cox's noses that had been put out of joint. Cox had been negotiating for months with Umbro over a new kit deal and the terms were agreed in the weeks before Ireland were due to play Iran in a two-leg play-off for the right to go to the 2002 World Cup. Ireland were strong favourites to beat Iran, and Delaney knew qualifying for a World Cup would at least double the number of replica Ireland jerseys the sports company would sell.

Jonathan Courtenay, the son of Umbro's Irish representative, worked on the 2001 FAI deal with his father. When Delaney met the

Courtenays to sign off on the new agreement, he told them there was 'a bit of a problem'.

'This Iran thing; we need someone to pay for the plane,' Delaney said. 'If you can pay for the plane we can sign the deal now.'

Umbro's Irish distributors decided they had no alternative but to stump up for the cost of the chartered flights – estimated at between £30,000 and £50,000.

'It's not an easy one to swallow – fifty grand – but how do you say no at that point?' Jonathan Courtenay asks. 'That would have been one of the first interactions I had with him. It goes in the memory bank.'

Less fraught were the financial negotiations with the Irish players' representatives that began once qualification for the 2002 World Cup was secured. The run-up to the 1990 tournament had been marked by a dispute when players refused to attend an Opel function in a marquee at Lansdowne Road because the sponsor hadn't made a contribution to the players' financial pool. For the next one, in 1994, the players made sponsorship deals separate from the association's. Better teamwork was required if both sides were to cash in fully on qualification this time.

Delaney dealt with two veteran players, Niall Quinn and Steve Staunton, accompanied by their lawyer, Michael Kennedy, who also represented the Ireland captain, Roy Keane.

An agreement between the FAI and the players' representatives on a joint approach to sponsorship and a player bonus scheme was quickly reached. Advised by Ciarán Medlar of BDO accountants, the players would later successfully argue that their FAI World Cup bonus payments should be exempt from taxation in the UK, where they all played club football. The players cited a precedent set by the victorious 1966 England World Cup team, whose win bonuses went untaxed owing to the one-off nature of a World Cup victory. Her Majesty's Revenue and Customs service ultimately accepted that the same principle applied to the Ireland players.

That same month – December 2001 – it was announced that Ireland's staging post for their trip to the World Cup in Japan and South Korea would be the Pacific island of Saipan, a US protectorate most famous for bloody battles between American and Japanese soldiers during the Second World War.

The interest of the Irish public was intense, and some of Menton's colleagues reckoned that the communications side of the FAI needed to be beefed up in order to keep pace with the explosion of media coverage. In the months leading up to the finals themselves, the Aer Lingus spin doctor, Declan Conroy, offered his services but was rebuffed.

Shortly before the team's departure, Roy Keane had pulled out of Niall Quinn's testimonial, citing a persistent hip problem. He was also angered that he had been asked to work on a piece for the testimonial programme with Cathal Dervan, the journalist who had encouraged supporters to boo Keane over his alleged lack of commitment to the Ireland team in one of Mick McCarthy's first matches as manager. The Ireland captain was clearly in a bad mood travelling out of Dublin airport for the long-haul flight to the Far East.

A week on a tropical island was supposed to iron out some of the worry lines before the real work for the World Cup began in Japan. 'Saipan was for R&R, and we only sent a few [FAI] people there, along with all the fuckin' journos,' says Eddie Cox. 'Otherwise it would have been the case of the blazers having a junket. It was all about the lads playing a bit of golf and having a few pints.' Keane didn't play golf.

Menton remained at his desk in Dublin working quietly, but Cox was about to shatter the peace. The list of twenty-three names for Ireland's World Cup squad had been submitted by fax well in advance of FIFA's midnight deadline. However, Cox received a tip-off over the phone from somebody at Umbro, informing him of an urgent order from Saipan for a new No. 6 shirt, with the name 'HEALY' on the back.

Colin Healy was a Cork-born midfielder who played for Celtic. The Ireland No. 6 shirt belonged to another Cork-born midfielder, and the team captain: Roy Keane. What was going on? Cox's Umbro source claimed that Ireland's captain had decided to leave the World Cup before it had even begun, for reasons that were initially unclear.

Cox sounded the alarm. Menton got on the phone to the Hyatt hotel in Saipan. It was 2 a.m. Saipan time and he couldn't rouse the

FAI President, Milo Corcoran, at the team hotel. Mick McCarthy couldn't be contacted either, having switched off his phone. Menton finally got through to Chris Ryan, the manager of the FAI's international department and his most senior staff member in Saipan. After initially being fobbed off, he finally established that Keane was coming home after a furious row with some members of the coaching staff, relating to issues ranging from the late arrival of the team kit in Saipan to the poor quality of the training pitch and what Keane saw as the low standard of the work that the players were doing on it.

The decision to quit the World Cup was Keane's, and McCarthy, whose relations with his captain had always been strained, wasn't standing in his way. The manager had even sent a revised squad list to FIFA with Healy's name on it rather than Keane's, while trying to keep leaky Merrion Square in the dark, so that the change could be presented as a fait accompli to both the blazers and the wider public.

Menton phoned Keane's agent, Michael Kennedy, and McCarthy's agent, Liam Gaskin, both of whom expressed their shock at the news. Then he informed the four senior FAI officers who remained in Dublin: Casey, Hyland, Vice-President David Blood and Delaney. They were supportive of Menton's decision to bypass McCarthy and try to keep Keane in the squad for now, but only Delaney decided to weigh in and get involved in the effort.

A series of phone calls ensued amongst Menton, Delaney, Gaskin and Kennedy. Eventually, a message was relayed to McCarthy through physiotherapist Mick Byrne that Keane had had a change of heart and would remain with the squad.

Just when it looked as though peace had dawned, Keane surfaced again, baring his teeth in a lengthy interview with Tom Humphries in the *Irish Times*. In the 5,000-word piece, he took large chunks out of McCarthy, his fellow players and the FAI's World Cup preparations. Menton was getting on a plane to Japan when the interview was published, having finally parked a League of Ireland issue involving player registration.

'Delegation wasn't one Brendan's strengths,' says his friend Brendan Dillon, who was serving on the FAI Board of Management at the time. 'With the World Cup, he was trying to take on too many things.

He was delayed going out there because he was trying to sort out a row between Pat Dolan at St Pat's and Ollie Byrne at Shelbourne. He should have had nothing to do with that.' As a result, instead of being in Saipan, 'He's on a plane when all the shit hits the fan.'

As Menton waited in Amsterdam's Schiphol Airport for the KLM connection to Tokyo, he learned that by the time he joined up with the squad in Japan, Roy Keane would not be amongst its number, as McCarthy had sent him home. McCarthy had arrived at a 'clear-the-air' team meeting with the offending copy of the *Irish Times* interview tucked under his arm. In front of all the players and staff, he sought clarification about what Keane's problem was. Soon accusations were being swapped. Keane launched a furious and insulting rant at McCarthy, calling him a 'fucking cunt' and a 'fucking wanker'. McCarthy brandished the red card, just when it appeared the captain was about to walk out anyway.

The *Sunday Tribune*'s chief sportswriter, Paul Howard, was travelling out to Japan on the same flights as Menton. 'The impression was that he was behind the story,' Howard recalls. 'He found out when we found out. We were talking to him at Amsterdam airport and there was the sense of him being beleaguered. He just wasn't up to it. This story was too big for him.'

Howard thought the same of the rest of the FAI people, with one exception. 'The FAI top brass were never an impressive lot, so if anybody came along who was in any way smart they suddenly seemed like the smartest person you had ever met in your whole life,' says Howard. 'When John Delaney came along he kind of looked like a Messiah, because he wasn't useless, or he certainly didn't appear useless at the time.'

With Menton in mid-air, a crisis committee quickly gathered in Merrion Square: Des Casey, John Byrne (deputizing for Menton) and Delaney, who had driven up to Dublin for the fire-fighting mission. This was very quickly becoming the biggest controversy in the history not just of Irish football, but of Irish sport. Those who passionately supported Keane and those who felt he was letting his country down could at least agree on one thing – that the FAI had messed up, again. Bungling and incompetence had directly led to the departure of the team's only world-class player, while making Irish football a laughing stock around the globe.

Merrion Square was besieged with fans and media wanting an explanation of what had gone wrong and, more importantly, some idea about how the association was going to fix the mess. With the news media gathered in the boardroom downstairs for a press conference, Casey, Byrne and Delaney met upstairs to agree on their approach. They decided they would back the manager in his decision to send Keane home, without condemning the player.

John Byrne recalls, 'To my eternal regret, I said, "There is only going to be one speaker in this press conference." I looked to Des as the senior person – he was the Honorary Secretary and a Deputy Vice-President of UEFA – and the next thing yer man [Delaney] says "I will handle it." And Des agreed: "That's fine, John, you handle it."'

Grasping the poisoned chalice, Delaney did extremely well in front of the national and international press, displaying composure and disarming the media with his frank admission that it was 'madness' that Ireland's best player was leaving the camp after having done more than anybody else to get Ireland to the finals.

With the majority of Irish football correspondents over in Saipan or en route to Japan, there were just three regular football writers amongst the media throng. Delaney made sure to look after them. After the press conference finished, Delaney brought the three journalists into a private briefing. They left with their notebooks bulging with quotes and stories.

'We were winging it a bit, but John thought he had done a fantastic job,' Byrne recalls. 'Next thing his phone starts ringing and Eamon Dunphy and Vincent Browne were looking for him. The following day I said to Casey, "We're after launching this guy now." He was on the phone to [Keane's agent] Michael Kennedy and he wouldn't tell me what was going on. "I'm the fuckin' guru here." I could see what was coming.'

Menton, having arrived in Japan, met McCarthy after the official welcoming ceremony. Keane had gone home to Manchester and McCarthy told Menton that the matter was closed. Having got up to speed on the nature of Keane's verbal assault, Menton assured the manager of the full support of the FAI.

Menton then spoke to Casey and Milo Corcoran, the FAI President. They concurred that there was nothing more to be done and decided to travel as scheduled to the pre-World Cup FIFA Congress in Seoul. However, in the South Korean capital, Menton learned that Delaney was trying to broker a deal with Kennedy to get Keane back. Again, Menton was in the wrong place at the wrong time. 'If I had been advised by the FAI in Dublin that talks were ongoing, I wouldn't have gone to Seoul,' Menton says.

Menton phoned Delaney, who told him that all was quiet. Several hours later, at 3 a.m. – with his wife Linda sleeping beside him in the Seoul hotel – Menton was woken by a phone call from Delaney, informing him that the situation had changed: negotiations were ongoing and there was a chance Keane would return to the squad. Keane was going on RTÉ television the following evening and it was thought that he would apologize, a step that could have been enough to get him back in the squad.

'I would love to know when contacts resumed between Delaney and Kennedy,' Menton says. 'The FAI officials were not being kept up to speed. In addition, I believe there was no contact between the FAI in Dublin and Mick McCarthy in this reopening of negotiations. The people involved in this were John Delaney, Michael Kennedy and Niall Quinn. Mick McCarthy was not consulted, except by Niall, and neither Milo Corcoran nor I was either consulted or briefed. We had given our total backing to Mick and were not moving on this.'

Keane's interview with RTÉ's Tommie Gorman turned out to be a damp squib. Despite some indications of regret, there wasn't the apology that would probably have forced McCarthy to take him back.

What followed was arguably the most shambolic moment in the whole sorry saga. Having read a transcript of the Gorman interview, McCarthy met the players and told them he didn't want Keane back under any circumstances. McCarthy was planning to make a statement to that effect in the hope of drawing a line under the affair, and the players agreed to issue a subsequent statement backing McCarthy. However, McCarthy's press conference was delayed, as Menton was still en route from Seoul. The players' statement was then released prematurely by the FAI press office, effectively undermining McCarthy and pitching Keane against his teammates.

The furious public reaction back in Ireland prompted Quinn to make a final effort to get Keane back. Meanwhile, Menton had a meeting with McCarthy. 'There was a danger that Mick could walk away if he felt his position was being undermined by the association,' says Menton. However, 'The fact that I had been caught so far off guard by developments, being in Seoul, persuaded McCarthy that the "official" FAI were acting in good faith.'

The efforts of Delaney, Kennedy and Quinn to get Keane to return were all in vain. The captain finally confirmed ahead of Ireland's first game that he was not returning, citing the hostility of his teammates as the reason.

*

By the time Delaney made it out to the World Cup, Ireland's campaign was transforming into a good news story once more. Spirited second-half comebacks against Cameroon and Germany gave Ireland two draws from two tough games and put them in a strong position to qualify for the knockout stages.

The players had their post-match meal after the Germany match in a private upstairs room at the New Otani hotel in Chiba. Meanwhile, downstairs, the Honorary Treasurer, without consulting anyone, threw the bar open for free drink to all comers. The bar bill came to the equivalent of about €20,000, by conservative estimates.

On the morning the team was due to move on to Yokohama for the final group game, against the Saudis, Delaney, the FAI Head of Finance Peter Buckley and Menton sat down with the Chiba City representative, Tatsumi Ono, to reconcile the hotel bill. Ono initially said that the local authorities would not cover the bill for the free bar, although eventually he was persuaded to change his mind as Ireland were under-budget in other areas. As with the flights to Iran, Menton was embarrassed, but felt powerless to stand in Delaney's way. 'Chiba

City Council had treated us brilliantly and it was highly embarrassing trying to extract this money from them,' says Menton. 'It allowed Delaney to claim that the boozing sessions had not cost the FAI, but he did not know that when he decided to throw open a night-long free bar.'

McCarthy had been amongst those enjoying a few free drinks. According to an explosive affidavit later sworn by his agent, Liam Gaskin, McCarthy was approached at the bar by Delaney, who wanted to dispense even more largesse. The Honorary Treasurer told McCarthy that, given the team's almost certain qualification for the knockout stages, he should renegotiate the terms of his new contract, which had already been verbally agreed with the FAI.

The following day Gaskin met Delaney for coffee, and Delaney confirmed that he had made the suggestion of an 'exceptional performance bonus' to McCarthy.

'How much are you talking about?' Gaskin asked Delaney.

'A hundred thousand pounds sterling,' came the reply from Delaney, according to Gaskin's affidavit. 'Mr Delaney then indicated to me that he and I would need to meet with the President Mr Milo Corcoran and the General Secretary Mr Brendan Menton to formalize the aforementioned exceptional performance bonus ... Mr Delaney then suggested that I should not mention the amount of the bonus to either Mr Milo Corcoran or to Mr Brendan Menton prior to such a meeting.'

Gaskin had met Corcoran and Menton a couple of days previously. The respective parties to McCarthy's new contract had assured each other that there were no problems with the latest draft of the agreement; the sticking point of McCarthy wearing Adidas boots when the team was sponsored by Umbro had been resolved. It was just a question of finding the right moment for McCarthy to sign amidst a busy World Cup.

As Menton would put it in *Beyond the Green Door*: 'Imagine our surprise at the subsequent officers' meeting on 10 June when Delaney stated that it was his information that Mick McCarthy would not sign the contract without the payment of an additional bonus for exceptional performance.'

Gaskin's affidavit painted a similar picture:

It was thereafter represented by Mr Delaney to the President, Mr Milo Corcoran and to the General Secretary, Mr Brendan Menton, that I had indicated to Mr Delaney that my client was refusing to sign the contract agreed by the parties in February 2002 unless an exceptional performance bonus of Stg£100,000 was appended to said contract. I say that at no time was a demand made of the Football Association of Ireland for any sum additional to those sums agreed in the original contract concluded in February, 2002, and I say that the signing of the said contract was at no time made conditional upon such a payment.

Gaskin met Delaney, Corcoran and Menton in Seoul, where Ireland were based after beating Saudi Arabia and qualifying for the last sixteen. Delaney mentioned the bonus without stating the amount. Gaskin said nothing about his one-to-one with Delaney eight days earlier and the Stg£100,000 suggestion. Menton and Corcoran, operating on the basis of what Delaney had told them, did not intervene. A hand-written addendum to McCarthy's contract stated that the bonus sum was to be agreed 'within seven days of Ireland's return from the World Cup', and was signed by all four people.

Some details of the bonus emerged in the press the following day, 16 June, as Delaney had shared at least part of the story with three journalists he had invited to join him at the team hotel: John O'Brien, from the *Sunday Times*, Paul Howard of the *Sunday Tribune* and the *Sunday Independent*'s Dion Fanning.

'Delaney was very media-savvy,' says Howard. 'So, he would say, "This bit is off the record, but I don't want you to say you got this from an FAI source. I am giving you this as deep background." John briefed me and Dion and John O'Brien off the record about McCarthy's bonus at the team hotel in Seoul, and I am happy to confirm this because he later denied that he had briefed us.'

The journalists searched for a motive for this extraordinary step. They were still under the impression that McCarthy's new contract had been signed months previously, when in fact there remained only a verbal agreement. Howard reported that the bonus was 'a reward for bringing Ireland through to the knockout stages of the finals. Officials hope that the bonus will sweeten future negotiations and that the manager will stay on until after the European Championship in 2004.'

O'Brien quoted a source: 'It was done as a goodwill gesture. He wasn't asked did he want it, he was just given it.'

In the last sixteen, Ireland were knocked out by Spain in a penalty shoot-out. A crowd of 100,000 gathered in Dublin's Phoenix Park to welcome home McCarthy's team. Westlife headed an impromptu concert for the fans. It was reported as the biggest crowd in the park since Pope John Paul II's Mass there in 1979.

Delaney, Gaskin, Menton and Corcoran met at the Red Cow hotel and agreed on the bonus figure. 'At the meeting I was asked by Mr Delaney if Stg£100,000 would be an appropriate exceptional performance bonus . . . I indicated that such would be acceptable to my client,' Gaskin's affidavit stated.

In late September, Gaskin learned that at a meeting of the FAI Finance Committee, Delaney asserted that the £100,000 bonus had been a consequence of the lengthy delay in getting McCarthy's contract signed. This was news to Gaskin and McCarthy, who were furious that it was portrayed that they had held the FAI to ransom over the delay.

McCarthy at the time was coming under renewed pressure following a poor start to the European Championship qualifying campaign, and this false portrayal of him as a greedy mercenary was not what he needed.

Menton, who hadn't attended that finance meeting, wasn't happy either that he was now in the firing line of national opinion for not having fully processed McCarthy's contract before the World Cup. 'I was in effect being accused of being responsible for the cost of this bonus to the FAI, when in truth the Honorary Treasurer had offered it to Mick,' Menton says.

*

It was a fevered time in Irish football. In an initiative led by Delaney, the FAI had commissioned Genesis, an Edinburgh-based consultancy group, to carry out an independent review of the Saipan affair. Roy Keane was amongst fifty people interviewed. The pressure was growing on Menton, particularly over the delay in getting training gear out to Saipan.

'Before the Genesis report came out, Brendan had kind of given up,' says John Byrne. 'The shit that used to go on at council meetings and the Board of Management; Delaney would come into the room with all his acolytes from Munster asking this question and that. Brendan was bombarded. I remember taking a council meeting when Brendan was sick – there wasn't a single question asked. The following meeting it was back to being a tsunami. There was a long game, which I didn't detect at the time. It was only really in 2004 that I saw the ultimate ambition.'

After one board meeting, Brendan Dillon wondered if the fight had gone out of Menton. 'When Delaney says "it's all Menton's fault", you are thinking, "Brendan, stand up for yourself." But Brendan at that stage was such a beaten docket and was so undermined,' Dillon says. 'He knew that something didn't add up, but the contract hadn't been signed so he wasn't able to say it was signed. He put up quite a meek defence, which certainly didn't impress me. I came out of that meeting with an absolute conviction that Brendan was just dead in the water.'

In Keane's absence, Ireland made a terrible start to their European Championship qualifying campaign in the autumn of 2002, being beaten 4–2 in Moscow by Russia and then 2–1 at home to Switzerland at Lansdowne Road. McCarthy had been booed loudly at the first home game after the World Cup, which hurt him deeply. His friend Cathal Dervan, who had ghost-written McCarthy's bestselling World Cup diary, now wrote that he wouldn't be surprised if the Ireland manager took the vacant job at Sunderland. Keane was intimating he might return if McCarthy was out of the way. Like Menton, McCarthy had the air of a beaten man and his resignation looked like only a matter of time.

Gaskin, meanwhile, was on the warpath about the way the bonus story was being reported. He seized on an article by John O'Brien in the *Sunday Times* on 3 November which claimed McCarthy 'had held them to ransom when they moved to secure his signature before they played Spain in the last sixteen of the World Cup'.

McCarthy resigned two days later, on 5 November, only four months into his new two-year contract. Gaskin negotiated a three-month pay-off with the FAI, which was considered highly restrained. McCarthy just wanted out, and his sense of disappointment with the association increased when details of a farewell dinner he was to have with the FAI board were leaked to the media as Gaskin and McCarthy were driving to the location, Kilkea Castle hotel in Kildare.

'That was leaked to Tony O'Donoghue,' says Gaskin, who remembers a flurry of phone calls at the time. 'Then I got a phone call off Cathal Dervan saying, "I'll see you down at Kilkea Castle." We turned the car around.'

O'Brien reported in the *Sunday Times* that 'Delaney insisted that McCarthy's side had played hardball to extract the [Stg£100,000 bonus] payment and used it as an argument against any significant resignation package'.

Delaney was quoted as saying: 'Two weeks ago I opened up the paper and saw a piece saying we were going to pay Mick off £250,000. I'm not saying where it came from but the figures were tallying with what we were hearing from Mick's side. And that annoyed me.'

The idea that Delaney was now taking credit for McCarthy not getting a bigger pay-off, and accusing McCarthy's side of leaking, further antagonized Gaskin. In his affidavit, Gaskin said it was a matter of grave concern that there should appear in the media 'apparently emanating from an official or officials of the Football Association of Ireland suggestions that I sought in an unprofessional, cynical, mercenary and unconscionable manner to resile from an agreement negotiated by me in good faith . . . my client, Mr Mick McCarthy, similarly has the gravest concerns.'

★

The Genesis report was published on 11 November 2002, less than a week after McCarthy resigned. It was highly critical of the management structures in Irish football. There was no mention of the Delaney/McCarthy bonus fiasco.

The report's author, Alistair Gray, was preparing to address FAI members at a meeting in the Burlington hotel when he had a quick word with Menton. 'Brendan, I'm really sorry for you but it's not going to look good,' he told him.

'I wanted him to prepare because he was under a lot of pressure,' Gray says. 'His wife was saying to me, "He's a lovely man, Alistair." I said, "I'm sure you're right, Mrs Menton. But the last thing the FAI needs right now is a lovely man." He was overwhelmed by it all.'

Menton resigned. It meant that he was left on the outside for the denouement of the McCarthy bonus affair.

Gaskin's affidavit, served with a demand for an apology in January 2003 as the FAI was looking for a new manager, threw the spotlight firmly on Delaney. Menton also swore an affidavit. Delaney's position as Honorary Treasurer was on the line going into a meeting of the FAI's Board of Management at the Red Cow hotel in west Dublin on 24 January 2003. The media was waiting outside, anxious for any news about the identity of McCarthy's successor and growing increasingly intrigued about the bonus row.

The President, Milo Corcoran, consulted the FAI's solicitors, A&L Goodbody, and the meeting got bogged down in procedure. Only a handful of the twenty-two board members actually read the affidavits. Brendan Dillon, who was Delaney's most trenchant adversary on the Board of Management, recalls 'all the loudmouths' on the board getting very animated as Corcoran insisted he would follow fair procedures to deal with the allegations made by Gaskin against Delaney. Ollie Byrne, the owner of Shelbourne FC, whose club had benefited more than most from FAI grants, was shouting at Corcoran, and in the mayhem Delaney found some wriggle room. 'There was nothing about how our Treasurer has handed the manager a hundred grand and knifed Menton,' Dillon says. 'I spoke at one stage and said that this was clearly causing huge division and the meeting had to be adjourned. You could scan-read the affidavit in two minutes and see that this was absolutely unbelievable stuff, but we needed time to consider it.'

The unruly meeting had at least managed to establish clarity on another matter: that Brian Kerr would be the next Ireland manager.

'John made a bolt for the door, where all the journos were going for him to talk about the bonus,' recalls John Byrne. 'He pushed me back slightly and said, "It's Kerr, lads, it's Kerr." They all went, "What?" He said, "Kerr got the job." I don't think Brian Kerr himself even knew he was getting it. Hit them with a story and get out. This was the news now, not the hundred grand for Mick McCarthy.'

Another board member, Paddy McCaul, also witnessed this exchange. 'I was following John out. "It's Kerr," he said. The news wasn't supposed to be released till the following week.' The leak, McCaul says, 'snookered our contract negotiations with Kerr'.

The government became alarmed at the prospect of yet another FAI scandal and moved to stop any more bloodletting. Con Haugh, then the Assistant Secretary at the Department of Sport, called John Byrne and invited him in to see the minister, John O'Donoghue.

'John O'Donoghue was literally tearing his hair out: "For fuck's sake, John, after Saipan you need to sort this out, the public can't expect the government to pay," ' Byrne recalls.

With O'Donoghue's words ringing in his ears, Byrne asked a number of colleagues not to force the Delaney issue. 'We had a board meeting in Citywest and everybody had been rung,' Brendan Dillon recalls. 'We all agreed to bury the hatchet. Noel Kennedy, who [later] became a fully signed-up member of the Delaney fan club, went ballistic and railed against it; said there had to be due process. We all said, "Noel, we hear what you are saying, but this has to be done for the greater good." '

Delaney was in combative mood at the next board meeting, two weeks later, at which he complained about the effect the McCarthy bonus controversy had had on his family. 'I would say within five minutes it became obvious to me that Delaney hadn't learned a thing,' Dillon says. 'Talk about not being conciliatory. I remember thinking, "Oh my god, what have we done?" '

At a special Board of Management meeting in late February, an independent facilitator was appointed to resolve the McCarthy bonus matter, and after a meeting of the relevant parties in the Four Courts a statement was issued:

The FAI is happy to clarify that at no time before during or after the Korea/Japan World Cup 2002 did Liam Gaskin or Mick McCarthy bring any undue pressure to bear on the association regarding the payment of a bonus. Indeed the contrary is the position and the FAI was prepared to offer and pay the bonus to Mr McCarthy.

The Association acknowledges that the awarding of the bonus was a collective decision and that John Delaney acted at all times in the best interests of the Association. The FAI apologizes for any distress or upset which may have been caused to either Mr Gaskin or Mr McCarthy by these media reports. The FAI has no hesitation in confirming that Mr Gaskin and Mr McCarthy, at all times, acted in a professional and honourable manner in all their dealings with the Association.

For his part, Menton ended up in Malaysia, working for the federation there on behalf of FIFA. He concluded that Malaysia would have been the ideal stopover point for McCarthy's team, rather than Saipan. The former FAI man had certainly found out the hard way.

3.   Fran the Baptist

As the heat faded on the Mick McCarthy bonus affair, Delaney and the other senior officers were also under some pressure as a result of the Genesis report into preparation and planning for the 2002 World Cup.

The report detailed the poor planning and budgeting for the World Cup and the absence of 'basic management discipline'. It recommended greater professionalism, and reforms that would ensure players and coaches were put first. Genesis also called for the creation of five new management roles, including that of a Chief Executive who would be a director on the Board of Management, which would be much reduced in number.

The day after the report was published, RTÉ's Brian Farrell went through the Genesis findings with Paul Lennon of the *Irish Daily Star* on *Prime Time*, RTÉ's flagship current-affairs show. Lennon, a seasoned veteran of the soccer beat, predicted 'a major shift in power from elected officers to paid employees, to senior executive staff'.

Brief footage of Brendan Menton's resignation speech was aired. Back in studio, bow-tied Farrell moved off his high-chair to a round-table discussion featuring John Delaney, Eamon Dunphy and Pat Dolan, the Managing Director of St Patrick's Athletic. On a screen behind them was the former Ireland international Tony Cascarino, live from RTÉ's London studio with a backdrop of the Houses of Parliament. Farrell asked Delaney why he wasn't also resigning. Delaney pointed out that he had been Honorary Treasurer for little more than a year and had been largely responsible for instigating the Genesis review.

'I demanded that we have an independent review, there was no difficulties from my officers, they accepted it,' said Delaney. 'I stated that if they didn't do it I would have resigned, no doubt about it, no question about it.' He was building up a head of steam. 'Paul Lennon hit the nail on the head. There will be a change of power in the association from my point of view. I think the officers will take less of a role, and highly paid chief executives and, you know, key executive positions will be filled.'

Cascarino then served up some entertaining tales about FAI officials being on foreign trips for 'the beano', sitting up in first class while the players scrunched up in economy. Then Ireland's most colourful football pundit stepped in.

'John Delaney has a commitment to change things and he is a key player in this if they are going to reform the association,' said Dunphy. For once, Dunphy appeared to be singing off the same hymn sheet as everybody else. 'If you take power away from people who have no business holding it and give it to paid executives with responsibilities and accountability, that will be the key to change.'

Farrell asked who was going to be responsible for recruiting these executives.

'Well, the people who are damned in this report,' Dunphy replied with a smile.

'Well then, no change?'

'I think that there is a change because they have been identified as a problem. The press will keep on their case. We would expect a real Chief Executive, and others in key positions supporting him.'

Dolan disagreed: 'If we are saying that there is going to be one resignation [Menton], and the same people who are damned in this report have the power to influence Irish football, we won't get change, because those people will stay there with the trapdoor open waiting for the paid officials to fail.'

*

For all the talk about a hard-hitting report, there was much about Genesis that was woolly sentiment. One important recommendation, though, was that a number of specialized committees be set up. Another was that the twenty-three-person Board of Management be made dramatically smaller. Genesis also recommended that 'consideration be given to the appointment of at least two non-executive directors from outside Irish football'.

Again, Delaney was insistent, coming out with a quote which would be thrown back at him years later: 'If these recommendations are not implemented in full in one year, I will be out of this place. End of story.'

Reducing the numbers on the board was a difficult proposition to sell, never mind the prospect of independent directors. For Brendan Dillon, who had been appointed chairman of the League of Ireland, it involved telling his member clubs that they needed to accept a curb in their influence on the board, which would now consist of the FAI's five office-holders along with the chairmen of a number of new committees: Domestic Affairs, Development, Legal and Corporate Affairs, Finance and International.

'Having twenty-three people on the board was a joke,' Dillon says. 'It was too unwieldy. You had all sorts of factions and I did feel that a ten-man board would work better. I was very instrumental in developing the whole committee thing, naively not realizing to what extent Delaney could completely monopolize the whole system.'

*

In January 2003 there were joyous scenes when Brian Kerr was unveiled at the Shelbourne hotel. People from all walks of life turned up to join in the giddy celebrations, as Ireland once again had a home-grown manager, a real Dublin football man at the helm. The FAI hoped that Kerr would be able to go some way towards matching the phenomenal success he had enjoyed as manager of the international under-age teams, and Kerr himself talked about coaxing Roy Keane out of international retirement. Delaney had wanted the former Manchester United captain Bryan Robson to be manager, but the two other men on the management selection committee – Milo Corcoran and Kevin Fahy – went for Kerr. It would be the last defeat Delaney would suffer at the FAI for quite some time.

The next big appointment would be that of Chief Executive, with beefed-up powers as recommended by Genesis. The Chief Executive would now sit on the board and have a vote, even though this was a practice which went against the recommendations of FIFA's statutes aimed at maintaining a separation of powers between the decision-makers (who, ideally, came from the grassroots of the game) and the administrators. While the FAI worked to recruit a high-powered CEO, the man at least notionally at the top would be the new Honorary Secretary, Kevin Fahy, a deputy head teacher.

As one of the senior officers, Fahy had tried to protect Menton in the wake of Saipan; but his efforts, which included arranging a meeting with Delaney at the Davenport hotel, were in vain. 'I was trying to talk sense into him,' says Fahy. 'There had been enough turmoil and it was time to steady the ship for the sake of the association. I didn't get very far with that. In the middle of our meeting, coincidentally, he got a phone call from his dad and they were chatting away jovially. Then he handed the phone to me. Joe just passed the time. That was the end of the meeting. Anything I said to him [John] in relation to calming things down went in one ear and out the other.'

From there, relations only deteriorated. Along with Dillon, Fahy was posing some awkward questions to Delaney about the accounts. Delaney had been spending heavily as Treasurer, pledging money to clubs and affiliates even though he knew that money was needed for a new technical plan for player development. 'Every time you asked John a question at a board meeting about the accounts, it was a little bit like you had accused him of some horrendous crime,' Dillon says. 'There were sulks: "How dare you?" And there were the throwaway remarks – "You can ask Peter Buckley that"; "You can ask such and such that"; "I have answered that question".'

Even getting Fahy to replace Menton on an interim basis had proved problematic. He needed to take a career break from his school, and the FAI agreed to match Fahy's teaching salary, but Delaney opposed matching his employer pension contributions.

'We had a man taking over because the rules say he has to, and we are saying it should cost him money,' says Dillon. 'Delaney fought tooth and nail to stop Kevin getting his pension. He was incredibly difficult about that.'

Eventually, Fahy got his pension contributions, and his six months as interim General Secretary were relatively trouble free – up to the point where it came to appointing the new CEO. Pricewaterhouse-Cooper (PwC) was hired to headhunt the best candidate, and the field was narrowed down to two: Gary Owens, the Chief Executive of Hibernian Insurance, and Fran Rooney, who had made his fortune with his computer security company Baltimore Technologies – and then lost much of it just as rapidly. Rooney had left Baltimore in 2001 after overstated earnings had led the firm to issue two profit warnings. Rooney had a footballing background, having played at Shamrock Rovers and managed the women's national team, but had spent much of the previous decade in the United States and therefore was a relatively fresh face in Irish football.

Owens, a business executive who had played amateur football in Dublin up until his mid thirties, was considered a safe pair of hands. The €250,000 salary on offer from the FAI was higher than he was being paid to run Hibernian, one of the largest insurance companies in Ireland with a €400 million turnover and 2,000 employees.

Delaney was on the interview board, along with Fahy, Corcoran and John Treacy from the Irish Sports Council. They were leaning towards Owens, but Declan O'Neill of PWC was very keen on Rooney. At the second interview stage, Rooney impressed the panel with his slick PowerPoint presentation and was offered the job.

Rooney started the job early in May 2003, before signing his employment contract, which led to another furious internal battle. FAI President Milo Corcoran received a letter from Rooney's solicitors, Ivor Fitzpatrick, about the terms of the contract.

Fahy, who was on the Remuneration Committee, found it hard to resolve the wrangle. 'I wasn't going to the meetings because I would get less than twenty-four hours' notice,' he recalls. 'It was being set up to give Rooney whatever he wanted, but later it occurred to me that it was John setting it up for himself. There was no way he was going to give up on his ambition to be CEO just because Fran Rooney was there. By hook or by crook, he was going to get it after Rooney.'

Brendan Dillon agrees: 'Delaney didn't give a shit because he had eyes on the job, so the higher the better when it came to the money.'

The five senior officers were split on the issue, with President Milo Corcoran supporting Fahy and Dillon. Rooney appeared to have the support of Delaney, most of the press and Brian Kerr. It was portrayed in the media as a battle between the traditionalists and reformers led by Rooney, and a board meeting set for early September was crucial to the outcome.

At the Citywest hotel, before the meeting began, Rooney and the FAI officers met to thrash out their differences. It was decided to deal with the sticking points one by one. Rooney wanted to use his Mercedes 500-series car rather than drive the Alfa Romeo provided by the FAI's sponsors, Fiat. Delaney had been dead set against Menton driving his own car, but seemed relaxed about Rooney's demand. A compromise was reached whereby he could use his Mercedes, but would partly pay for the running of it himself.

Dillon was particularly struck by the dynamic between Rooney and Delaney in the meeting. During the debate over the car, Dillon recalls, 'Rooney looks at me and then looks at Delaney as if to say, "What do you advise me to do?"'

Rooney says he only brought in his lawyers when the FAI 'tried to row back' on what they had offered.

'One guy was hiding behind the other guy,' Rooney says. 'I said, "Can we get everybody who is going to make this decision together?" That was very difficult. It was messy and kind of amateurish and all played out in the media. I very nearly walked away because I was suspicious at that stage.'

A disappointing draw against Russia at home three days after the meeting set back Ireland's hopes of qualifying for Euro 2004, but at least there was a result in November when the Genesis recommendations were formally adopted at an FAI EGM. The one exception was the recommended appointment of two independent directors: that was no longer on the agenda.

*

Rooney's appointment had finally been made official, but what followed was an unprecedented year of bloodletting that would culminate in the departure of the Chief Executive himself.

Brendan Dillon remained Rooney and Delaney's most formidable opponent. In December 2003 Delaney sent Dillon an email suggesting that he use the Christmas break to 'consider a less combative approach in the interests of Irish football'.

Rooney, for his part, took exception to how Dillon spoke to him. 'Brendan was quite abusive towards me and used some expletives, so that was the end of the relationship with Brendan,' he says.

Another major source of tension was a request by Milo Corcoran to become a full-time employee rather than perform his duties in an honorary capacity. Corcoran was having problems combining his role as FAI President with his day job as a sales representative for Heineken, but Dillon told him that only the Chief Executive could be paid under the articles of the association.

In January 2004 Dillon resigned from the FAI board to concentrate on his burgeoning legal practice. Several weeks after his departure, he wrote a fourteen-page letter to Corcoran. 'I grew increasingly disenchanted with the level of interference in the League by both the CEO and Honorary Treasurer of the FAI and I had grave concerns regarding various decisions made by the FAI over a period of time and the lack of information, transparency and openness in relation to the financial and operational workings of the association,' Dillon wrote. He also wrote that Delaney had projected a loss on non-World Cup activities of €1.45 million for the year ending 31 March 2003, but the figure in the end was €2.7 million, a €1.25 million difference.

The financial queries continued for page after page. With the help of his brother, an accountant, Dillon had even created charts to highlight the large discrepancies between projections and outcomes. He requested documents dealing with money paid to specific clubs and what had happened to public money coming in to the association.

With Corcoran's request to be paid in mind, he also asked for information regarding payments made to officers 'by way of salary, honoraria or expenses'.

When his letter was ignored, Dillon wrote again on 30 March 2004, saying he was duty-bound as a former director and was now passing on his letter to the company's auditors, Deloitte & Touche. He also went a step further, making a complaint to the Office for the Director of Corporate Enforcement (ODCE), Ireland's company-law watchdog. Dillon met the ODCE but says that the body was concentrating on 'low-hanging stuff. This was too big a story.'

With Dillon out of the way, Delaney had Fahy in his sights. This meant that another board member, Michael Cody, had Fahy in his sights also. Although he had sided against Joe Delaney following the earlier ticketing scandal, Cody had now formed an alliance with the younger Delaney.

On Des Casey's retirement, Cody had been unexpectedly beaten to the post of Honorary Secretary by Fahy at the AGM in July 2002. Delaney had campaigned for Cody, but Fahy gained huge support from the League of Ireland, which might have been expected to support Cody, a representative of Cobh Ramblers.

Despite the setback, Cody continued to be a regular presence around Merrion Square. He had taken an early-retirement package as General Manager of the insurance company FBD and was never slow to remind people how far he had risen in the commercial world.

John Byrne, who had taken a role as the FAI's Planning and Development Officer, was another who left the association, saying that he couldn't work with Rooney. He had witnessed Cody's metamorphosis into Delaney's right-hand man. 'Everything that was said and everything that happened, he reported back to Delaney,' Byrne recalls.

Fahy as Honorary Secretary was refusing to sign off on the accounts until the issues raised in Dillon's marathon letter were addressed, including the thorny question of whether Corcoran was actually being paid by Heineken or the FAI. Rooney was reported to have told the board that Heineken had submitted an invoice for €39,000, and that the payment had been approved by a 'senior official' at the FAI. Rooney insisted in the press at the time that he wasn't the senior official – so who was? 'I believe that Delaney probably cut a deal with Milo,' Rooney says. However, Fahy and Dillon insist that Rooney also knew about the arrangement.

Corcoran also accused Fahy of being 'adversarial' and undermining the position of the Honorary Treasurer, amongst others, by voting against the adoption of the annual accounts 'without any acceptable reason'. Corcoran informed Fahy that he was facing expulsion at a special meeting of the board the following month.

Fahy sent a stinging reply a week later, pointing out a number of things Corcoran had failed to act upon – all relating to Delaney. The list included 'a compensation payment of €10,000 (and €15,000 for our insurers) as a result of the Honorary Treasurer giving information to a newspaper about an incident at the World Cup which resulted in a defamation case against the paper and a threat to join the FAI into litigation', plus 'the cost of the Stg£100,000 to the FAI payable to Mick McCarthy which was the result of the Honorary Treasurer's actions which he initially denied and subsequently had to concede after Liam Gaskin swore his affidavit'.

Fahy refused to attend the meeting at which the FAI Council dismissed him. Afterwards, he remarked: 'I have done nothing wrong. All I did was ask questions at meetings and sought answers to those questions. So much for openness and transparency. The Genesis report was for openness, but that is not happening.'

Council also voted to approve, retrospectively, the deal for Corcoran's salary to be paid by the FAI. Thus Corcoran became the first paid FAI President – and the last.

On 17 September 2004, Cody was elected, unopposed, to replace Fahy as Honorary Secretary – a post that he felt should have been his two years earlier. A cornerstone in the Delaney empire had just been put in place.

*

This decisive swing in the FAI power struggle resulted in a reality check for Rooney. 'I thought it would make life easier,' Rooney says. 'Then, what I realized is "Wow! Delaney has now lost his biggest opponents. So, he has actually built quite a power base now." He would spend a lot of time driving around meeting people and make all the phone calls. He was the only board member who had contact with all these people on a daily basis. I was very conscious of that. He would have been like a consummate politician at that stage, rather than a businessman.'

Rooney upset some of the blazers with a plan to outsource ticket sales to Ticketmaster. Rooney was surprised when the matter was raised at an FAI Council meeting by Charlie Cahill, a Leinster Senior League stalwart who had been FAI President from 1978 to 1980. Rooney says that Cahill, on behalf of the league, got a small cut of the ticket-selling revenue. The only person Rooney had informed about the Ticketmaster plan was Delaney.

Cahill, according to Rooney, challenged the idea. 'He said I was giving away "our" tickets to Ticketmaster,' said Rooney. 'And then I kind of started to look at that. There were a number of people who had built up a right to have a bundle of tickets here for each game and they would come into the ticket office in the FAI and they will be printed off and they literally walk away with a bundle of tickets in an envelope.' At one point Rooney found himself locked out of the ticket office in the basement of Merrion Square amidst a climate of suspicion about the use or abuse of the ticketing system.

Rooney was involved in supporting Brian Kerr's efforts to bring Roy Keane back into the squad. Keane had returned for a friendly in May 2004 against Romania, and Kerr wanted to pick him for qualifiers in September, but Alex Ferguson was resistant to letting the ageing midfielder play competitively for his country again. Rooney recalls, 'We had a match on the Saturday. After the game Delaney came over and asked what was happening with Roy. I said, "Look, confidentially, he's coming back and it will be announced next week." Within ten minutes Dion Fanning came up to me and asked me for a quote about Roy being available. I'm relying on senior board confidentiality, but within ten minutes a journalist is looking for a quote and we haven't even agreed how we'd announce it yet.'

As Rooney became increasingly isolated, it was reported that he had been told by Delaney, over a drink in Jury's hotel in Ballsbridge, not to get involved in the politics of the FAI, but had ignored the advice.

Rooney had come in with some good ideas, such as devising a new FAI logo and properly marketing the international games. Another of Rooney's ideas was a bespoke FAI clothing range. Rooney put considerable effort into organizing fashion shows and commissioning FAI-branded clothing, much to the chagrin of the FAI's existing kit sponsor, Umbro, whose Irish supplier threatened legal action if the merchandise went on sale.

Instead of fashion shows, staff were looking for decisions on important issues such as running UEFA training courses. Rooney became known as Two-Day Fran, a label he insists was misleading. 'I had to have meetings with various people, including Brian [Kerr], and we wouldn't always be meeting in Merrion Square,' he says. 'I was pretty much 24/7. But if I wasn't in the office it was said I wasn't doing my job.'

At times, Rooney didn't help himself. He enjoyed briefing the press, particularly on away trips, sometimes over a couple of drinks in a hotel as he smoked a cigar, reassuring them that the reform process was on track and that he was on top of everything.

Some believed the CEO was trying to talk his way out of a job. At the pre-match meal with visitors from the Faroe Islands in October in Jury's Ballsbridge, Rooney told an outrageous joke concerning Northern Ireland football which caused some offence.

There were other issues swirling around Rooney. He was unhappy that his Mercedes was constantly being scratched and bumped in the tiny car park at the back of Merrion Square. Also, his mansion in Castleknock, Nirvana, had been burgled while his teenage daughter was on her own in the property. He blamed the *Evening Herald* for identifying the house and its location in an article and wondered who had put the paper up to it.

Matters came to a head when three senior managers – Head of Finance Peter Buckley, HR man Tadhg O'Halloran, and Pat Costello, who was in charge of communications – drafted two letters, one nine pages long, detailing complaints to the FAI board about Rooney.

Amongst the allegations was that Rooney had yet to settle a bill for a long farewell lunch he hosted for the old twenty-three-man Board of Management in Restaurant Patrick Guilbaud in Dublin months earlier, reported to have cost around €2,000. Questions were also raised about the amount owed by Rooney's office to the ticketing department. And there was a complaint that merchandise costing €150,000 was ordered at Rooney's behest, but couldn't be sold because of the existing deal with Umbro. (The FAI would quietly give away this gear to clubs and supporters for a number of years, and Umbro shipped some of it to charities in Africa.)

Buckley, O'Halloran and Costello also revealed that contracts with two of the association's biggest sponsors, Eircom and Fiat, had not been signed, despite having been agreed many months earlier.

Rooney was also under fire for the failure to implement a number of Genesis recommendations, including the filling of four key management posts. Rooney countered he was being blocked in his efforts to advertise for some prominent positions, particularly that of Finance Director, a job which the senior officers wanted to give to Buckley, who was already heading up the department. Rooney thought differently and the FAI was split on the issue, with Delaney, Cody and Corcoran lined up against him going into a meeting with the Irish Sports Council about funding. 'This is the first time that the three of us were at complete odds with what Fran was saying,' Corcoran said afterwards. 'Fran had a totally different impression of what went on at that meeting to what we had. If I was on my own, I would have thought I was on a different planet, but three of us can't be wrong.'

Rooney still had plenty of grassroots support, as a standing ovation when he addressed a centenary dinner at the Athletic Union League demonstrated. The Dublin football folk stayed in their seats when Corcoran followed. However, Rooney was isolated and losing the battle within 80 Merrion Square, so he decided to appeal to a wider audience with an appearance on RTÉ's *Liveline* on 28 October 2004. It took up Joe Duffy's entire show. Rooney alleged he was the victim of a 'witch-hunt' and addressed a number of the allegations made against him.

'There's a spin going around about tickets,' Rooney said. 'Depending on which newspaper you read I owe anything from €10,000 to €50,000. That's simply not true. I don't owe a cent. Fran Rooney doesn't owe a cent to the FAI for tickets.'

And the bill for Restaurant Patrick Guilbaud? 'I dropped a cheque in to Patrick for that and that's the end of the story,' Rooney said. 'It's nothing to do with the FAI. It's a personal matter between myself and Patrick.'

Duffy tentatively asked about Rooney's socializing habits. 'I like a pint as much as the next man,' Rooney said, but explained that long days in the FAI left him with little down time.

The legendary centre-half Paul McGrath was amongst those who called in offering their support for Rooney. 'He's someone who wants to do the job and do it properly, and I just don't understand why the FAI are not allowing this man, a genuine guy, do the actual job.'

Most of the other callers were also supportive of Rooney, but within the FAI those arguments were falling on deaf ears. The FAI Council was considering the complaints made by the three senior employees, and Rooney was completely outmanoeuvred by Delaney when it came to getting the votes in the room.

Rooney says he was assured by many FAI Council delegates that they would not vote for the proposal to set up an internal committee to investigate complaints against him. He recalls that just seventeen out of the fifty-six entitled to vote actually voted in favour of setting up the committee. 'So I think, "It's not going to pass,"' says Rooney.

He was shocked when it was announced that just three had voted against the proposal. There were some thirty abstentions. He was left to conclude that the abstainers had 'all been got at'.

The three-man committee to investigate the complaints was made up of the Vice-President, David Blood, Cody and another board member, Eddie Murray. The committee was dismissed in the *Sunday Times* as merely adding 'another list of puppets to the central casting'. A lengthy piece by John O'Brien was illustrated with a picture of Brian Kerr shaking hands with John Delaney and both men grinning wildly, with the headline: 'Meet the most powerful man in Irish football: he's the one on the right.' The one on the right was Delaney.

'Offstage, where the main plot unfolds, the masters can spin away to their heart's content,' O'Brien wrote. 'And in the forums and bar-stool discussions of Irish football, one name looms large when the FAI enters the arena: John Delaney.'

O'Brien painted a picture of a man who had been chastened by his defeat over the appointment of Kerr, but who had silently been regrouping: 'What rankles many is this: for fifteen of the past twenty years a Delaney has controlled the purse strings of the FAI and in an organization where finance has always been a testy subject, that constitutes an endless source of acrimony.'

Rooney thought about mounting a legal challenge to the internal investigation, but instead decided that he wanted out, and engaged a top employment barrister, Ercus Stewart SC.

Rooney remembers his exchange with Stewart as follows:

'How much do you want?'

'Two years' salary.'

'What's your salary?'

'Two hundred and fifty thousand euro.'

'They won't pay half a million!'

'They will.'

And they did, bringing an end to seventeen fractious months of Rooney rule, at a huge price.

*

Cody, as Honorary Secretary, should have stepped into the role of interim CEO under the terms of the FAI's constitution. However, he made it clear he was not interested. Nobody tried to persuade him otherwise. And he had an outstanding candidate in mind.

Everyone assumed that Delaney wanted the job, but he gave the impression of not being sure. He told some people that his hands were already full, or that he did not know whether it was the right time. On his regular trips to Dublin from Waterford, Delaney had developed a habit of ringing five people from the grassroots of the game on the way up and another five people on the way back – just for a chat and to see if there was anything he could do for them. This was the constituency which now wanted him to run the association.

Delaney had sold off most of his business interests in the previous year, including a coffee-vending machine operation and a waste-management company in Waterford, and his furniture business in Athlone. The divestment had been done relatively swiftly. But then there was the curious case of Novian International, trading as Healthcare Waste Management Services.

Businessman Brian Rogers set up the business in 1998, to collect and dispose of medical waste from private clinics and care homes. When he was seeking a financial expert who could help him raise funds and run the financial side of the business, an acquaintance pointed him in Delaney's direction.

After meeting him and hearing about his varied business experience and accountancy background, Rogers offered Delaney a 49 per cent stake in the new company. Delaney helped to get a commercial loan from AIB in Waterford, and provided invoice and revenue collection services.

However, Rogers began to have concerns after Delaney sent him the first set of annual management accounts for the business. He was shocked to discover that Delaney was not a chartered accountant. 'The accounts were signed off by a guy in Ballinasloe,' says Rogers. 'I asked John why he hadn't done them. He told me he hadn't done the certificate, so although he'd done the numbers he couldn't sign off on them. I said, "Christ, John. No cert? That's why you're here."'

Rogers let it pass. But he became increasingly wary. 'I remember seeing €5,000 or €6,000 coming out [of our bank account] to sponsor Waterford in the League of Ireland,' Rogers said. 'John had said, "We must do some sponsorship of Waterford," and I might have said, "Sure, we could do something." I felt he had taken advantage, as I wasn't personally asked. I let it go.'

The final straw came when Rogers served notice to quit on one of his main customers, whom he felt was unwilling to pay a fair price for the provision of nine trucks and drivers servicing the contract. Rogers was furious when he discovered that Delaney had negotiated to do the same deal with his former client on behalf of a different logistics firm.

Rogers threatened to sue and make public his grievances with Delaney. A meeting was set for the Dolmen hotel in Carlow town. Delaney resigned his directorship of the company, and agreed to hand over his 49 per cent stake in the profitable company for free.

But there was a sting in the tail for Rogers. New accountants for the company found it had not paid tax on Delaney's director's fees. 'We owed Revenue €27,000,' says Rogers. 'I went down to Revenue and agreed to pay it over sixteen months. The company was liable. He was gone. He had handled the finances. I was then the sole shareholder. It cost me a lot of money.'

It wouldn't be the last time Delaney's actions would leave an employer facing a hefty Revenue bill.

*

Brian Rogers believes he 'survived' Delaney because he 'faced him down'. There was nobody left around in the FAI to do the same.

However, opposition came from outside the association. The Chief Executive of the Irish Sports Council, John Treacy, who had been having meetings on virtually a monthly basis with the FAI about the implementation of the Genesis report, expressed his unhappiness about the pace of change.

Following Rooney's departure, the government announced it was suspending €500,000 in annual public funding because of the lack of progress in reforms. Over at Government Buildings, sports minister John O'Donoghue was tearing his hair out again. In his view, the FAI needed to 'grow up'. 'They have lost three chief executive officers appointed in the last four years,' he told reporters. 'The general public has lost confidence in the FAI and formed the view it is in disarray.'

The FAI kept digging. On 11 November 2004, the FAI Council met at the Citywest hotel and Delaney was formally offered, and accepted, the post of interim Chief Executive. 'How long is interim?' Milo Corcoran was asked by reporters on the steps of Merrion Square: 'How long is a piece of string?' he replied. On the same day, the Department of Sport officials said that neither the government nor the Sports Council would hold any meetings with the FAI unless the association agreed to advertise the posts of Chief Executive and Finance Director before 1 January 2005.

In a Q&A with Dion Fanning in the *Sunday Independent* on 28 November, Delaney promised his leadership would herald the end of chaotic times in the FAI, while admitting he saw himself in the job on a long-term basis.

'The problem has been the administration of 80 Merrion Square and the difficulties that have surrounded it,' Delaney said. 'What I'm hoping we can do over the interim period and, if I'm successful, over a longer period, is go back to being a more quiet, business-like, professional organization, as simple as that.'

He insisted that almost unanimous support from grassroots organizers had persuaded him to seek the job. 'There was also the view that I was in the shadows and it was time to step up to the plate,' he said.

'There is an idea that the reason you withdrew your backing [for Rooney] was because he was putting pressure on people close to you,' said Fanning.

Delaney replied, 'The only thing I'll say on this subject is that it was not a political row within the organization, at all.'

Fanning put it to Delaney that he was taking the job because there was something to hide in the FAI's financial records. Delaney rejected the charge, pointing out that the FAI's finances were audited by Deloitte & Touche, the second largest accountancy firm in the world.

'We've been audited and audited and audited,' he insisted.

The advertisement for the CEO position appeared in the press on 30 and 31 December:

> The Chief Executive will be responsible to the board for managing, operating and developing the Football Association of Ireland. He/she will lead a management team within the organization to oversee and deliver the necessary changes required to enhance the effectiveness and efficiency of a modern, international sporting organization. The Chief Executive will have overall responsibility for a significant number of staff and for managing the Association's finances . . . The remuneration and benefits package will be set to attract candidates of the highest calibre.

State funding was restored, but at the highest level of government there was still considerable unease about the interim CEO. This was relayed to John Byrne, who had returned to the FAI fold after Rooney left and was trying to sell Delaney's appointment to the government.

Bertie Ahern and John O'Donoghue had concerns about Delaney, but Byrne had Delaney's back in private chats with the senior ministers. 'I said, "Well, he's the man for the job at the moment,"' Byrne recalls. 'Bertie had more doubts than O'Donoghue. Bertie could sniff a wide boy just like that. He had a sixth fuckin' sense. It's nothing that you could put your finger on. Bertie would say: "Ah, Jaysus Christ, are you fuckin' sure about this fella?" One night, Delaney hooked Bertie at a match, he was hugging him after a goal. I was having the cup of tea at half time and Bertie gave me the eye [as if to say] "Get that fuckin' eejit away from me."'

Eight candidates were interviewed for the post. The government took the unusual step of putting the powerful Assistant Secretary at the Department of Sport, Con Haugh, on the interview board, along with an independent chairman – the Dublin City manager John Fitzgerald – and a representative from the Sports Council. The FAI, represented by Cody and Corcoran, were in a minority.

Delaney had given himself a good head start over his rival candidates. As interim CEO he had tied up a new kit deal with Umbro Ireland, patching up the relationship with the company that had been so strained by Rooney's botched apparel scheme.

If Ahern had serious doubts about Delaney, he was in a minority. It took only one set of interviews for John Delaney to be confirmed as Chief Executive on a permanent basis on 11 March 2005. The salary was €290,000 per annum. He was thirty-seven years old.

4. 33,000 Millionaires

'I'm going to shock you here now,' says John Byrne, 'but in the first eighteen months he was brilliant. Everything was done for the right reasons.'

After being out in the cold under Rooney, Byrne was back, and other changes were afoot. David Blood was the first person from the United Churches League to become FAI President, which made him a trailblazer, in one way. Blood had the right demeanour for somebody coming from the 'altar boy' league and he quickly found the moral high ground by announcing that he would not be taking a salary. He didn't want his hand greased, but he wouldn't be hands-on either.

Succeeding Delaney as Honorary Treasurer was Eddie Murray, a personable retired garda superintendent from Monaghan. Delaney had asked Murray to be his replacement, and no one else had put himself forward for the historically powerful role. It was clear that Murray had neither the aptitude nor the desire to be as hands-on as his predecessor. All this was agreed at the FAI's 2005 AGM in Waterford, at which no elections were needed for the posts to be filled.

'Everyone should get a chance to have a senior position in the organization and that's what happened today,' Delaney explained, full of patrician goodwill on his home patch. 'It's just democracy. It just shows the sense of maturity about the organization.'

The important work was done by Delaney in weekly meetings with Byrne and Declan Conroy, who had previously worked as an adviser to Delaney and was now on board as director of communications and strategy.

The consultants Genesis were also back, with a report on the future of the League of Ireland that recommended a complete merger between the domestic professional game and the FAI, which would include strict participation agreements and tight wage controls. Again Delaney agreed to implement all the recommendations. It helped that Delaney developed a good relationship with Fran Gavin, the head of the Irish professional footballers' union the PFAI.

The players wanted standard contracts to protect them over issues such as non-payment of salary, image rights and disciplinary processes. Despite years of pressure up to 2006, the PFAI felt the FAI had never engaged seriously on the issue, with various committees forming and disbanding before making progress. Stephen McGuinness, a League of Ireland veteran who was active in the PFAI, felt it might take a strike to force the issue until Delaney arrived on the scene.

'When Delaney got into power and got speaking to Fran the contract was implemented within six weeks,' says McGuinness. 'Done. There was no red tape any more. There were no more bullshit meetings. I was thinking, "This is the guy who's going to pave the way for professional football in Ireland. He sees it. He gets it."'

Delaney was so impressed with Gavin that he hired him as the FAI's Director of the League of Ireland shortly after agreeing to implement a standard players' contract. McGuinness then took over as PFAI General Secretary.

The most important piece of business on the agenda remained the vexed question of finding a home for Irish football – preferably one the FAI would not have to pay for. That ambition was dealt a fatal blow by hostility to the 'Bertie Bowl' from the powerful junior party in government, the Progressive Democrats. Instead, the government made a commitment to subsidize a new stadium at a venue yet to be confirmed. All signs pointed to the redevelopment of the dilapidated Lansdowne Road, the home of the IRFU, where the FAI played most of its senior internationals. Public money would be released to part-fund the redevelopment of the stadium if the landlord/tenant relationship changed and the FAI was given a major stake in the new stadium.

This was an area where Rooney had been proactive, and in January 2004 the IRFU and FAI announced plans for a €250-million redevelopment of the stadium. By October 2005, the FAI and the IRFU had agreed a number of upgrades – including a VIP car park under the stadium – which raised the cost of the stadium to €410 million; the government stake was €191 million, with the rest to be provided by the two sporting organizations.

How could the FAI afford its commitment, which was around €90 million? One source of income was the impending sale of the Merrion Square headquarters to the businessman Lochlann Quinn for €9 million. Based on projections for advance season-ticket sales, the FAI secured a bridging loan of €40 million from National Irish Bank, with interest payable at the bank's prime rate, for the development of the stadium and the administration and marketing costs of ticket sales. There was a further €10 million 'revolving loan' to fund general working capital requirements.

That level of detail wasn't publicly known at the time, but Delaney's dealings with the banks were seen as impressive manoeuvring. He then displayed his decisiveness in another piece of business: ending Brian Kerr's tenure as Republic of Ireland manager.

Kerr remained a popular public figure, but he had a spiky side that didn't endear him to everybody in the association. When managing the youth teams on away trips, Kerr had alienated some accompanying board members by complaining they were taking up places that could have gone to players. Kerr also objected when Delaney as Honorary Treasurer curbed the budget for under-age internationals, which had been increasing in number and cost as the teams became more successful. Kerr knew that Delaney had been against his appointment as senior manager and the relationship remained cold.

As manager, Kerr liked to get his hands dirty with the development side of the game, touring the country with the Technical Director Packie Bonner as they devised a new plan for Irish football. When the plan was launched at the Burlington hotel in June 2004, Delaney was conspicuous by his absence.

Kerr sought to mould Irish football, a responsibility he felt came with the job of being senior team manager. He wanted the under-21 manager Don Givens replaced, because of his poor record in the job, but instead Delaney gave a new contract to the former Ireland international, one of his go-to men in the association.

Delaney turned to the FAI kit man, Johnny Fallon, who had known Kerr for twenty years and was also friendly with Joe Delaney. 'I was driving with my missus to our holiday home in Wexford,' says Fallon. 'My phone rang. It was Delaney.' They exchanged pleasantries, then

Fallon remembers Delaney asking: 'How are you getting on with Brian?'

'We're friends a long time, John.'

'What's he like in the dressing room?'

'John, don't put me in this spot.'

'I heard he is a little bit weak with the lads.'

'I wouldn't say that.'

'Do you think he is more suited to dealing with younger players?'

'Look, he's the senior manager. He's my boss.'

'No, I'm your boss.'

Fallon recalls: 'He always said that. I told him I was uncomfortable with the conversation, but I never told Brian.'

In March 2005 the senior team travelled to Tel Aviv for a game against Israel, accompanied by the under-21s, who had a match of their own the night before. The travelling FAI party attended the under-21 match and sat under one of the stands while Kerr and some members of the senior team watched from elsewhere. Delaney showed fellow directors angry texts he said were from Kerr, berating him because the blazers were in the shade while the senior team watched under a hot sun.

After a 2–0 victory in the Faroe Islands in June 2005, which left Ireland top of their World Cup qualifying group with three games left, Kerr complained that he had been left 'dangling' over a new contract, with his present one due to run out at the end of the campaign. It was clear that the FAI was going to wait until the conclusion of qualifying before deciding whether to offer Kerr a new two-year term.

In late September, Kerr posed for a GOAL charity event, alongside some other prominent sporting figures and Bertie Ahern. Kerr was wearing the jersey of his old club, St Patrick's Athletic, which was emblazoned with the logo of the club's sponsor, Smart Telecom. A complaint was apparently made by the FAI's flagship sponsor, Eircom, and Kerr was spoken to by Delaney. Kerr made it known that he was deeply upset by the episode and felt undermined.

The campaign ended on 12 October with a disappointing home draw against Switzerland, leaving Ireland fourth in the group, well short of qualification for the 2006 World Cup in Germany. Ominously, there was no communication between the CEO and the manager in the immediate aftermath. A week later, the Board of Management assembled at the Great Southern hotel, Dublin airport.

Kerr's fate was decided in the Abbey Conference Room on the ground floor at the back of the hotel. Paddy McCaul, an FAI board member, says that Delaney and Michael Cody were the main instigators of Kerr's removal, but Kerr's supporters were only about three in a group of ten.

McCaul remembers Delaney and Cody coming into the meeting with a 'dossier' about Kerr. The St Pat's jersey he'd worn, with the Smart Telecom logo, was mentioned. There were a few people genuinely not so happy with him. Martin O'Neill's name was being bandied about. He was then on a sabbatical. There was a feeling that if Brian had to go, then someone like O'Neill we could live with. But there wasn't a vote. [Delaney] never wanted a vote. The word consensus was always used. He didn't want anyone outside thinking there might be anyone against it.'

Delaney rang Kerr's agent, Fintan Drury, to tell him that his client's contract was not being renewed. The media had been waiting in the lobby and hallways of the hotel for hours, confident that the board members were hemmed in. As the meeting came to an end, the assembled media were ushered into the Aviation Room for a press conference. Hotel staff had set up three or four chairs at the top table for the press conference. Somebody from the FAI then told them only one was needed. A balding head peeped out from the Abbey Room. Was the coast clear? Not quite.

Delaney then swept in to meet the press, sucking in a couple of stragglers, and the door of the Aviation Room closed behind him. The same head peeped out of the Abbey again. An empty corridor. Out from the Abbey hastened the nine other members of the board, fixing their coats and hats as they stole off into the night; amongst them was David Blood, the official head of the association who as FAI President would normally have been expected to lead the press conference.

John Delaney was more than capable of dealing with the press on his own. Speaking to the media, Delaney was pundit one moment – 'The style of person I'd like to see would be somebody who can get the best out of the players we have, somebody who can make tactical adjustments when required at the highest level' – and disgruntled fan the next – 'There was no fear in their eyes,' he said of the Swiss team. 'The most interesting remark came from Damien Duff, who said we were playing like a pub team.'

Delaney quoting Duff in such a manner was rubbing salt into the wounds, as the winger had come through Kerr's highly successful youth teams and was considered one of his protégés. Kerr was angry that he hadn't been given the opportunity to address the board at the airport before they booked him a one-way ticket to oblivion. He complained that the FAI's attitude towards him had changed since March, which happened to be the month when Delaney's appointment became full time.

Ousted from his dream job, Kerr was too big to go back to the League of Ireland, while in Britain his profile was that of failed Ireland manager. It was thought there would be a role for him in UEFA, where his achievements at under-age level meant he was frequently called upon to address coaching seminars. He was friendly with Andy Roxburgh, the former Scotland manager turned UEFA Technical Director. However, Emmet Malone in the *Irish Times* reported that when Roxburgh pencilled Kerr in for a place on a UEFA technical analysis group, the move was vetoed by the FAI.

*

As well as a 'world-class' new stadium at Lansdowne Road, Delaney now promised a 'world-class' manager to succeed Kerr. The day after Kerr's sacking, Delaney sat down with Blood and Cody in his office in Merrion Square. There were two blank sheets of A4 paper in front of them. On one, they jotted down the qualities they were looking for in the next Ireland manager; on the other they wrote down a list of people they thought fitted the bill. At the top were Alex Ferguson, who was going through a rocky period at Manchester United, and Martin O'Neill. Further down were the likes of Terry Venables, David Moyes and Steve Bruce, Premier League managers whose jobs were under threat. Towards the bottom were former Ireland players like John Aldridge, Frank Stapleton and Kevin Moran. Steve Staunton, an assistant coach at Walsall in the English Midlands, a side in the third tier of English football, was also on the list – quite high up on Delaney's, because of the leadership qualities he had shown in Saipan, when he had taken over the captaincy from Keane and successfully galvanized the players.

The Ferguson dream evaporated instantly, and O'Neill quickly ruled himself out of the running when he came over to Dublin to promote the launch of a bookmaker.

Johnny Fallon, the kit man and scout who had worked with Terry Venables at Spurs, says he was asked by Delaney to approach Venables. 'I knew Venables would be interested, but he doesn't apply for jobs,' says Fallon. 'I rang Venables and said I wasn't sure which way it was going, but it looks like the Irish job could be a very interesting project.'

Fallon told Venables to expect a phone call, but it never came.

The three FAI men went to see Staunton at his home in Birmingham in November. 'Passion' had become the buzzword. And having spoken to Staunton, Delaney had come to the conclusion that the Louth man had it, albeit he needed an older hand at his side. He suggested to Staunton that he work with a mentor.

Niall Quinn was another big backer of Staunton at the time, also citing the 'passion' that was missing under the previous regime. When he was contacted by his former teammate, Quinn put forward the name of the former England and Newcastle manager Sir Bobby Robson to guide the novice along. Quinn, once more the go-between, then made the phone call to Robson, who was seventy-two and had recovered from two serious bouts of cancer, but was still keen to come on board. The reservations of the Technical Director, Packie Bonner, who felt Staunton didn't have the experience for the job, were ignored.

Kerr's unveiling at the Shelbourne hotel had felt like a coronation. Staunton's three years later around the corner in the Round Room of the Mansion House was very different. A supporter who had brazened his way into the press conference stood up and delivered a eulogy to the new manager and berated the press, who were sceptical about what was now being described by the FAI as a 'world-class management team' and wondered who was really in charge. The knight of the realm was asked by reporters did he want to be called Sir Bobby or just Bobby. 'Bobby will do,' Robson said. A nervous

Staunton declared his own title. 'I'm the boss. I'm the gaffer. At the end of the day what I say goes – the buck stops with me.'

Staunton's tenure started with a series of three friendly matches. Eamon Dunphy called for his head after the third, a 4–0 defeat at home to Holland.

Staunton got a free pass for Ireland's first competitive game under his tenure – a single-goal defeat to Germany in Stuttgart in a European Championship qualifier. In the build-up to the next game, against Cyprus, Delaney backed Staunton: 'We have appointed a manager for four years. We welcome his use of younger players and we have to support the manager, who is there for the long-term strategy of the game. He's been given a four-year contract to see the next two campaigns out and I see no reason why he shouldn't.' However, disaster struck in Nicosia, as Ireland were thrashed 5–2 by a country they had beaten in their six previous encounters.

Roy Keane had described Staunton and Quinn as 'muppets' over Saipan, so the *Irish Sun* now depicted the Ireland manager as Kermit the Frog on its front page. A *Sun* reporter came to the training ground dressed as Miss Piggy.

Not to be outdone, the *Irish Star on Sunday* portrayed Staunton and Delaney as Laurel and Hardy below the headline 'Another Fine Mess'. Builders whistled the Stan and Ollie theme tune at Staunton on the street. 'Stan', as the Ireland manager was popularly known, was under huge pressure, but there was some relief when his team managed a 1–1 draw at home to a strong Czech Republic side four days after the Cyprus debacle and Delaney came to Staunton's aid, sort of.

'The media need to be questioned. There were new standards and new lows again this week, Kermit the Frog stuff, muppeteering,' Delaney wrote in the *Sunday Tribune* on 15 October 2006, before reminding everyone: 'I'd like it noted that I wasn't the only one to appoint Stephen Staunton. There was a sub-committee that was ratified and the people who were involved and had an important role in the appointment were really disappointed in the overreaction from some sectors. They were saying if John Delaney's getting stick, so should we.'

Regarding the Laurel and Hardy jibe, Delaney sent a solicitor's letter to the *Irish Star on Sunday*. Its editor, Des Gibson, asked if Delaney would meet him. They hammered the problem out so thoroughly that they ended up agreeing to collaborate on Delaney's autobiography. Delaney would keep regular written notes of his time as CEO over the next decade, often telling people they would get the full story on the controversy of the day when his book was published by Gibson's publishing firm.

It didn't go quite so swimmingly for Delaney at the annual Soccer Writers' Association of Ireland (SWAI) banquet held at the Park Inn, Dundalk, in January 2007. SWAI President Neil O'Riordan, the *Irish Sun*'s football writer, delivered a critical speech on the state of the Irish game in front of Delaney, Staunton and others. O'Riordan spoke of 'a steep learning curve for Steve Staunton'. He also referred to the new system where League of Ireland clubs weren't supposed to be given a licence to play unless they were financially viable: 'One licensed club went out of business mid-season [Dublin City] and another [Shelbourne] went on to win the league, but was unable to pay its players.' After mentioning some Irish club success in Europe, he said he 'wanted to end on an upbeat note before the League's new director, Fran Gavin, hits the bottle wondering what he has let himself in for'.

Delaney, fuming, refused to speak to O'Riordan when he returned to his place at their table, but the riposte was not long in coming. In an email addressed to O'Riordan, with the seventy-odd SWAI members copied in, he said:

> I particularly took grave exception to your specific remarks about League of Ireland Director Fran Gavin and Senior International Manager Stephen Staunton . . . I do not believe that the President of the Gaelic Writers' Association, the Rugby Writers' Association or the Golf Writers' Association would have allowed their guests from the IRFU, GAA or GUI to be treated in the manner that those representing the Football Association of Ireland were subjected to on Friday night.

Shelbourne, the League of Ireland champions, had seriously breached the club licensing rules and were facing relegation after a huge points deduction – a punishment Delaney wanted to avert. Delaney asked John Byrne to get on the phone to the chairman of the licensing committee, Donagh Morgan, who was also a civil servant in the Department of Sport, on secondment at the national sports campus. Byrne refused, telling Delaney: 'You will rue the day you take him on.'

Delaney phoned Morgan himself. Morgan recalls: 'He was basically making the point that if we were to deduct points from Shelbourne it would put the club in a non-viable situation, and with the business deals that were going on in the background this really shouldn't happen. I responded that my understanding was that this would be an independent role and that if that was inconvenient for him I was happy to step aside.'

Delaney retreated and the League of Ireland champions were duly relegated.

The national team's next game was away to San Marino, who had suffered a record 13–0 defeat in their previous home game, against Germany. Staunton's side made hard work of the minnows and a growing number of supporters who travelled to the microstate near the Italian city of Rimini had come to the conclusion that the buck stopped with Delaney, despite his protestations to the contrary. The Chief Executive sat uneasily in his VIP seat in the tiny Stadio Olimpico in Serravalle. There were chants of 'Delaney Must Go', and a 'Delaney Out' banner was unveiled. Abuse was directed at the players afterwards as Ireland scraped to a 2–1 victory with a goal in the ninety-fifth minute.

A crowd of 72,539 turned up for Ireland's first game at Croke Park in March 2007, a European Championship qualifier against Wales. The record attendance for an Irish soccer match demonstrated that there was still huge interest in the game in Ireland, though it cost the FAI around €1.5 million a game to rent the facility from the GAA, which had changed its rules to allow soccer and rugby to be played at the ground while Lansdowne Road was being rebuilt.

The IRFU Chief Executive, Philip Browne, and Delaney gave a joint press conference in September 2007 to report on the redevelopment of Lansdowne Road, where the old stands had now been reduced to rubble. Both associations were relying largely on the sales of ten-year tickets to finance their share of the construction costs. Browne announced that the IRFU's ten-year ticket offer had sold out, over-subscribed only months after being offered to the market.

The FAI was nowhere near that point. Delaney had engaged a company called Comperio to conduct market research, and he said the initial findings showed strong demand for premium seats and boxes. He told the press the FAI would announce the findings of the research in late October and begin marketing tickets at the beginning of 2008. It was the first in a series of FAI stadium targets that weren't to be met.

Later that month, in Slovakia for a Euro 2008 qualifier, Delaney and other FAI directors experienced the growing anger of some Irish supporters. 'The car was taking us to the match behind the team bus,' says Paddy McCaul. 'And the fans nearly turned over the car. The Irish fans were rocking the car back. John was visibly shaken that night.'

The match was a 2–2 draw. Midfielder Stephen Ireland left the squad immediately after the game, saying his grandmother had died. He was flown home in a private jet, paid for by the FAI. He gave the FAI her name and the association released the details. When Ireland's granny piped up to assert she was still alive, Ireland said it was his other grandmother. 'I was up half the night [sorting it out],' Staunton told the media. 'It's not on his mother's side, it's on his father's side. We were given the wrong information.'

Hardly ideal preparation for a game against the Czech Republic in Prague four days later, which Ireland lost 1–0. Afterwards, it emerged that neither of Ireland's grandmothers had died, but his partner had suffered a miscarriage. Everybody agreed to leave it at that.

*

That Irish football was once again a laughing stock while rugby had seemingly gotten its act together in the professional era was a source of some frustration to three figures lunching at the Hôtel Ritz in Paris on 21 September 2007, the day Ireland took on France in the Rugby World Cup. They were David O'Leary, the former Republic of Ireland international who had managed in the Premier League with Leeds United and Aston Villa, Eddie Jordan, the Formula 1 impresario, who was also enjoying a period of leisure, and Denis O'Brien, a billionaire businessman from south Dublin.

O'Brien was grappling with the IRFU over a home for his rugby club, Wanderers, whose clubhouse at Lansdowne Road had been demolished as part of the redevelopment, and he was keen to help the FAI. Jordan felt that what was needed was for the FAI to pay top dollar to get a top manager – such as O'Leary. Raising his hands, O'Leary demurred, but O'Brien liked the idea in principle.

'Denis felt the team was going the wrong way and he could do something to improve it,' O'Leary recalls. 'All he wanted to do was put something into the pot to help the FAI. His attitude was, "I might like somebody, i.e. David O'Leary, but that is not my place." It wasn't a case of "I'm coming in here and I have all this money, but it has all those restrictions with it." No. The man has got more class than that.'

When O'Brien returned to Dublin, he got Delaney's number from his friend Kieran Mulvey, the chairman of the Labour Relations Commission. Although Delaney initially thought it was a prank call, the two men met and O'Brien was impressed by Delaney and what he was trying to do – so much so that he agreed to subsidize the appointment of a world-class manager, if one could be found.

By the time Cyprus came to Croke Park on 17 October, it was clear that Staunton's side would have to win, convincingly, if he was to have a chance of staying in his job. Instead the team stuttered to an embarrassing draw. The 'Delaney Out' banners reappeared, but this time they were removed by stewards.

The Chief Executive effectively washed his hands of the manager afterwards. 'It's unfortunate that I've been personally linked to the appointment [of Staunton],' he said. 'It was a sub-committee of three, which was ratified by the board of the FAI, which is a committee of ten.'

People didn't buy it. Delaney was now being mocked up in the *Irish Sun* as Gonzo from *The Muppet Show*. 'When people do things like that, they should consider people like your mam and dad,' Delaney told Marian Finucane on RTÉ. Finucane asked him how his mother had taken it. 'Not well, to be fair to her.'

A week later, the media were tipped off that the FAI board were
meeting at the Crowne Plaza hotel in Santry, north Dublin. At
the hotel, two conference rooms were booked in the name of the
Finance Director, Mark O'Leary, according to the electronic moni-
tors in the hotel. In Room 14 were twelve leatherette chairs set
around a large conference table; two large plates of chicken tikka and
ham salad sandwiches were on a side table alongside four pots of
steaming coffee.

While journalists gathered at the Crowne Plaza, the real action
took place two miles away. Steve Staunton was staying in Room 322
of the Radisson hotel at Dublin airport, also booked in the name of
Mark O'Leary, and minded by the FAI's security man, Bobby Ward.
He was visited by an FAI delegation of Delaney, Blood and Cody.
Staunton insisted that he be allowed to address the board, which was
assembling surreptitiously at Bewley's airport hotel, just as a live
report from Tony O'Donoghue was being broadcast on RTÉ's *Six
One News* outside the Crowne Plaza.

At Bewley's hotel, Delaney addressed the board and admitted he'd
made a mistake in the appointment of a rookie manager. Staunton
himself was admitted to the room along with Alan Kelly, his goalkeeping coach. Staunton addressed the meeting. 'He went around
each person at the table and asked "Why do you think I shouldn't be
the manager?"' says board member Eamon Naughton. 'I idolized
Steve Staunton. I travelled around Europe supporting the team. I
found it to be very hard and I felt sorry for him, but the general
consensus was he had to go.'

Staunton left the board meeting. Then, when the meeting ended,
Delaney, Blood and Cody met Staunton in another room formally
to relieve him of his duties, discuss compensation and agree on the
release of a statement, which would say that Staunton's contract was
being terminated 'by mutual consent'.

Finally, the FAI trio set off for the Crowne Plaza. It was 1.15 a.m.
and some reporters had been waiting for more than ten hours. The
prelude to the arrival of the FAI delegation was the sight of two
waiters emerging from Room 14, one carrying a tray of curled sandwiches, the other the four wasted pots of coffee.

Delaney was asked how a repeat of the Staunton disaster could be avoided. 'We're going to try to find the people with the right professional expertise to go and make the appointment if you like,' said Delaney. 'They will come up with one name. We will then ratify that regardless of any reservations. It will be completely external.

'It allows people like myself to get on with administrating the game. I regard myself now on reflection as a good strong administrator in what I do and the proof is there of that. But certainly getting involved in the process of appointing a new manager I wouldn't see as a core competency for me.'

*

What *was* Delaney's core competency? He was starting to make waves in UEFA, having been elected to their Disciplinary Committee. In the summer of 2007, he helped UEFA President Michel Platini with the arrangements for a three-week English-language course at Trinity College. Platini attended the official opening of the new FAI headquarters in Abbotstown in December 2007 and was given a tour by Delaney and Packie Bonner.

Delaney showed Platini his office, a three-room suite, by far the biggest in the building. Inspecting his private bathroom, Platini remarked half-jokingly that this must be the FAI President's office. No, Delaney assured him, it was his. Platini raised an eyebrow. In UEFA's eyes, the elected President was still the most powerful figure in any football association and the allocation of office space should reflect as much. Des Casey, the former UEFA Vice-President, could have explained to Platini that things were now working differently in Ireland; but Casey hadn't been invited to the opening ceremony, and he watched Platini's visit on the news from his home in Dundalk.

The opening ceremony for the Abbotstown HQ was due to be performed by the sports minister Séamus Brennan, but Delaney had a late change of heart.

'At 4.30 p.m. that afternoon he told me that he didn't want Brennan to perform the opening, he wanted Platini to do it,' says John Byrne. 'I lost it and said, "This is fucking crazy, John. The government are after providing us with suites of offices. This is the minister who funded it and you want Monsieur Platini to come over." '

Delaney wanted Byrne to smooth it over with the ministry's civil servants. Again, Byrne refused. 'He rang Con Haugh [Secretary General at the Department of Sport] because I wouldn't ring him. Con just blew him out of the water and told him there would be nobody from the government there and there would be no more fuckin' money either.'

Delaney's sphere of influence was clearly not as wide as he wanted it to be. Byrne recalls: 'I got on great with Bertie [Ahern] and I don't think I ever asked him for anything that he didn't give me. That used to drive yer man fuckin' mad. There were a couple of times we ran into problems and I would ring Bertie and we got it sorted. John couldn't abide that. Nobody could have an "in" unless he [Delaney] had an "in". That's what started the drift. He wanted to be the guy going round the country giving out the grants and the good news. I said, "You can't be promising money that isn't yours," and he didn't like that either.'

*

Bolstered by O'Brien's financial pledge, which was a secret at that time, the FAI was thinking big when it came to choosing Staunton's successor. The RTÉ panellist Liam Brady sounded out the legendary Italian manager Giovanni Trapattoni.

Johnny Fallon was asked to sound out Terry Venables again, which he did, though reluctantly this time, having done so to no apparent purpose during the previous managerial vacancy. Venables agreed to be interviewed by the FAI's official head-hunting committee, which consisted of the former Ireland international Ray Houghton, the under-21 manager Don Givens and the former England and Arsenal coach Don Howe.

Venables was the choice of a large rump of the players when Delaney canvassed their opinion. But when Eamon Dunphy, who knew Venables from their days together as players' union delegates, launched a scathing attack on RTÉ regarding his history of dubious financial dealings, it resonated strongly with Delaney and others in the FAI.

'They'd no intention of hiring Terry,' says Fallon. 'I remember meeting the late Milo [Corcoran] at the airport hotel. I said at long last we might get a big-name manager. He asked who and I said "Terry Venables."'

According to Fallon, Corcoran said, '"He's no chance of getting it."'

The three official headhunters were directed towards Austria. There, the sixty-eight-year-old Trapattoni – no longer an A-lister in European club management terms – was manager of Red Bull Salzburg. The three men ended up in Trapattoni's luxury apartment overlooking the River Salzach sipping wine, nibbling slices of salami and chatting to the manager with one of the best CVs in world football. An agreement was reached that Trapattoni would take over when the Austrian league season ended.

The appointment was greeted with astonishment back in Dublin, and it was only when Givens and Houghton held a press conference at Abbotstown in the company of Delaney that Denis O'Brien's involvement emerged. It was revealed the millionaire would be paying a substantial portion of Trapattoni's reported €2 million annual salary. Trapattoni was eventually released from his Salzburg commitments early and was unveiled at a lavish launch at the RDS Concert Hall. Trapattoni wasn't a big man, but he filled the huge stage with his presence. Strangely, Delaney wasn't up there with him, but sat in the front row of the audience, grinning widely.

*

Delaney felt the time had arrived to push the button on the ten-year season-ticket scheme that he hoped would pay for the majority of the FAI's €90-million outlay on the new stadium – and even leave the FAI with plenty of spare change, if everything went according to plan. The plan was to sell around 10,000 such tickets – nearly twice the number the IRFU had sold.

The FAI rehired the global sports management company IMG to handle the sale through a London-based offshoot, ISG (International Stadia Group). In the interim, ISG had made a success of selling the ten-year ticket scheme at the rebuilt home of English football in a scheme called Club Wembley, confounding widespread scepticism by finding ready buyers at premium prices from amongst what Roy Keane had once labelled 'the prawn-sandwich brigade'.

Coming back for a second attempt at cracking the Dublin market was a high-flying Irish executive called Diarmuid Crowley, who had worked on the Eircom Park project in tandem with another IMG executive, Rory Smyth, who was now the FAI's Commercial Manager. Back in the day, Crowley had been invited by Bernard O'Byrne to address the FAI executive and found his most hostile interrogator to be Delaney.

The relationship was still a somewhat uneasy one. When IMG's involvement in the Lansdowne Road project emerged, it was in the context of reports, later confirmed, about a proposed deal for the company to pay a flat fee of between €80 and €90 million for exclusive rights to the 10,000 ten-year tickets. Others involved in the consortium were the American bank Wachovia and Clearbrook Capital. The deal was never done, with Delaney later blaming the 2008 financial crisis for scuppering the interest from the American banks. Instead, Delaney gambled on the association being able to sell the tickets itself, using IMG/ISG as an agent.

Con Haugh, Secretary General at the Department of Sport, had written to both the FAI and the IRFU looking for assurances that their finances were still in place for the stadium build. The Fine Gael spokesperson on sport, Olivia Mitchell, noted that the cost of the overall project had risen from €365 million to €466 million. She raised doubts about the FAI's ability to raise its share of the cost, and she was worried the taxpayer was going to have to foot the bill.

Delaney's response, a few days later, was furious: 'Olivia Mitchell's claims are wrong, false, inaccurate and untrue . . . If we have to write the cheques tomorrow morning the credit line and ability to pay is there – full stop.'

That month, June 2008, the Economic and Social Research Institute forecasted that Ireland was heading for a mild recession. With dividends being cut and people being laid off, the summer was marked by a severe economic chill. Even the ISG people who had moved over from London to take up an office in the old Sweepstakes building in Ballsbridge could feel it. They were there for a 'soft launch' of the ticket scheme, but it was clear that they were set for a hard landing when the pricing scheme for the season tickets was reported in the press in late August, three weeks before the official launch.

The FAI's plan was to raise €185 million from the sale of ten-year tickets at the new stadium, charging more than twice as much as the IRFU for the most well-appointed seats. The ten-year seats around the halfway line would cost €32,000 each. This would comprise an upfront 'membership fee' of €12,000 followed by an annual fee of €2,000 for ten years. Should the FAI sell all the seats in this category alone, it would raise €76 million.

Sideline seating was priced at €19,000 for the ten years, corner seating €14,500, and seats behind the goal €12,000. By contrast, the IRFU's less ambitious ten-year scheme, in which 5,000 seats were offered, all at €15,000, had already sold out. Ten-year premium seats at Croke Park cost GAA fans €11,600.

Disquiet was felt at an FAI board meeting held at Eircom headquarters around that time. The meeting was addressed by ISG and Delaney. At the end of their presentation, the ISG agents got up to leave the room and Delaney and Cody went with them. The rest of the board now felt free to talk. The FAI Vice-President, Paddy McCaul, a hotelier and chairman of Athlone Town, knew all about the difficulty of selling season tickets, even in the sunniest of economic climes. Paraic Treanor, the manager of an EBS branch in Naas, was also uneasy. Concerns were expressed, particularly about the €32,000 price tag for the most expensive tickets.

Delaney and Cody returned to the room and, according to one former board member, David Blood raised his hand: 'We don't really think that . . .'

'Delaney said: "Look, lads, we've paid these guys good money. Are we going to contradict what they are coming back with?"'

Not for the last time, the directors agreed not to disagree.

The FAI launched the Vantage Club, as the ticket scheme was called, on 18 September 2008. The timing could hardly have been worse: three days earlier, the giant American investment bank Lehman Brothers had collapsed, and it was clear that a global financial crisis was underway. The venue was the terrace on the roof of the

Watermarque building in Ringsend, Dublin 4. Guests marvelled at the Aviva Stadium taking shape just a few hundred metres away, and there were plenty of footballing celebrities to eyeball: Trapattoni, Bonner, Houghton, Paul McGrath and Angie Best, the former wife of George, who was chatting animatedly to Gerry Ryan, a presenter with RTÉ.

Amidst the broad smiles and the waiters circling with trays of canapés, it seemed disloyal and even unpatriotic to be sceptical, but there was no escaping the doubts, despite the reassuring words of Delaney and the ISG Chief Executive, Andrew Hampel, who had travelled over from his Wembley base.

'We took in €15 million worth of orders in the last month,' Hampel said. 'It is a grim financial situation, but I am confident because we have done our homework. There are 33,000 millionaires in Ireland and they have not all ceased to be millionaires as a result of the recession. They benefited from fifteen years of boom and they still have disposable income and still want to be seen at the front of the aeroplane. These seats are the front of the aeroplane.'

'Some people said the stadium wouldn't get planning [permission],' Delaney said. 'Some people said it wouldn't get built, some people said we wouldn't have the money to pay for it, and now some people will probably say we won't sell the seats – let me tell you, we'll do it, not a problem.

'There are 33,000 millionaires in this country,' Delaney echoed, 'and we have a database of 80,000 people we're chasing – we only need 3,000 to say "yes", because the average sale is three to four seats. We'll do it. We'll be fine.'

Days after the glitzy Vantage Club launch, the Irish government bailed out the six main banks. It was not a time for ostentatious spending on luxury items such as match tickets, but Delaney was making bullish noises nonetheless, claiming six weeks later that sales were into 'four figures'.

'I've had lunch with some big corporates and they've bought ten on the spot,' he said. 'In fact, the most seats sold to date are the €32,000 ones. That's straight-up.'

5.   Bend It Like Blatter

In May 2008 the actor and impersonator Mario Rosenstock received an invitation to Giovanni Trapattoni's first game as Ireland manager, a friendly against Serbia, along with a personal note of welcome from John Delaney. Rosenstock was intrigued, given he had been parodying Delaney since 2001, so he decided to go along. In one prophetic sketch on Today FM Delaney gave a press conference from a bus that had broken down on the way to a party in a brewery held to celebrate qualifying for the 2002 World Cup.

'He was introduced to me,' Rosenstock recalls, 'and he put his arms around me with the same kind of Sepp Blatter/Platiniesque hug which meant "Welcome to the football family, Mario," and I literally said to him, "If you think this is going to stop me doing sketches you have another fuckin' thing coming." He burst out laughing: "I love the sketches, they're great." He was really charming, a front-of-house man. A guy that would let you in on a plan: "Come on in and I will show you this, wait till you see this."'

Rosenstock was enjoying the post-match hospitality with Gerry Ryan when Delaney asked, 'Would you like to go down and meet the man himself?' As they descended through the Croke Park stadium 'under John's arm', Rosenstock recalls, 'I felt like Ray Liotta passing through the back kitchen in *Goodfellas*. My voiceover would be, "Everybody seemed to love this guy, he got special treatment everywhere he went." And then who did I meet, only the Don himself, Don Trapattoni. He is a legend in the game and I am hugging Trapattoni. This was down in the changing area. It isn't a one-on-one, there are five or six of us. It is an open hugging scene. It is like Joe Pesci being made, minus the shot in the back of the head.'

For Johnny Fallon, getting 'whacked' was not a laughing matter. Shortly after Trapattoni was appointed, the kit man had his FAI phone taken from him. He was accused of briefing journalists, a charge he denied. On secondment from Umbro Ireland and based at Abbotstown, he took a case for unfair dismissal against the FAI, but kept working for Umbro. There, his boss, John Courtenay, warned him that Delaney would 'bury him' if he proceeded with the case.

Fallon retorted: 'Bring two shovels, as I'm going to bury him.'

Fallon had another side role in the FAI. 'I was very good at forging Roy Keane's signature as not everyone would ask him,' Fallon says. 'We used to sign lots of shirts. I don't want to break any charity's hearts, but I used to sign it in such a way that I knew it was mine. I'm looking at a picture of Bertie one day in a programme and he is giving the thumbs up and I'm looking at the shirt framed behind him in his office and it's one of mine. They were called Johnny Fallon Specials. Once or twice, Delaney came down to me and said, "Here, Johnny, sign a few of them, will you?"'

In the conversation with John Courtenay, Fallon said that if the case went to a hearing, he would reveal that Delaney had asked him to forge autographs – 'and the Taoiseach has one hanging behind him'.

Ireland internationals Lee Carsley and Gary Breen flew over from England on the day of the hearing to give evidence on Fallon's behalf. Fallon settled for a figure just short of €15,000 – a decision he has regretted ever since.

*

Long the preserve of committee men, the FAI AGM was rebranded a week-long 'Festival of Football'. The event brought out the best and worst of Delaney. On one level, it was a good idea, bringing some razzmatazz to GAA strongholds, where football people had long felt ignored by the FAI and local media. The first was held in 2007 in Killarney, and it was ramped up further for Castlebar in 2008, where Trapattoni was the star attraction, taking a trip up Croagh Patrick and dispensing advice to young people as though it were a papal visit. On one occasion, Delaney even brought Trapattoni to visit his parents at the family home in Tipperary.

The downside was Delaney's behaviour on the road: 'Every night became a session,' says one of his entourage. 'We'd stop off in some pub and he'd buy everyone a drink. That was the way. He became a celebrity.'

Delaney also developed something of a comic routine which involved belittling FAI President David Blood. Delaney regurgitated the same speech at one club after another and made Blood the butt of his jokes. When Blood was making his speech, his phone would ring and he would look up to see Delaney grinning at him mischievously.

'Have you not turned off your phone?' Delaney would chide.

A more sinister trend was developing. For the 2009 AGM in Monaghan, the 2008 annual accounts were withheld till the day of the event – in contravention of company law, which dictated that they be released a minimum of twenty-one days in advance. 'I find it ironic that senior people within the body, such as John Delaney and Michael Cody, were once much to the forefront in arguing about openness and transparency,' said Brendan Dillon, a lone voice crying from the wilderness.

Two delegates stepped forward at the Monaghan AGM. One was Paul Cooke, the Waterford representative, who had previously had a run-in with Delaney when they were making rival bids to take control of that club. The other was the vice-chairwoman of the League of Ireland, Caroline Rhatigan, a legal secretary who was also the chair of Kilkenny City FC and regarded as a bright prospect within the game.

The night before the AGM, as delegates were getting ready for their dinner, they were addressed by Delaney, Cody and Blood. Rhatigan made some notes of what the three men said regarding the delay in publishing the accounts:

> 2008 was really a one-off year in terms of the association and part of those losses is one exceptional item which will be talked about again tomorrow. We didn't want you as members reading two weeks of rubbish. The IRFU are going to be €40 million to €50 million in debt and no one gives a toss about that. Croke Park is in debt and nobody talks about that. I'm sure these journalists who are reporting this all have mortgages on their homes . . . we would ask what you

have heard now to keep confidential and respect the information that you have received.

The accounts were handed to delegates as they entered the room for the start of the AGM, and the figures were grim. A profit of €10 million in 2007 had turned into a €16 million operating deficit in 2008. Delaney blamed much of the deficit on overspending by the technical department. This infuriated the Technical Director, Packie Bonner, to the point where he marched out to the car park, and had to be talked down by John Byrne and others from resigning on the spot.

There was also a sum of €5.2 million, put down to 'exceptional costs' concerning the new stadium. The huge figure stuck out like a sore thumb, but no further explanation was contained in the accounts. 'I spotted the exceptional item charge, asked a question and was not given an answer of any description,' says Cooke. 'I think I was the last one to ask a question in 2009. Somebody might have asked one in 2014, but that sums up the culture; one of secrecy. It surprised me that no external bodies picked up on the accounts only being made available just before the AGM. There was no questions in the Dáil. Nobody else raised a query.'

Nor was Delaney actively pursued by the media over the unexplained €5.2 million payment; instead it was Vantage Club sales and a new contract for Trapattoni that occupied minds. The Chief Executive had suddenly become very coy. 'I don't talk about managers' contracts and I don't talk about the sales to date because we have a confidentiality agreement in place with ISG and IMG,' said Delaney. 'But we'll be OK, we'll be fine.'

Had there been more of a pushback, perhaps Delaney might have had second thoughts about his next act of self-aggrandizement.

A month after the Monaghan AGM, Delaney wrote to the UEFA General Secretary David Taylor, copying in Alistair Gray of Genesis, portraying the FAI as a role model for other associations throughout Europe and spelling out how it had modernized its leadership, governance and coaching methods since the 'challenges' of the 2002 World Cup. 'We believe it would be valuable for us to share the FAI story with our fellow member nations, perhaps through a UEFA supported seminar or contribution to the UEFA Top Executive programme,' wrote Delaney. 'I would be happy to contribute to this personally along with other key executives in my management team.'

*

In Trapattoni's first qualifying campaign, Ireland were unbeaten, with four wins and six draws – good enough to finish second behind Italy and earn a place in a qualifying playoff. FIFA suddenly decided shortly before the draw to seed the playoffs on the basis of the teams' world rankings, leaving Ireland unseeded. The move favoured France – ninth in the world rankings – the team Ireland subsequently drew in their playoff. Ireland started the two-legged tie as firm underdogs. Trapattoni complained to Platini, a friend from their time together at Juventus in the 1980s, and was met with a Gallic shrug.

The underdog tag was wholly justified by Ireland's poor performance in the first leg at Croke Park on 14 November 2009, which they lost 1–0. Nobody gave Ireland a realistic chance in the second leg in the Stade de France four days later, but Ireland went from insipid to inspired and led after ninety minutes through a Robbie Keane goal, forcing the game into thirty minutes of extra time. One more goal, or victory in a penalty shoot-out, would be enough to send Ireland to the World Cup in South Africa.

The tie turned on an incident in the 104th minute, when the French striker Thierry Henry deliberately tapped the ball twice with his hand on the dead-ball line to stop it going out of play, and then crossed for William Gallas to score. The view of the referee and his assistant was restricted and neither saw the handball, so the goal stood, even though Henry's offence was instantly obvious to millions of television viewers across the world. Ireland were unable to score in the remainder of extra time and lost the tie.

In the subsequent furore, the Taoiseach Brian Cowen promised to raise the matter with Nicolas Sarkozy, the French president, at an EU meeting. Henry suggested a replay, an idea Delaney latched on to as he rode a wave of public outrage. 'This wasn't Bohemians against Waterford in the cup,' Delaney said. 'The whole world was watching last night and if FIFA really care about fair play and integrity they have a chance to show it.'

Listening in from his vantage point as manager of Ipswich Town was Roy Keane. The Corkman dismissed all the outrage and was at his most caustic when the FAI CEO's name was raised at his weekly press conference. 'John Delaney?' he said. 'He's on about honesty and integrity? I wouldn't take any notice of that man.'

FIFA boss Sepp Blatter, however, was anxious to take the heat out of the situation and agreed to see Delaney. On 27 November Delaney flew to FIFA headquarters in Zurich accompanied by Cody and the FAI's legal adviser, Sarah O'Shea. Strategizing on the way over, the FAI team knew there was no case for a replay as the referee's decision was final, but decided they would try to squeeze FIFA for compensation.

At the meeting, Delaney and the others quickly detected that Blatter and the FIFA General Secretary Jérôme Valcke were concerned that the FAI might appeal to the Court of Arbitration for Sport, which would jeopardize the draw for the World Cup finals five days later. As part of the negotiations, Cody put forward the idea of Ireland being given a wildcard into the finals, but that idea didn't gain much traction. FIFA listened to Delaney's complaints about loss of income. No offer was made at the meeting, but the two parties agreed to meet again.

The FAI team went back to Ireland while Blatter headed for South Africa. It was agreed that everything would remain confidential, but Blatter couldn't help himself when he was asked about it at a Soccerex event in Johannesburg two days before the draw.

'They have asked, very humbly, "Can't we be team number 33 at the World Cup?"'

The audience in Johannesburg laughed and Blatter sniggered.

'They asked for that! Really! I will bring it to the attention of the Executive Committee.'

Blatter was being condescending and Delaney took offence. 'He insulted us as a country,' Delaney complained. 'I tried to impress upon him last Friday the hurt that was in our country over how the whole Henry incident had affected our ability to qualify for the World Cup, and he clearly didn't understand.'

Blatter quickly apologized for any offence caused, but Delaney was determined to make him pay.

'When Blatter made that faux pas, John saw dollar signs,' says Paddy McCaul, who was the FAI's Vice-President at the time.

The FAI team returned to Zurich on 12 January. Delaney was ill with a stomach bug on the way over. It was a tense meeting. The FAI presented Blatter with projections for its financial loss and Blatter made sympathetic noises about the losses and stadium repayments. At one point the advisers were asked to leave and Delaney and Blatter had a one-on-one discussion.

After the two men emerged from the meeting, Delaney embraced Blatter warmly. Even by Delaney's touchy-feely standards it seemed over the top, but Delaney told people afterwards he just wanted Blatter to catch his bug. On the way out of FIFA headquarters, Delaney informed his colleagues of the amount of compensation he had agreed with Blatter: €5 million.

The money was classed as a loan, to be repaid only if Ireland qualified for the next World Cup – which it didn't. The board and senior staff were sworn to secrecy about the payment, and Deloitte were consulted on how the money could be presented in the annual accounts without drawing anybody's attention to it.

*

While cash-rich FIFA were something of a soft touch, ISG found the recession-hit Irish market hard to crack. The Dublin professional classes were proving distinctly unenthusiastic about joining the Vantage Club, so ISG and the FAI reached out to the 'football family', concentrating efforts on selling the tickets through the hundreds of clubs throughout the country. Rather than reduce prices, they offered a number of incentives, chief amongst them a voucher worth €2,500 over ten years for Umbro sports equipment. Tickets could be paid for entirely by instalments. The FAI and ISG claimed at a series of presentations that special arrangements had been made with credit unions to facilitate loans, though the Irish League of Credit Unions said normal lending rules would apply. The plan was pitched to the clubs on the basis that they could raffle off the tickets and therefore recoup their money, perhaps even be left with a profit.

Even before ISG's eighteen-month contract ended, the burden fell on the FAI's Development Officers to try to sell the tickets on their visits to clubs in their area, though there was no mention of that role in their job description. Packie Bonner was dispatched to Donegal to make a presentation on the Vantage Club to the leagues there, and an acquaintance of his bought a couple of €19,000 tickets.

The Leinster Football Association sold off their headquarters on Parnell Square for €1.125 million, and took office space in the FAI headquarters in Abbotstown. It pledged in the region of €600,000 for the purchase of about sixty tickets.

The LFA Treasurer David Hearst later admitted to the *Irish Independent* that he ring-fenced €100,000 of the remaining proceeds of the sale into a secure, long-term account to prevent 'prying eyes getting their hands on whatever we have left'.

'If anyone wanted to progress in football, you had to play ball with the CEO,' Hearst said. 'I don't know of anyone in the amateur ranks who didn't play ball. It was felt that the CEO could walk on water. People feared putting their head above the parapet.'

The FAI's Monday executive meetings became dominated by Vantage Club matters. Delaney would throw out a figure about how many he had sold, and then challenge senior executives to say how they had performed. The Commercial Manager, Rory Smyth, was given a particularly rough ride, bullied even, according to several other senior members of staff.

'John was under pressure, but it was all about saving himself,' says one former senior executive. 'He didn't want people [outside the FAI] to know there was a problem.'

There was renewed focus from Delaney at the management meetings on controlling costs, but some FAI staff said they were never given annual budgets for their departments.

One staff member whose work involved promoting League of Ireland matches used to splurge on hiring attractive models for photoshoots and renting out hotel rooms for press conferences. 'I was never told what my budget was,' he says. 'Just hand the bills to

Finance. It seemed very unprofessional. I used to hire Georgia Salpa [one of Ireland's top models at the time] from Assets Model Agency to promote Bohs games. I was never told if that was OK or not or if I was spending too much.'

The Law Library football team, which consisted mainly of young barristers, was invited to attend a presentation on the Vantage scheme by Delaney, Bonner and Ray Houghton in the Westbury hotel in Dublin and asked to bring along 'heavy hitter' senior counsel. The FAI laid on free drink and canapés for about twenty lawyers as Delaney gave a PowerPoint presentation in a private room on 19 March 2010, a Friday night.

Bizarrely, Delaney made it personal. 'What is this? It's ten years of my life,' he told the twenty assembled lawyers. It didn't work.

'There are barristers who come from privilege, but most of our guys hadn't a bean at that stage in our careers,' says one barrister who was present. Plates were cleared and bottles emptied, but no sales were made.

Amidst the catalogue of arm-twisting and failures there was something of a coup, when Delaney did a deal with corporate ticket reseller Marcus Evans, who was regarded even by his own employees as one of the most unscrupulous operators in the murky world of sports corporate hospitality. Evans ran one of the biggest secondary ticket operations in the world and was persona non grata as far as UEFA, FIFA and a host of British sporting bodies were concerned. In 2011 the *Daily Mail* would describe Evans as the 'world's biggest ticket tout'.

On 26 April 2010 the FAI signed a contract with Marcus Evans Ltd (MEL) regarding hospitality packages at the Aviva Stadium. The five-year contract provided MEL with exclusive rights to sell the restaurant seats and all match-to-match corporate box seats, plus 1,000 tickets for the 2011 Europa League final, which was to be held in Dublin, including all 635 restaurant section seats. There was also an option to purchase up to 25 per cent of any ticket allocation the FAI received for any World Cup or European Championship finals involving the senior national team, subject to UEFA and FIFA agreement. The deal was worth a minimum €1.6 million to the FAI.

Delaney also struck deals with a number of international match agents, which also proved controversial. International friendlies were to be arranged through Kentaro, a company with close links to Jerome Anderson, the former stadium announcer at Highbury and a London-based agent who had brokered the deal that brought Trapattoni to Ireland. The match agents Endemol were given sole licence to organize club friendlies involving big European sides coming to Ireland.

Details of these deals emerged only when the association refused a request for a friendly game at Thomond Park that Limerick FC had organized with Barcelona for the summer of 2010. There was widespread disbelief and anger that the FAI wouldn't allow a game involving one of the biggest clubs in the world to go ahead. Platinum One, the company run by Brian Kerr's agent, Fintan Drury, who had brought Real Madrid to Dublin to play Shamrock Rovers the previous year, was also barred from organizing any friendlies at the Aviva Stadium. The deal with Endemol diverted a revenue stream from the clubs and traditional match agents to the FAI. The sow was eating its piglets.

FAI Director of Communications Peter Sherrard rubbed further salt into the wounds when he said the deal with the agents did not apply to the first football match played at the new Aviva, between Alex Ferguson's Manchester United and a League of Ireland XI on 3 August 2010. This was a money-spinning event for the association, but somewhat inappropriate as it was not an international game.

That game sold out and everybody assumed that the visit a week later of Argentina, with Lionel Messi guaranteed to be in the side, would do likewise. However, the attendance for the first Ireland international in the new stadium fell 5,000 short of capacity.

'John was pissed off,' says a member of the management team. 'He had worked so hard to build the stadium. His senior management team had let him down.'

*

The row with FIFA over the Henry handball didn't stop Delaney, Blood and Cody attending the 2010 World Cup that summer, spending a week in Johannesburg and attending the FIFA Congress. This was Blood's farewell tour. At the 2010 AGM in Wexford, Blood handed over the chains of office to Paddy McCaul, who was thought to be one of the few directors to be sceptical about Delaney's methods.

Rather than repeat the cloak-and-dagger approach of the previous year, this time the annual accounts had been circulated in advance, and the report in the *Irish Times* on the day of the AGM should have led to serious questions being directed from the floor to the top table. Pointing out that the association's borrowing had grown by some €50 million in the previous year as payments towards the cost of construction of the Aviva Stadium became due, one delegate was quoted as saying the figures 'would make you cry'.

However, the FAI's Finance Director, Mark O'Leary, gave a glowing account of the association's finances, and a succession of delegates stood up at the meeting to hail the delivery of the new stadium and to praise Delaney's stewardship. The FAI, said one, was a bigger success story than Ryanair.

Delaney told the media afterwards that the association would be debt free by 2020 and that the overall debt figures being reported were inaccurate. 'The debt is not €76 million, absolutely not. I can categorically state that – we have sold new seats since January 2010,' Delaney said. 'Our debt to our bank is €38 million on the stadium at the end of 2009 and we're very comfortable with our bankers. We've borrowed our monies, we'll have it paid back in ten years and after 2020 the monies that will be derived from that will be huge.'

Delaney said that 6,300 of the Vantage Club seats had been 'allocated'. 'We have 3,700 seats to sell and we expect to sell them over the next couple of years.'

*

Ireland made a positive start to their European Championship qualifying campaign with a 1–0 victory over Armenia in Yerevan. But the travelling football writers were caught by surprise when it was announced suddenly that Mark O'Leary was leaving the association with immediate effect, despite having given such a glowing account of the finances at the AGM two weeks' earlier. O'Leary, the FAI said, had actually stayed on beyond his contracted period, but it was telling that the news of his departure was suppressed at the time of the AGM. The only public sign of potential financial trouble came in late 2010 when Delaney confirmed that he had taken a 'significant' pay cut, along with Trapattoni, due to the Irish financial crisis. Delaney's salary went from €431,687 to €400,000.

Such matters were of little import to the majority of Trap's Army, who were more concerned about how to get to the Slovakia–Ireland match in October 2010, the fourth game of Ireland's Euro 2012 qualifying campaign. At short notice, the game had been moved from the capital Bratislava to the town of Žilina, more than 200 kilometres away, much to the annoyance of the FAI. A week before the game, the FAI announced that it would charter a train for Ireland supporters between Bratislava and Žilina.

Not just free travel, but free booze. Crates of Carlsberg, the FAI's official beer, were loaded on to the train along with 800 fans, many of them already tanked up on strong Slovakian pilsner in the capital. Soon everybody was bouncing around to Pogues songs as the train wound its way through the Slovakian countryside. There to greet them on the platform at Žilina was the Chief Executive of the FAI, who was hoisted shoulder-high by boisterous fans.

Delaney, it was widely reported, had spent €5,000 of his own money on the beer. 'It's the least I could do for the fans who made the trip,' Delaney said. 'It's hard times at home and these lads have been messed around with the change of venue. If we show one tenth of the passion in the remainder of the group that these lads show, then we'll be all right.'

Delaney set himself up in the foyer of the Holiday Inn, beside the MŠK Žilina stadium, selling tickets to Ireland fans. These were tickets to the corporate end – the only ones available apparently at a face value of €80 – and so the great and good of Žilina society were joined by Ireland fans enjoying beef stroganoff at half-time and free beer and wine, before, during and after the match. Fans wrapped in tricolours staggered round the press box, singing 'Oh John Delaney, used to be a wanker but he's all right now.'

A poll in the *Sunday Independent* found that 73 per cent thought

Delaney had done the right thing in chartering the train. Supporter David Dunne was not amongst them: 'We had booked through Abbey Travel and were assured that, despite the rumours, the game wouldn't be moved outside the capital. We then had to endure a two-hour bus journey to get there. We were getting updates from my friend's cousin who was on the train. They were having the time of their lives while we were stuck on a coach without the use of the on-board toilet and the driver refused to stop. This almost caused a punch-up on the bus. We'd gone through the official FAI channels and had a terrible journey while fans without tickets were having the time of their lives.'

Amongst those who disapproved was the new FAI President, Paddy McCaul, who remembers Delaney boasting that 'they carried me shoulder high'. 'That was John going full circle from the car nearly being overturned,' says McCaul, remembering what had happened to the FAI party on the previous visit to Slovakia. 'Then the culture set in that we'd meet and greet the fans the night before [away games] with the sponsors. Down to the pub.'

★

The FAI organized a 'Celtic league' – the Republic of Ireland, Northern Ireland, Scotland and Wales – to play a series of friendlies in the new Aviva Stadium in February and May 2011. It had a sponsored name, the Carling Nations Cup. Scotland drove a hard bargain before agreeing to take part, securing a £2 million flat fee for the tournament. In September 2010, the Scotland FA had a new Chief Executive, Stewart Regan, and one of his first jobs was to host a meeting with Delaney in Glasgow, where the FAI man wanted to rip up the deal. Delaney told Regan that he had to renegotiate their fee because ticket sales for the tournament were not expected to be as 'robust' as previously projected.

'I sat and listened, then made my point very clearly that we actually had a contract and had budgeted for that income after he had signed that contract,' says Regan. 'Needless to say, John wasn't very happy. He started to talk about how football federations needed to work together, saying something like "this is how the football family behave and treat each other".'

Delaney offered the Scottish FA a share of the tournament proceeds, insisting the FAI could not pay the agreed £2 million fee. Rather than pull out of the tournament at short notice, the SFA agreed to accept a reduced fee of £1.2 million.

Delaney was right about one thing: the tournament was a flop. The highest attendance was 19,783 for the opening game between the Republic of Ireland and Wales. Just 529 people turned up for Wales v. Northern Ireland. The Scots sent dozens of reminders and considered lodging an official complaint with FIFA before the FAI finally paid the agreed reduced fee in 2012.

'Given what we now know about the FAI finances, it all makes sense, but at the time it just seemed amateurish and petulant for a CEO to be behaving in this way,' says Regan.

As a former Celtic player whose family was based in Glasgow, the FAI's Technical Director, Packie Bonner, might have been used to smooth things over, but Bonner's relationship with Delaney was fraught.

Bonner's stature in Irish football was huge in more ways than one. He had been involved in all four major tournaments that Ireland had qualified for – three as goalkeeper and the fourth as a coach. He had achieved Irish footballing immortality when he saved Daniel Timofte's penalty in the 1990 World Cup penalty shoot-out against Romania, which saw Ireland reach the quarter finals in Italy.

Bonner became Technical Director in February 2003, when Kerr took the Ireland manager's job, but was disappointed to be excluded from the business of hiring and firing of senior Ireland managers, particularly in the case of Steve Staunton. It was speculated that he was undermined by the arrival of Wim Koevermans as International Performance Director in July 2008. However, Bonner had actively encouraged his appointment and worked well with the Dutch coach.

While Bonner was an astute politician as well as a respected coach, it was clear that he and Delaney co-existed in a climate of mutual suspicion. Bonner's friendship with John Byrne didn't help, especially once Byrne was effectively cut adrift. 'Packie and myself were getting close and we were seen out a lot,' says Byrne. 'This was feeding back to Delaney. We were mixing and drinking with [Taoiseach]

Brian Cowen. This type of thing Delaney couldn't hack. If he wasn't there, who the fuck were we to be there?'

Bonner was coming to the end of his second contract and felt he had been left dangling about his future, but he finally managed to corner Delaney, in November 2010, after a meeting in Abbotstown. The two men retired to Delaney's office. There Delaney explained that in such straitened financial circumstances the FAI couldn't afford to keep both Bonner and Koevermans.

Bonner subsequently signed a non-disclosure agreement. Once, when he made a very mild comment which might have been construed as critical – namely that he would be disappointed if Koevermans didn't have his contract renewed – he received a sharp letter from the FAI's lawyer, Sarah O'Shea, saying he was in breach of the confidentiality agreement.

*

It was Bonner's friend John Byrne who eventually became a whistle-blower of sorts, even though he found the paymasters in Irish sport hard of hearing. Much to Delaney's chagrin, Byrne had joined the board of the Irish Sports Council in 2009 when he was still an FAI employee. Byrne says Delaney wanted Cody to take the position, but Brian Cowen insisted that Byrne should get the job. Byrne joined the board at the same time as the ex-Ireland rugby international Jim Glennon, a former Fianna Fáil TD.

In April 2010 the Chief Executive of the Sports Council, John Treacy, wrote to Delaney expressing 'regret' that access to information that had been agreed in advance of an audit of the FAI was subsequently withdrawn. Delaney replied that copies of board minutes could not be supplied to the auditors 'because these were strictly confidential and had highly sensitive commercial information in them'. He added that this information was unrelated to the projects supported by the council, which were mainly grassroots programmes and developing the women's game.

In March 2011 the board of the Sports Council – according to its minutes – discussed 'the necessity for the executive to ensure that any [council] funding allocated to the FAI be ring-fenced and protected from any claims by a creditor should the FAI end up in financial difficulty'.

The concerns arose when it was revealed that the association was only paying the interest on the bank loans for the Aviva Stadium. The Sports Council considered paying the FAI's annual grant of around €3 million in monthly instalments and setting up a bank account into which the grant would be paid.

Delaney was then asked to appear before the Sports Council in November 2011 to be questioned about the association's finances and development plans. It was usual in such circumstances for the board members to get some papers in advance to study.

'On the day of the meeting,' Glennon recalls, 'we got a big brown Jiffy bag around the table and inside it was a sheaf of loose leaves which was some kind of shite he had taken out of a drawer somewhere and they were handed out to us. I may have made a point about this being so unprofessional and unsatisfactory that I don't believe we should take a presentation. I was told Delaney was outside and we should pay him the courtesy. And he came in and he talked down to us for about an hour.'

According to the minutes, Delaney told the board he 'was comfortable with the FAI's ability to meet its debt obligations over the coming years and did not feel this sense of comfort was in any way aspirational'.

Glennon remembers asking Delaney: 'How can you justify a salary that is more than the combined salaries of the Taoiseach and the Chief Justice?' Delaney, Glennon says, 'was livid'.

Some of this was reported by Joe Humphreys in the *Irish Times*, on the back of a Freedom of Information request that he had submitted. The FAI managed to get its hands on the same documents – by submitting an FOI request of its own, it is believed – and the paper trail led to John Byrne. He had left the FAI in 2011, but before doing so had sent a series of emails from his FAI account to Glennon and two other Sports Council board members, Susan Ahern and the former Dublin Gaelic footballer Brian Mullins.

In the emails, Byrne called the presentations made by Delaney to the Sports Council 'claptrap' and 'more smoke and mirrors'.

Mullins asked Byrne whether they needed 'to mount pressure on the chairman and CEO to undertake a deep examination of the presentation and the strategy document'. Byrne replied: 'Something needs to be done, Brian.'

By the time Delaney saw the email correspondence from his former friend, Byrne had left the FAI; but he remained on the board of the Sports Council and had taken a new job as CEO of the Community Games. On 8 June 2012 he received a letter from FAI President Paddy McCaul saying his 'negative comments' were 'actionable' and 'we are now very concerned about the implication being made by you with regard to Sports Council funding'.

The FAI also wrote to the Sports Council chairman, Kieran Mulvey, complaining about Sports Council 'bias'. Mulvey then ordered an investigation into Byrne's activities to be conducted by Paul Appleby, the former Director of Corporate Enforcement. Byrne sought a High Court injunction saying that Mulvey was acting beyond his powers, as only a government minister had the authority to order such an investigation. Justice Michael Peart agreed. 'The setting up of an investigation and the appointment of a former Director of Corporate Enforcement carries with it the whiff of sulphur,' Peart said as he ruled in Byrne's favour.

Delaney wasn't prepared to let the matter rest there. He then wrote a letter of complaint to the then Sports Minister, Leo Varadkar, charging that Byrne had been involved in 'a grave and improper interference in the funding process'.

Byrne was angry that he had to put his house on the line to defend his name in court. He was even more angry that Mulvey had targeted him rather than try to get a handle on what was happening at the FAI.

Glennon recalls meeting Delaney at an RTÉ awards night. 'He said to me, "Any more questions, Mr Glennon?"'

Mulvey says he felt that Glennon, Byrne and the others did not approach the FAI's funding issues with 'clean hands' and were acting as a 'cabal' outside normal board meetings. He insists that any concerns raised about the FAI were examined by the Sports Council and proper oversight of state money was maintained.

'I felt there was an agenda there,' he says. 'There were constant leaks, particularly in the *Sunday Independent*. I knew who was leaking. It doesn't take rocket science. I confronted board members. I asked could they own up and stop it. I then sent a letter reminding them of the obligations of confidentiality, particularly as it related to financial matters. I found out in the emails that Byrne and Glennon were laughing about it.'

Delaney met a senior official from the Sports Council on the Abbotstown campus soon after Byrne's departure from the state body, and made it clear that his former friend had outlived his usefulness to the FAI. Delaney said: 'Sure, what the fuck would I need him for now Fine Gael are in?'

*

Another parting from the association was that of the Head of League Marketing, Noel Mooney, who took the rap after a disastrous first running of the John Giles Walk of Dreams in March 2011.

Some 25,000 football club members, including thousands of children, took part in walks around the country, and €360,000 was raised, to be split evenly between the John Giles Foundation, which would disburse its funds to grassroots clubs, and the clubs that raised the money. However, the marquee event in Dublin was a shambles, with children forced to urinate in the streets because of a lack of toilet facilities and parents complaining of a lack of bottled water and rip-off prices for hot food at the walk's endpoint in the Aviva Stadium. Also missing were the Ireland players, who were in town for a friendly and were supposed to be waiting at the stadium along with free entertainment when the hordes arrived. Trapattoni gave the players a day off instead, and the entertainment was limited to three football jugglers. All this was aired on RTÉ's *Liveline*. Giles had to come on air to apologize to irate parents and coaches for the mistakes and assure people that it wouldn't happen the next time, if there was to be one.

What the public would not learn until much later was that the FAI was contracted to pay over €500,000 for the 'concept' of the John Giles Foundation and the fundraising walk. The bizarre deal came about from a friendship between Delaney and Giles.

Giles, who normally regarded the FAI blazers with a healthy degree of suspicion, got to know Delaney when the FAI invited all living former Ireland internationals to a pre-match reception before the first soccer international at Croke Park against Wales in March 2007. Delaney roped in the FAI's travel agent and former international Ray Treacy to approach Giles about coming on the organizing committee.

Giles asked Treacy, 'What's the catch?'

Treacy said there was none.

'Any time I had seen John Delaney he was never friendly with me,' Giles recalls. 'So I went to see John. I said, "What's the catch?"'

'No catch.'

'I said, "Are we going to be sitting at a table with people who are paying?"' Giles recalls. 'Usually there's a sponsor. You sit beside them and have a terrible night. You're not with the lads at all. I said: "Is the press going to be there?"'

'No, just the lads,' insisted Delaney.

Giles recalls, 'I'd never heard of this before and it was genuine. He did do it. It was a great night. All the players from the different generations, we all mixed; nobody to bother us. John had me from that day.'

Con Martin Snr, who was at the reunion, was one of Giles's heroes. Mick Martin, Con's son, was a close friend and former international teammate. Giles had also got to know Mick's brother, Con Jnr, an insurance broker who had played for Bohemians. Con Jnr shared a passion for golf with Giles and became part of his circle.

'I got so friendly that I lent him money,' Giles says. 'I'm OK most of the time, but when it comes to money I can be an eejit. I lent Con Martin [Jnr] €60,000. He was crying. He said he was going to have to sell his house and give me back the money.'

Con Martin Jnr was, in Giles's words, an ideas man, 'a schemer'. He had applied to become FAI Chief Executive in 2003 but was politely knocked back. He ran golf classics for football-related causes, using Giles's name, up to 2007, and then came up with the idea of the John Giles Foundation, incorporating the sponsored Walk of Dreams plus a kit-wear scheme whereby all the football clubs in Ireland would get their kit from the same manufacturer. Giles was receptive to the idea, and the two men approached Delaney.

From the perspective of Con Martin Jnr, the meeting with Delaney, Cody and Giles in November 2007 could hardly have gone better. Delaney wrote to Martin the following day outlining the agreement that would be put to the board:

> The Association will, from its own funds, pay you annually 1 per cent of all monies received by the John Giles Foundation in the preceding twelve month period subject to a minimum payment of €100,000 and a maximum payment of €150,000. If the FAI decided to abandon the project it would pay you €25,000 for the remainder of the five-year period.

A trust agreement establishing the John Giles Foundation was signed by Giles, Delaney and Blood in a document prepared by A&L Goodbody on 28 April 2008 and witnessed by Sarah O'Shea, the FAI's in-house solicitor. The foundation was established as a not-for-profit trust with the aim of raising and distributing funds for grassroots football.

In a separate agreement signed by Delaney and Giles in July 2008, the former Leeds United star handed over his image rights to the FAI free of charge.

Delaney signed a contract with Martin in September 2008 that led to the FAI paying him €300,000 in sixty tranches of €5,000 over five years on top of an initial €200,000 lump-sum payment, all in return for his 'concepts'.

In 2009 Martin sent Delaney a proposal for developing his sponsored-walk and kit-buying ideas across Europe. It claimed that by harnessing the fundraising ability of each registered footballer across all fifty-three UEFA countries, billions of euro could be generated annually. The proposal suggested €50 million could be raised from his schemes in Ireland in one year. If France copied the idea and set up a Just Fontaine Foundation, named after its legendary striker, the French Football Federation could raise €250 million a year. These were outlandish projections, but what was even more nonsensical was that Delaney signed a contract compelling the FAI to pay Martin hundreds of thousands of euro for his concepts.

It was only years later, reading about it in the *Sunday Times*, that Giles learned the FAI had drafted a deal with Martin that purported to include payment for his 'personality rights'.

Following the shambolic first Walk of Dreams in 2011, there were critical articles in the newspapers the following day, though the account in the *Irish Independent* was glowing. The newspaper and its sister publication the *Evening Herald* were official 'partners' of the foundation. Stephen Rae, the editor of the *Herald*, where Giles wrote a column, became one of the foundation's trustees alongside Giles and Delaney. Independent Newspapers had reached a settlement with Delaney over an article which Paul Hyland had written in the *Evening Herald* back in 2009. Hyland had heard through his sources that Joe Delaney had participated 'in a presentation to key FAI staff and board members about poor ticket sales', held in the Clarion hotel at Dublin airport. The father of the FAI Chief Executive, Hyland wrote, 'is back and apparently involved in a decision-making process about, of all things, international match tickets'.

Joe Delaney – an honorary life member of the FAI – had been at Dublin airport all right. He and his son were taking Denis O'Brien's private jet to the Champions League final in Rome between their beloved Manchester United and Barcelona. However, there was no proof to the allegation that Joe was in the hotel room in question. Delaney's solicitor, Paddy Goodwin, pounced. Lengthy negotiations resulted in an apology running to 275 words, which Delaney's lawyers insisted be published above the fold on the inside back page. Goodwin wrote to the Independent Newspapers legal team on 11 March 2010, setting out the contents of a discussion between Delaney and the Chief Executive of Independent News Media in Ireland, Joe Webb:

> He [Delaney] instructs me that the following was agreed between himself and Mr Webb:
>
> In relation to the positive articles there are to be two articles published in relation to the good work that the FAI are doing in relation

to 'Grassroots Football'. One of these is to be published in the *Evening Herald* and the other in the *Independent*. In addition to this there is to be a positive article relating to John Delaney himself which is to be published in the *Sunday Independent*.

Mr Delaney also instructed me last night that the amount of damages due to himself is €62,500 and not €62,000 as outlined to you in my letter of 9 March. Mr Delaney instructs me that an agreement has been reached with Mr Webb that Mr Paul Hyland will not write any articles about Mr Delaney or his family.

Webb remembers the conversation with Delaney, which was held at Abbotstown, slightly differently: 'Most of that rings true,' he says, 'except the bit about the *Sunday Independent*. I don't think I would have agreed on a positive story in the *Sunday Independent*. It would have been like broadcasting to the nation.'

The *Sunday Independent*'s coverage at the time remained critical of the FAI; indeed, it attacked the FAI vociferously over the cancelled Barcelona friendly with Limerick FC on the day the positive story stipulated by Delaney's solicitor was supposed to go in. However, Hyland, Delaney's most outspoken critic in the media, had been silenced. Rather than continue as a lame-duck football correspondent, he left the *Evening Herald* in due course and pursued his passion for fishing instead.

The legal actions continued. Delaney went after RTÉ over an interview Des Cahill had conducted with Roddy Collins, then the manager of Monaghan United and a fierce anti-Delaneyite.

On the day of the 2011 AGM, there was a heated debate on RTÉ between Collins and Damien Richardson, the former Shamrock Rovers player and manager, mediated by Cahill, in which Delaney's salary was discussed as well as the Aviva Stadium debt. After the debate, the association's staff were instructed not to do interviews with Cahill. Delaney and the FAI then jointly filed a High Court action against RTÉ.

Collins eventually employed a legal team – headed by none other than Fran Rooney, now working as a barrister – as he skirmished with Delaney in and out of the courts. Monaghan United had gone bust while he was manager there and he was fined again when he called the League of Ireland a 'shambles' in his *Daily Star* column.

'A Delaney wingman called me and told me to shut my mouth and Delaney would have me back in work within a month,' says Collins. 'I said I would rather dig holes in the road.'

★

Tony Dignam, who joined the FAI as Finance Director in July 2011, quickly took on the appearance of a man with the weight of the world on his shoulders. Dignam sometimes snapped at board members who came in to get cheques issued to cover their FAI travel expenses, asking did they not understand how bad the FAI's finances were. After Dignam sent a presentation to the FAI Finance Committee about how far the Vantage scheme was off target, he received a text from Delaney criticizing him for sharing sensitive information. From then on all paperwork for the committee had to be signed off by Delaney first. Cody warned the finance team not to put too many figures in Treasurer Eddie Murray's presentations for council meetings, as he 'struggled with the figures'. The finance team got so wound up about complying with this suggestion that for one presentation Murray's slides had no figures at all.

Although the Vantage scheme was supposed to be a huge revenue generator for the FAI, it turned out to be a disaster. By 2011 the FAI was owed up to €6 million by those who had signed up to buy ten-year tickets but who had defaulted on their direct debits. Those who were paying for their tickets soon realized that sitting beside them in their premium seats were fans who had bought individual tickets at discounted prices, or, in the case of some friendlies, had got them for free. Delaney authorized discounting to generate revenue, and give-aways to amateur clubs to fill seats at the less popular matches. In a bid to keep those who had signed up paying their annual bills and to encourage those who had refused to pay to play ball, the FAI quietly decided to top up the ticket allocations of Vantage Club members, based on the value of the ticket or tickets already paid for – so that, for example, the holder of a single €32,000 halfway-line ticket would be awarded five additional ten-year tickets.

The failure of the Vantage scheme to bring in the revenue that had been forecast meant the FAI was effectively insolvent from 2010, according to a senior source who worked in the association at the time. However, Delaney kept pulling rabbits out of the hat, usually from the FAI's future income, to stave off the day of reckoning.

6. I Come Amongst You

Delaney's charm offensive with the fans went into overdrive in Moscow at the Euro qualifying match against Russia in September 2011. On the night before the game he engaged in a raucous sing-song with Ireland fans in Katie O'Shea's pub in the centre of the city, holding a microphone in one hand and embracing Ray Houghton with the other. Hovering by the bar was Robert Finnegan, Chief Executive of team sponsor Three, who was buying drinks for the fans. Houghton grabbed the microphone and made a speech: 'John Delaney, in my opinion, epitomizes what the FAI is about today. John is here, in amongst you. That's one good thing about John. He wants to be amongst the Irish supporters, enjoying nights like tonight because we know tomorrow is so important.'

Thanks to a heroic rearguard performance led by centre-half Richard Dunne, Ireland grabbed a goalless draw the following night. After the game, Delaney had what one pitchside photographer described as his 'rock-star' moment. An emotional Delaney, accompanied by the photographer Dave Maher, entered the pitch at the Luzhniki Stadium, removing his green tie as he ran towards the Irish supporters and threw it into the end where the green army had congregated, honing a routine he had first performed a few months earlier when Ireland beat Macedonia in Skopje.

Delaney had taken to travelling around Dublin with a large entourage, such as when he turned up for a public Newstalk interview with twenty supporters who had been called by Joe McGlue, the FAI's Head of Security, with the promise of a free drink. Presenter Eoin McDevitt compared Delaney to P Diddy.

Amongst those Delaney regularly invited to enjoy FAI hospitality at home matches were Susan Keegan, a childcare worker who became his girlfriend, and Mark O'Hare, a professional George Best lookalike from Co. Down. Delaney and O'Hare became regular drinking pals. On his website where he takes bookings, O'Hare has a photograph of himself with Delaney's arm around him as they clink pints of Guinness under the headline 'catch up with friend and mentor John Delaney'. In interviews, O'Hare would credit his 'good friend' Delaney with introducing him to celebrities such as Rosanna Davison, a former Miss World, at Ireland games.

Ticket sales continued to disappoint. When new Commercial Manager Max Hamilton admitted they were 'challenging' in an interview with the *Sunday Business Post*, he was collared by a furious Delaney the following day: 'How dare you!' There was to be no public or even private acknowledgement that the FAI was struggling.

Ireland reached the playoffs for Euro 2012 and got the best possible draw: Estonia. After an emphatic 4–0 victory in Tallinn in the first leg, the qualification celebrations could commence and Delaney was at it again, striding across the pitch after the final whistle and bowing and clapping towards incredulous Ireland supporters. 'There were even more reasons for fans in Tallinn to smile after FAI boss John Delaney dropped a wad of cash behind a bar for loyal supporters,' the *Irish Daily Mirror* reported. 'The footy boss forked out around €2,000 as fun-loving fans toasted a historic performance by Trap's boys.'

At least that didn't overshadow the performance, but the same could not be said for Delaney's behaviour at the tournament in Poland. Headquarters for the squad and supporters alike was the resort of Sopot on the Baltic Sea, which had sweeping beaches and was crammed with cheap bars, restaurants and small hotels; the perfect base for a large portion of the 10,000 Ireland fans who had travelled there intent on holding a huge party, whatever happened on the football pitch. The surprise was that the FAI chose to house the team in a hotel right in the centre of Sopot, the Sheraton, which overlooked the town square on one side and the beach on the other. Damien Duff was somewhat bemused: 'You think, "Who goes over and chooses these things?"' he said in 2016. 'They're obviously going three or four months beforehand when it's not busy, but it was like staying in Ayia Napa or Playa Del Ingles.'

The team could hear the fans whooping, hollering and singing 'Come on you boys in green' late into the night.

Delaney was at the heart of the socializing in Poznań, where Ireland played two games, and in Sopot. Senior FAI managers, notably the Legal Director, Sarah O'Shea, and Max Hamilton, were at times required to accompany him. Delaney also openly consorted with his girlfriend, Susan Keegan, who then had to make herself scarce when his wife Emer came out for a few days.

If you went into one of Sopot's bars in the main square, there was a good chance that Delaney would be there buying drink, with O'Shea or Hamilton instructed to use their FAI credit cards to pay. After bringing Sport Ireland representatives out for dinner and bank-rolling functions for council members and players' wives, the FAI staff had to ring back to Abbotstown to get their credit-card limits extended. Paddy McCaul was horrified.

'Before we went it was decided by the board that the team would be isolated from the fans,' McCaul says. 'I told Delaney I was concerned this would turn into a bit of a circus. I was assured that that wouldn't happen. John said tickets will be scarce. The opposite happened.'

In the first game, against Croatia in Poznań, Ireland were soundly beaten 3–1 and it was clear that the team was seriously out of its depth in a group which also contained Spain and Italy. Four days later, Ireland were trounced 4–0 by Spain in the city of Gdańsk, near Sopot, which became an orgy of lament and defiance for the last twenty minutes as thousands of Ireland fans repeatedly sang 'The Fields of Athenry'. The following night, Delaney was again out in the bars of Sopot, returning to his hotel at around 3 a.m., accompanied by the FAI security man Joe McGlue, who was smiling sheepishly.

Delaney appeared hardly able to stand or talk as partying fans milled around him singing, pulling at his hair and taking photos and videos on their phones. For further amusement, they then asked Delaney to make a speech. The CEO took a deep breath and somehow found the words: 'All I can say is thank you for supporting our country, and our team. You have been absolutely fucking brilliant. You were fucking magnificent last night. I am sorry that the team couldn't do what you wanted them to do.' Closer to the hotel, Delaney made another speech to another group of fans and was then hoisted shoulder-high towards the hotel, with his shoes having been removed by fans.

Kept awake by the din, the players fumed. One senior member of the team is said to have thrown a bucket of water at somebody out the window late at night, annoyed at being denied his sleep.

Ireland lost their final match 2–0 to Italy. Some fringe members of the Ireland squad, such as Darron Gibson and Darren O'Dea, were disgusted about how they were treated by Trapattoni, stuck in the hotel without getting any game time, and treated like training cones. Several players broke the curfew imposed by Trapattoni to join in the revelry. However, the inquiry back at home focused more on Delaney's behaviour.

Delaney agreed to do a post-tournament interview with Dion Fanning in the *Sunday Independent*. The CEO arrived with an armful of folders documenting the FAI's preparations for the event. But the interview focused on his behaviour, and was accompanied by a large photo of Delaney in Sopot looking completely wasted. Delaney produced a particularly weird quote which became the headline: 'Fans carried me head-high home. Now if that's a crime, I'm not guilty. Trust me.'

A week after Ireland were knocked out, McCaul and Delaney attended the funeral back in Ireland of a twenty-one-year-old Ireland fan, James Nolan, who had died when he fell into a river in the Polish city of Bydgoszcz. McCaul was still upset by what had happened in Sopot and the way that he felt Delaney had tried to usurp his role at one of the UEFA functions. 'On the way back home I rang him [Delaney] and I just let him have it. I said I was disgusted with the carry on,' he says.

McCaul wanted Delaney reined in and he asked Tom Jordan to mediate. Jordan, who listed conflict resolution in Northern Ireland on his CV, had helped set up the FAI's HR department and he had the ear of board members as well as of Delaney.

Jordan had been in Sopot himself and had been shocked by some of what he had seen and heard. He felt that senior staffers should have spent less time in the pubs with Delaney, and he got a handle on how unhappy the players were with both the preparation and the tournament itself. He had also been talking to senior executives within the association – including Peter Sherrard and the Finance Director Tony Dignam – who were concerned with the financial direction the association was taking even before the Euros, but were too scared of Delaney to confront him themselves.

McCaul spoke to the Honorary Treasurer, Eddie Murray, who was also unhappy with Delaney's behaviour, but advised that McCaul raise his issue directly with the CEO rather than bring it to the board.

On 26 June, eight days after the defeat to Italy, Jordan set up a meeting at the Alexander hotel off Merrion Square. McCaul and his friend and fellow board member Eamon Naughton were on one side of the table, with Delaney on the other and Jordan in between as mediator. McCaul spoke first, talking about the poor team performance, which segued into disappointment at the behaviour of some senior executives, particularly Delaney, in the bars of Sopot and elsewhere. 'You're our CEO,' he reminded Delaney. Naughton mentioned Delaney's tie-throwing routine, which both he and McCaul were particularly unhappy about, though Jordan tried to keep the meeting focused on matters relating to what happened in Poland.

If they expected a mea culpa from Delaney, they were disappointed. The CEO fired back, criticizing McCaul. 'If he had anything on you, he'd nail you,' McCaul says. 'I was having a bad time with business. We were in receivership here and lost a good bit of property. He said I wasn't available, which was probably true to certain extent, but I was there when I was supposed to be. He felt we were wrong to question him.'

Delaney also turned on Jordan. 'He got very upset with Tom,' Naughton recalls. 'This was the first time someone said you're wrong or out of line.'

Unused to being challenged, Delaney asserted his authority. The exchanges took a sinister turn, according to the two board members present.

'In that meeting with us he said he'd bring down the FAI,' says Naughton.

McCaul recalls: 'He said, "You bring this to the board and I'll bring down the FAI." It was alarming. We were in a precarious financial position and we didn't want to be the architects of the demise of the FAI.'

How could Delaney bring down the association?

'He was referring to his connections [with sponsors]. He would clean us out.'

The meeting broke up after about ninety minutes. Delaney said he had to meet John Giles in another part of the hotel. There was clearly no meeting of minds; in fact, Delaney from then on started to be 'really shitty' towards McCaul, as one senior FAI official put it.

Other directors say they only heard of the post-Euro 2012 confrontation between McCaul, Naughton and Delaney years later and wonder what might have happened if it had been brought to the board.

There was more fallout from Poland, this time from one of Ireland's most famous players, Shay Given. The goalkeeper's father, Seamus, had been in Sopot venting his frustrations in a bar along with some other supporters about Delaney's salary, unaware that his comments would be overheard by a tabloid reporter and splashed all over the papers.

During a meeting with senior players – Robbie Keane, John O'Shea and Given – over bonuses, Delaney made a jibe about Given's father.

'If John Delaney had a problem with me he could have called me to one side before the meeting or after,' says Given. 'I was raging, really angry, and I told him so. It's just as well there was a big table between us.'

★

The 2012 AGM was held in Letterkenny, Co. Donegal. As was now tradition, a former international was paid to accompany the FAI delegation as they visited clubs around the county. Ray Houghton provided the star power in Donegal. Towards the end of the week staff held a mock awards ceremony in a pub and Houghton was given the 'best supporting actor Oscar' award for his ability to laugh on cue every time Delaney made the same jokes in his stock speech. Staff were delighted the following day to see the statuette, an empty Corona bottle covered in the gold wrapping from chocolate bars, peeping out of Houghton's jacket pocket when he got on the FAI bus.

At the AGM, the FAI's accounts showed that total debt stood at €63 million and Delaney announced he was taking a further pay cut to 'show leadership'. That had an ominous ring, and sure enough the FAI then announced job losses and further pay cuts for staff of between 10 and 15 per cent. The FAI said the cuts were necessary because of the economic 'climate'. Delaney pointed out that his pay had dropped twice in the previous years; from a peak of €431,687, it was now at €360,000. For some FAI staff on €30,000 a year, Delaney's huge salary, even after the cut, caused disgust, and it was pointed out in press reports that the CEO still earned more than the combined total of his counterparts in Spain and Italy, the two countries that had just contested the Euro 2012 final.

In September, a female staff member made a complaint of harassment against the FAI Vice-President, Tony Fitzgerald. Her solicitor's letter of complaint said that the harassment 'continued despite our client's clear upset and the perpetrator's actions were obvious to other members of staff'. It also said that 'despite her complaint your organization has failed to deal with it under your policy of bullying and harassment. Instead, the CEO in a letter has attempted to set up a committee that is not provided for under the policy of bullying and harassment.' The letter complained that the woman had suffered stress and anxiety as a result of Fitzgerald's actions. Once the employee produced text messages that she had received from Fitzgerald, the FAI decided to settle, paying a low five-figure sum.

The FAI committee investigating the complaint consisted of Michael Cody, Eddie Murray and Niamh O'Donoghue, a senior civil servant and veteran FAI Council member. Further to the committee's recommendations, Fitzgerald was required to make a written apology to the complainant, to attend a training course and to step aside temporarily from all FAI duties. But he retained his senior position on the FAI board.

The case of the FAI's Director of Football Support Services, Gerry McDermott, was also disturbing. In September 2011 McDermott was diagnosed with Hodgkin's lymphoma. He went on sick leave the following month.

In April 2012, after he had finished chemotherapy, he met Delaney in Castleknock for lunch. They discussed how, because of restructuring, he would return to his original role as Communications Manager. It was a pleasant meal. McDermott insisted on paying the bill.

In June 2012 Peter Sherrard called McDermott 'out of the blue' to say the FAI would be cutting his wages by 45 per cent. McDermott, who was on €90,000 a year, asked what would happen if he objected. He was told that if he didn't like it he would be made redundant.

McDermott, who was now on unpaid sick leave, agreed to return to work, but asked for a part-time role as UEFA Venue Manager, to facilitate the running of Champions League and Europa League matches. In December, three months after he had returned to work, he was told the board wouldn't sign off on the necessary forms. Delaney refused to engage with him when he tried to talk to him about it.

McDermott wanted a Return to Work interview with Delaney, who had been his line manager when he went off on sick leave, but there was no interaction with Delaney after he came back.

'That was the thing about John,' says McDermott. 'He always got other people to deliver his bad news.'

⋆

Following the disaster in Poland, Ireland squeaked a victory in their next competitive game, a World Cup qualifier away to Kazakhstan. Then came a 6–1 thrashing at home to Germany, a result which confirmed that Ireland were no longer able to compete against top European sides.

The deputy editor of the *Irish Independent*, Ian Mallon – who, along with the editor Stephen Rae, regularly socialized with Delaney – wrote that Trapattoni was about to be sacked, regardless of the result against the Faroe Islands in Tórshavn four days later.

'Trapattoni is heading for a fall from the vertiginous cliffs which frame these spectacular islands,' wrote Philip Quinn in the *Irish Daily Mail*. When Quinn and a colleague, Paul Lennon, approached Delaney in the tiny Tórsvøllur stadium before the match to see if he was prepared to share some information about Trapattoni, they were angrily waved away and told they were trespassing in the VIP area.

Delaney hurried back from the Faroes for a secret board meeting at Abbotstown the night after the 4–1 victory. Unlike other board meetings, there was no attendant media circus, as the football writers were still traipsing back from the Faroes. But two journalists who had remained in Dublin, John Fallon and Paul Rowan, got wind of the meeting and were waiting in the car park when it broke up.

Paddy McCaul was the first board member to emerge, pausing for a moment on the concourse to light a cigarette, but nonetheless anxious to make his getaway as quickly as possible. Then came Milo Corcoran. 'We've had a conversation and we're staying as we are,' Corcoran said as he prepared to step into his car. 'A statement for the media is being prepared.'

Rowan then entered the FAI reception area and had a conversation with a security guard, who asked him did he have an appointment. Rowan said he didn't, but the security guard buzzed him through anyway. Rowan knocked on the door of the boardroom and entered. Standing around the large oval table were Delaney, Sarah O'Shea and Naughton. Rowan extended his arm to shake Delaney's hand, but was rebuffed. Delaney led him back out of the room and handed him over to the security guard. 'Escort him from the building' was the instruction, which the security guard swiftly obeyed. Rowan then waited on the street for Delaney, who drove by shortly afterwards in his Ford company car without stopping.

Shortly afterwards, two gardaí from nearby Blanchardstown station pulled up and questioned Rowan. The reporter then drove home, receiving a phone call on the way from the *Sunday Times*'s Ireland editor, Frank Fitzgibbon, saying there had been a complaint made against him by the FAI's lawyer. The following day Rowan was questioned at length on the phone by a detective from Blanchardstown about what had happened the night before.

*

After further defeats in the crucial qualifying matches against Sweden at home and Austria in Vienna, Trapattoni was sacked during what Delaney described as a 'tearful' meeting at Dublin airport in September 2013. The fact that Delaney's long-time target, Martin

O'Neill, was in the job market after leaving Sunderland earlier that year probably had something to do with Trapattoni being shown the door. Before long it became more a question of when rather than if the former Northern Ireland captain would become Republic of Ireland manager. Denis O'Brien had made it clear he was prepared to subsidize the cost of employing O'Neill, as he had with Trapattoni.

What came as a surprise was O'Neill's demand that he bring Roy Keane with him as his deputy, having developed a rapport with the Corkman when they worked together as pundits for ITV. This presented Delaney with both a problem and an opportunity. Delaney had repeatedly expressed the view that Keane should 'get over himself' about Saipan, and he had even worked his feud with the former Ireland captain into his after-dinner speeches at the club dinners he attended up and down the country.

At the awards ceremony of the Combined Counties Football League on 1 June 2013 he heard somebody shout 'Keano, Keano' when he was called to the stage to make a speech. Delaney addressed the heckler: 'I hope it was Robbie, not that fuckin' Roy.' There were some cheers from the audience. 'Apologies for the bad language. It's OK to swear a small bit is it? Or is it too late?' He also recounted putting the 'two grand behind the bar' for fans during an away match against Estonia. 'It might fuckin' happen tonight, you never know,' he said.

There were clearly fences to mend, and Delaney met O'Neill and Keane at the Grosvenor hotel in London to finalize the deal for the new management team. Denis O'Brien had committed €1.3 million a year to cover most of the salaries of the new management team.

Delaney then went on Newstalk radio – owned by O'Brien – to announce the appointments.

'There should be a line drawn in the sand in terms of Saipan and what happened,' Delaney said. 'We were all younger people back then. I think we all say things in different parts of our life . . . But anything that would have been said by Roy or I to each other or about each other is irrelevant. Irish football and our country is bigger than anything.'

Keane's return to the Irish scene was huge news. The fact that it was exclusively revealed on Newstalk by Delaney, instead of at a press conference where all media could ask questions, caused consternation in RTÉ, the FAI's broadcast partner for international games.

Delaney agreed to come into RTÉ's studios for an interview on the *News at One*. In the corridor, Ryle Nugent, RTÉ's Head of Sport, tackled Delaney. How could he think it was OK to give one radio station an exclusive announcement on who the next Irish management team would be?

Delaney patted Nugent on his head and told him, 'You don't understand business.' Nugent turned and walked away. An RTÉ source said he was worried for a moment that Nugent might take a swing at Delaney over the demeaning way he had patted him on the head. Nugent later told colleagues it was one of the most difficult moments in his career.

While Delaney spoke about reconciliation with Keane, there were more draconian measures against other dissenters. Paul Cooke was barred from the 2013 AGM after criticizing the FAI on a *Prime Time* programme that again raised questions about the €5.2 million of 'exceptional costs' in the 2008 accounts which had never been explained.

Finally, in June 2013, that mystery was solved when the *Sunday Times* reported that, at the start of 2008, the FAI had identified a principal lender for the stadium and then approached Goldman Sachs to secure 'mezzanine debt' to make up the shortfall. After this initial deal broke down, Goldman Sachs was told its services were no longer required.

When the FAI returned to Goldman Sachs soon afterwards seeking mezzanine debt for a fresh deal with a different lender, Goldman agreed, but this time included a 'break' clause worth between €5 million and €6 million should the FAI again have second thoughts.

The FAI then secured a loan offer from Danske Bank covering virtually all of the construction costs, and again Goldman was told its services were no longer required. At this point, Goldman pressed for its break fees and a figure of €4 million was agreed. It still wasn't clear what made up the remaining €1.2 million in 'exceptional costs' in the 2008 FAI accounts, but legal expenses related to the mezzanine debt drama probably contributed to much of them.

Small fires were breaking out all over the place. In an interview published in October 2013, the PFAI General Secretary, Stephen McGuinness, told reporter John Fallon that the League of Ireland would remain in crisis unless the FAI extended their crippling loan-repayment schedule beyond the 2020 deadline and got 'young blood' into the upper echelons of power.

When Fallon arrived to cover the women's FAI Cup final at the Aviva Stadium in November 2013 he was informed by Peter Sherrard that his accreditation had been withdrawn because the board was unhappy with his reporting. Fallon went home but then filed a complaint with Sherrard. From checking with his own sources, Fallon was adamant that it wasn't a board decision and says he received an assurance from an apologetic Sherrard that there wouldn't be a repeat of the intimidatory tactics.

McGuinness got more personal feedback from Delaney. He had slowly risen up the list of Delaney's adversaries since the PFAI's move out to Abbotstown, where it shared office space with the FAI. Some weeks after the interview was published, Delaney arranged to meet McGuinness at the Crowne Plaza hotel in Blanchardstown, a short drive from Abbotstown.

McGuinness arrived in the hotel lobby first and sat near a large cage containing the hotel's resident lovebirds, Bubble and Squeak. Delaney walked in behind McGuinness and pulled a cutting of the interview with Fallon out of his breast pocket.

'What the fuck was that?' he demanded.

McGuinness said he had expressed his opinion. Delaney told him he hadn't a clue about all the work he had done for the league.

The PFAI boss will never forget how the meeting ended.

'He says to me, "You and your fucking organization can say what the fuck they like about the FAI, about the board and about me because you know what, Stephen?" '

Delaney cupped his left hand and pointed into it with his right.

' "I've the fucking board in there. And as long as I have them, it doesn't matter what you say." '

Delaney closed his hand and walked out the door, leaving a shocked McGuinness with only the chirping lovebirds for company.

7. The Ballad of John Delaney

Wearing a dark, loose-fitting T-shirt and sporting a tight salt-and-pepper beard, Roy Keane was the personification of serenity. A small fountain bubbled away as Keane purposefully led a team of helpers to arrange his own Zen garden. Using a small twig clipper, he daintily pruned a bonsai tree before directing his band of gofers to move ornaments and furniture with assertive but encouraging nods. A wall hanging of the yin and yang symbol unfurled to Keane's approval just as Martin O'Neill bungled in through the front door. The Ireland manager looked perturbed as he clattered his head off low-hanging wind chimes.

'What's all this about, Roy?' a bewildered O'Neill asked.

'It's feng shui,' explained Keane. O'Neill's assistant manager calmly elaborated. It was about 'creating space' and being 'calm and peaceful'.

'Breathe in, breathe out,' Keane instructed.

But O'Neill hadn't achieved a state of Zen. Instead, as he grappled with a large chair, he grimaced in agony after bashing his knee. Keane moved over to attend to the stricken O'Neill as the TV commercial's voiceover came in. Viewers could take the 'stress' out of applying for a loan by using their local credit union.

That advert, and another for the Irish League of Credit Unions, was filmed by a cast and crew of fifty-three over the course of one day in Dublin in July 2014. However, due to what representatives for the Credit Unions regarded as a 'complete clusterfuck' on the FAI's part, the adverts were never broadcast.

The Credit Unions initially approached the FAI while Keane and O'Neill were in America with the Ireland team to play friendlies in June 2014. The FAI was still on tenterhooks with Keane, given his track record. When a mistake on a train in America led to the team missing its stop, Keane texted one of the FAI operations team, 'This is worse than Saipan.'

Keane was joking. Everybody laughed.

O'Neill's and Keane's contracts required them to do promotional work for FAI sponsors. While they were still in America, the FAI agreed to the Credit Unions' offer of a €100,000 payment up front and a possible bonus payment of up to €150,000 if Ireland qualified for the 2016 European Championship. In return the Ireland management team would shoot two adverts for a new TV campaign. The concept for the commercials was to flip the public personas of the two men. 'Make Roy lovely and Martin horrible.'

The cast, which included players from Bohemian FC, and crew were ready to go when the FAI told the Credit Unions that O'Neill didn't want to do it. The problem was the script, which O'Neill got to see only on the eve of the shoot. He hated it. The FAI convinced O'Neill to do the adverts but told him he could veto them if he didn't like the end result.

All through the shoot, O'Neill made his distaste known. One of those in attendance told O'Neill she was a big fan of his. He responded by saying she wouldn't be a fan later, because 'I didn't sign up for this.'

Keane was in hysterics at times as O'Neill struggled with his lines. 'How the fuck did you get Martin to do this?' Keane asked.

At the end of the shoot, O'Neill thanked the crew. 'Pity it will never see the light of day,' he said, ominously.

The post-production work and booking of TV slots for that September would more than double the €100,000 filming costs. The FAI assured the Credit Unions that they could go ahead. The adverts were finished and the TV slots were booked. The Credit Unions were delighted with the end result, but O'Neill was not. The FAI said it would return the upfront payment, but the adverts could not be used.

The Credit Unions and their production company demanded that the FAI reimburse their full costs of some €230,000, inclusive of VAT. The FAI insisted it would return the €100,000 and no more. The Credit Unions then threatened to run the adverts as planned unless the FAI paid the full costs incurred. The FAI responded by threatening to go to the High Court to injunct the Credit Unions from broadcasting the commercials. The association feared that O'Neill would resign if they were broadcast. At one delicate stage of the drama, the FAI was unable to get instructions from Delaney as he was at the Galway Races.

Ultimately, the FAI backed down and paid up, although it would fight paying some €35,000 in VAT until 2016, when it was threatened with legal action. The affair was settled with non-disclosure agreements keeping the sorry mess from going public.

The debacle cost the FAI in excess of €300,000, through direct payments and missed sponsorship income. The Credit Unions, which had been keen to link in with the FAI as a major sponsor, vowed never to work with the association again.

'They were dysfunctional to their core,' says one source involved with the Credit Unions.

An FAI source empathized with O'Neill. 'He hadn't done this at Celtic or Leicester, so he just thought, "Why do I have to do this now?"' the source says. Delaney, for his part, didn't have enough pull with O'Neill to ensure he would approve the commercials for the FAI's benefit. 'John would ask Martin to do all sorts of personal favours with the grassroots, like attending functions down the country. Roy occasionally too. But it was at a cost of what the FAI needed from them. He used up his personal capital with them that could have been used to ask them to help with sponsors.'

*

Delaney's power base in the FAI was centred in the amateur clubs and leagues across Ireland. Many administrators in these clubs and leagues came to view Delaney as a messianic figure, such was his ability to help them to get government grants or to deliver FAI funds. He spent most weekends attending up to half a dozen events for clubs up and down the country. He would often promise an FAI grant of between €5,000 and €10,000 to assist clubs, or, if not money, then large numbers of tickets to upcoming Ireland games. Few clubs received more of Delaney's largesse than Clones Town in Monaghan.

Clones Town, which maintains that it is the oldest football club in Ireland, had always been forced to play home matches in rented roadside fields. Sarto Quigley, a labourer by trade and a left-sided midfielder with Clones Town in his playing days, was amongst the volunteers who went around with a rake and a bag before matches to lift cow pats and sheep dung.

In 2006 the club emptied its savings to buy a hilly five-acre site overlooking the town for €30,000. Major engineering and construction work was needed to excavate 200,000 tonnes of earth before two pitches could be created. A grant of €100,000 was secured from the Department of Sport, but the club risked losing this as it was unable to secure a contractor to do the necessary work.

When the FAI held its AGM in the Hillgrove hotel in Monaghan in 2009, Quigley took the opportunity to introduce himself to Delaney, who had already announced a €20,000 grant for the club. Quigley told Delaney that he needed ten minutes of his time. 'You wouldn't be in your position but for Clones Town Football Club,' said Quigley, who had done much research on his club's history. 'Clones Town was the gateway for soccer in Ireland.'

Although most would have dismissed Quigley's claim as hyperbole, Delaney liked it. He saw a man with a fervent passion for a long-established grassroots club.

Quigley got his meeting. He says he will never reveal exactly what was said in their private chat, but the upshot was that Delaney committed to helping Clones Town develop a permanent ground if Quigley would commit to seeing the project through.

'I would trust John with my life,' says Quigley. 'From what I know of John Delaney, he's never, ever broken his word. I asked if he would see it through and he asked if I would see it through.'

Delaney even arranged to have Giovanni Trapattoni attend a gala dinner for the club in the Hotel Kilmore in Co. Cavan in 2010. It was a huge success, with over 400 people in attendance and €37,500 raised, although most of that money went towards the club's running costs. The seventy-one-year-old Trapattoni made a speech and spent over an hour signing autographs and posing for photographs. Delaney donated some €4,000 of his own money.

Quigley also turned to local farmer and businessman Alo Mohan for assistance. Mohan, a poultry farmer, was chairman of the Irish

Farmers' Association's poultry committee and sat on the meat and livestock board of Bord Bia, a semi-state food promotion authority. He proposed a sponsorship deal between Bord Bia and the FAI.

A meeting was held in the Department of Agriculture between Mohan, Aidan Cotter, the Chief Executive of Bord Bia, Simon Coveney, then the Minister for Agriculture, and the FAI, represented by Delaney and Max Hamilton. A €50,000 sponsorship deal was eventually agreed. In return for Bord Bia's money, the FAI provided players and Trapattoni to promote Irish beef before and after the Euro 2012 tournament, with an emphasis on the Italian and German markets. The deal included Trapattoni having to attend a trade dinner near the Irish training camp in Italy ahead of the Euro 2012 tournament and making a short speech.

In return for his successful advice and introductions, Mohan got Delaney to commit to giving Clones a further €70,000 from the FAI over ten years. The club used an FAI commitment letter to get a €70,000 loan from Ulster Bank.

Delaney also provided match tickets and signed jerseys. Many of those working on the Clones pitches offered their labour voluntarily. Any tickets not used for fundraising raffles were given as gifts to those helping to build the club's new home.

Bowled over by Delaney's support, Quigley proposed in 2013 that the new ground be called John Delaney Park. There was no alternative proposal. 'He took a huge chance,' says Quigley. 'There was a lot of grief and turmoil in the club.'

Delaney did not accept the honour straight away. He asked Quigley to take over as chairman of the club to ensure there was no split amongst its members. He didn't want his name associated with a club that could break up. Delaney joked that the ground-naming was an effort to 'squeeze' more money out of him. But at the 2013 opening ceremony, Delaney had tears rolling down his face as he spoke about the honour.

Mohan regarded the job as half done: even with two pitches developed, the club needed more funds to build changing rooms. The name of the ground didn't harm the club's chances of getting further assistance. In 2014 Michael Ring, a junior minister in the Department of

Sport, announced one-off funding for football of €1.2 million to be split evenly between six projects chosen by the FAI. John Delaney Park was one of the six, and so another €200,000 helped finance an impressive new clubhouse.

The new facilities have helped Clones Town expand from having just one senior men's team and two juvenile sides to a position where the club now boasts a senior men's team, a B-team, eleven under-age teams, a women's team and a girls' team. All that in a GAA stronghold.

The name of the ground would become a source of derision for the club, but Quigley believes it should be retained. 'I know personally what John did for the people of Clones,' he says. 'The man committed no crime that I can see. In my dealings with him he certainly didn't cross any lines. I don't see any reason why it should be changed.'

★

A May 2014 article by Nick Webb in the *Sunday Independent* talked about the FAI's 'remarkable turnaround' under Delaney. Webb wrote that the FAI had been 'a joke', but that Delaney's emphasis was 'stability' and 'making the FAI less intentionally funny'.

That may have been Delaney's goal, but the FAI was soon to become synonymous with high farce. In the summer of 2014, Delaney had a meal with Paul Clarkson, the editor of the *Irish Sun* – something he did semi-regularly with certain newspaper editors. During the dinner, Delaney mentioned the secret FIFA payment over the Thierry Henry handball back in 2010. He also agreed to do an interview with the paper.

On 13 July 2014 the *Irish Sun* front-page splash was 'The €5m Hand-out of Frog – FIFA paid FAI to shut up about rat Thierry'. The story quoted an anonymous source. Other media tried to follow up the story, but the FAI refused to comment. Aloïs Hug, a spokesman for FIFA, told the *Sunday Times* 'we have checked internally and we are not aware of any such payment'.

On 17 July the *Sun* published the first part of an interview with Delaney in which he revealed that he had signed a new deal with the FAI to extend his contract to 2020. The following day the paper ran another Delaney exclusive, under the headline: 'I didn't score Nadia,

I'm her father figure'. The FAI's Chief Executive was referring to his relationship with Nadia Forde, a singer and model who had sung the national anthem in the Aviva Stadium in September 2013 before a match against Sweden, shortly after dancing with Delaney at a charity event.

'If you read what's written at times, you'd wonder what's going on between me and Nadia,' Delaney told the *Sun*. 'But listen, we're very firm friends – and just friends. I think I'm more like a father figure. I'm forty-six years of age, she is in her early twenties, to be fair.'

Irish supporters, FAI staff and board members were bemused by the rate at which Delaney was volunteering details of his personal life. There was much more to come. In September, FAI staff and council members were invited to attend the premiere of a short documentary about Delaney, *John the Baptist*. The film was made by the *Sunday Independent*'s showbiz correspondent, Barry Egan. The documentary amounted to a fawning celebration of Delaney as a celebrity football administrator.

An FAI staff member who had to organize the event told colleagues it was a 'low point in my life', such was her embarrassment. The premiere in Dublin's Sugar Club on Leeson Street cost the FAI some €5,000.

Denis O'Brien, the largest shareholder in Independent Newspapers, was the star interviewee in *John the Baptist*, which was later released on Independent.ie in three parts. O'Brien told Egan that the FAI was lucky to have attracted somebody of Delaney's calibre. 'John Delaney could run anything,' said O'Brien. 'John Delaney could run UEFA easily. He could run FIFA as far as I'm concerned, certainly better than Sepp Blatter, and more honestly.'

In a speech at the documentary launch, Delaney declared his love for his new girlfriend, Emma English. Delaney and English had met in May 2013 at the same *Strictly Come Dancing* football charity event where Delaney had danced with Nadia Forde. English, who is ten years younger than Delaney, was a computer programmer and model before she turned her hand to event organizing through Couleur Productions, a business she ran with her husband James English. Emma was not only responsible for producing the 2013 fundraising dance event, held in Citywest hotel, but also danced for the judges, who included Barry Egan. Emma and James English, who had four children, separated some time before Emma started dating Delaney in mid-2014. Their first date was said to be in the Doheny & Nesbitt pub in Dublin. English would soon become a constant at Delaney's side, whether it was at matches, UEFA meetings or dinner nights for local clubs and leagues across the country.

The week after the *John the Baptist* premiere, a close-up photo of Delaney adorned the front cover of the *Sunday Independent*'s Life magazine; the headline was 'The Guv'nor'. Inside, there was a full-page picture of Delaney eating a prawn sandwich, a nod to Roy Keane's famous dismissal of corporate types who attend matches.

Egan explained in the five-page feature why Delaney was the 'John the Baptist of the FAI'. 'He partly cleansed it of its sins and made it a much, much better institution,' Egan gushed.

The article concluded with Delaney telling a story about going drinking with Eric Cantona, the former Manchester United and Leeds striker, and the organizer of a fundraiser in Cork. The band of three met 'three lovely girls'. Delaney said a pal of his had showed up and was delighted to meet Cantona and the three women.

'Let's just say my pal was fourth in the queue,' said Delaney.

Emma English was now regularly accompanying Delaney to international football meetings and grassroots events, and visiting him in Abbotstown, and she became well acquainted with FAI staffers and directors. Board members who had known Delaney for over a decade were shocked to find Delaney and English kissing passionately at events or matches.

'It was like he turned into a teenager around her,' says one board member.

While English's presence at formal pre-match dinners and UEFA events raised a few eyebrows, as Delaney's star rose in UEFA other associations made sure she felt welcome. She was regularly given gifts: Germany, Turkey, the USA and Moldova all gave her jerseys with 'Emma' emblazoned on the back.

In September 2014 Dublin was chosen by UEFA as one of thirteen cities that would host matches in the Euro 2020 tournament. The

Aviva would host four games, a notable achievement for Delaney and the FAI, and he was not shy about claiming credit.

Arising out of his speech at the *John the Baptist* premiere, Delaney was invited to be a guest on a Saturday-night chat show on RTÉ television hosted by Brendan O'Connor, who was also editor of the *Sunday Independent*'s Life magazine. On 11 October, on live TV and with a studio audience, O'Connor introduced Delaney as a man who 'was never short of opinions', but added that his 'new girlfriend says he's a big teddy bear really'.

Under the noise of the applauding crowd, O'Connor could be heard calling Delaney 'the big teddy bear' as they shook hands. Delaney responded 'fuck you' while smiling and taking his seat.

In the interview, Delaney once again spoke about his new love, and about how English had turned his life around. 'Sometimes when you're not personally happy, or as happy as you should be, you throw yourself into the job a lot,' said Delaney. 'I was probably going down a track that I wouldn't have been happy about myself. I've met Emma and she's been absolutely fantastic.'

What track had Delaney been on?

'I wouldn't want to go into that too much,' said Delaney. 'I wouldn't have been in the best of places personally. But I met her . . . So, I'm very much in love with her. She's been a huge influence on my life. She's a terrific person. She's a beautiful person inside. She's really, really changed me and I'm very pleased.'

English, who was sitting in the audience, was asked if Delaney was a 'teddy bear'.

'Oh, for sure,' said English. 'Oh my God, honestly he really is. He's so romantic. But he has that big soft centre in him as well. He can never say no to people. It comes naturally to him to just do right by people. Just everywhere I go, he offers. He is always giving. He always wants to make people happy and do the right thing. It's incredible, actually, to watch him.'

*

In November, Ireland had to play Scotland away at Celtic Park in a European Championship qualifier. There was huge demand for tickets from Ireland's travelling supporters. When it emerged that the Scottish Football Association (SFA) had decided to limit Ireland's ticket allocation to the minimum-permitted 5 per cent of the capacity, all hell broke loose.

Many fans who had not missed an Ireland away game in years were told by the FAI that they would not be getting tickets. A fans' group, You Boys in Green (YBIG), demanded to know how the FAI had used its share of tickets, amidst suspicion that a large proportion had been allocated to friends and associates of Delaney.

Delaney admitted that the FAI had made a mistake in assuming that it would receive more tickets. The FAI bought 150 premium tickets to sell to loyal fans at a loss. However, Delaney was not taking personal responsibility for the ticketing mess. He publicly questioned the professionalism of the SFA and Stewart Regan, its Chief Executive, for limiting Ireland to the minimum ticket allocation. Delaney warned that this could create security issues, as Ireland fans would be forced to buy home tickets and would end up dotted amongst the Scottish crowd.

'This is a derby game, it's a Friday night in Glasgow and there'll be tension in the air,' said Delaney.

Stewart Regan was shocked by Delaney's response. 'As a result of his bleating, UEFA actually changed the category of the game to the highest category security risk,' says Regan. 'They put an inspector from UEFA on the game to basically watch over it. He [Delaney] ramped up the Scottish press and the Irish press.'

Regan, for his part, had no worries about Irish and Scottish fans fighting, given their long track records of good behaviour. The match passed off without any crowd problems and Scotland won 1–0.

Delaney insisted that the visiting FAI delegation would not attend the normal pre-match meal with the SFA. It was the only time in Regan's eight years in charge that a visiting association snubbed the traditional pre-match dinner.

If Delaney thought his high-profile attack on the SFA would take the pressure off him with disgruntled Irish fans, he was mistaken. Zeno Kelly had been going to Ireland matches since he was in primary school, and had missed just one away fixture since 2009. Like many dedicated Ireland fans, he had spent tens of thousands of euro following the team. As a St Patrick's Athletic supporter, Kelly had grown increasingly angry at what he saw as Delaney's lack of interest in the League of Ireland, and over the lack of transparency in how the association was run. In 2014 Delaney had labelled the League of Ireland a 'difficult child', infuriating many supporters.

The ticket allocation for the Scotland match was the least of Kelly's concerns, but he saw the Celtic Park fiasco as an opportunity to transform a spontaneous swell of anger into action. Kelly had got tickets for the Scotland game, but '95 per cent' of the independent supporters he knew did not. He posted on the YBIG forum and on its Facebook page calling for a protest to be held in the singing section of the Aviva Stadium against Delaney during the USA game on 18 November, four days after the Scotland match.

When the fans unveiled their banners and started singing their protest chants against Delaney, many match stewards and gardaí descended on Section 114. Posters and banners were seized with some force.

'For a lot of Irish fans, that was when the tide started to turn,' says Kelly. 'The protest was one way of getting a lot of people onside.'

Ger Keville, one of the YBIG forum's owners, was amongst the crowd.

'I saw a steward diving at a fella,' he says. 'There was a kid of about eight sandwiched in the middle. This guy was trying to take a flag. It was the first time I'd ever seen anything like this – very aggressive stewarding.'

The heavy-handed nature of the FAI's response to criticism, at a low-key friendly on a Tuesday evening, attracted a lot of media attention in the following days. But worse was to come for Delaney.

After the game, his retinue retreated to the Bath pub beside the stadium. Delaney sang 'Joe McDonnell', a ballad about an IRA hunger-striker. A grainy video of Delaney singing the song was circulated amongst Irish fans before it was posted on YouTube that Friday. Balls.ie ran a story about the video. The timing was awkward: Roy Hodgson, the England manager, had recently apologized for England fans singing anti-IRA songs in Celtic Park at a friendly against

Scotland, and both England and Scotland were due in Dublin the following summer. It would be England's first match in Ireland since
their fans ripped up wooden seats in the old Lansdowne Road in 1995
and threw them over the stands, causing the game to be called off.

Peter Sherrard, the FAI's Head of Communications, failed to
respond to numerous calls, texts and emails that weekend, but he did
contact Balls.ie. He warned the site that Delaney would take legal
action, because the man singing the song in the video was not him.
The website took down the video.

On Monday other media were still trying to authenticate the
video. Barry Egan had unwittingly given partial confirmation by
reporting in the *Sunday Independent* that Delaney and English had a
singsong in the Bath pub after the match. Egan named several former
footballers who had been present. His gossip item reported that Delaney and English, 'the romance of the year', were going to 'heat up
Marbella . . . with their passionate intensity' that weekend.

Unhappy with the advice he was getting from senior FAI managers
to come clean, Delaney sought counsel from Keith Bishop, a UK-
based PR guru who worked with Mike Ashley, the owner of
Newcastle FC and Sports Direct, a chain of sporting-goods shops.
Through Bishop, Delaney instructed London firm Debello Law to
issue legal threats to the *Daily Telegraph* and *Guardian* newspapers
after they intimated that they would report that it was Delaney singing in the video.

Eventually, Emmet Malone in the *Irish Times* was able to confirm
that it was in fact Delaney in the video. The story ran on the newspaper's front page on Tuesday, 25 November. It prompted a media
onslaught from Delaney. He did at least four separate radio interviews. Remarkably, he had not one but two front-page stories to talk
about.

English had put a Facebook post up complaining about 'vile and
abusive' posts that were made about her on YBIG's online forum. 'I
have had to sit with my eleven-year-old son, who cried his eyes out
that people were speaking about his Mom like this,' she wrote. On
the morning the *Irish Times* report about Delaney's IRA song was
published, several tabloids led with 'Delaney-girl: My troll hell'

stories. When Delaney went on Ryan Tubridy's RTÉ One radio show, RTÉ's highest-paid broadcaster opened the interview by asking Delaney did he want to deal with the cyber-bullying story or the IRA song first.

'I'll probably take the Emma one first as that's very much been on our minds for the last number of weeks,' said Delaney. He said he believed the derogatory comments about his partner were made out of jealousy.

'It's very hard, as a man who wants to protect his woman, it's very hard,' said Delaney. 'Every man wants to protect their woman. Cyber-bullying is very cowardly.'

Tubridy eventually moved on to the IRA song. He was about to play the clip for his listeners but changed his mind after Delaney asked him not to. Delaney explained he was not a violent person. 'My grandfather fought in the civil war, war of independence,' he said. 'I've said before I've a nationalist background.'

'We share that in common,' said Tubridy.

'Absolutely,' said Delaney. 'To sing a song like that, you don't believe in every word. I sing a large number of songs. Maybe five or six. It's normally done in a private way. A sing-song. A typical Irish thing to do. Unfortunately, on occasion people use camera phones in a sly way and try to make it bigger than it is. If the song offends anybody then I'm sorry. It's not in my nature to offend anybody.'

In his interview with Pat Kenny an hour later on Newstalk, Delaney broke down in tears talking about cyber-bullying. In a joint interview on the Niall Boylan show on 4FM, English spoke about how she and Delaney had never looked for the 'spotlight'. 'My life is extremely private, as is John's, his personal life,' she said.

Boylan, who didn't ask about the IRA song, concluded the interview by asking for an invite to the couple's wedding, whenever that might be.

After it was revealed that the *Guardian* and *Daily Telegraph* had received correspondence from lawyers acting on the FAI's behalf that claimed Delaney was not the man singing in the video, the question arose as to how the legal threats had come to be made on a false premise. Delaney issued a statement that did little to clarify the matter.

'I now understand that while I was travelling and uncontactable there was some confusion through a third party around the background of a video which appeared and where it happened which led to misunderstanding,' the statement said.

While the singing of the IRA song called into question Delaney's judgement, using lawyers to threaten newspapers on spurious grounds raised serious ethical questions about how Delaney was operating. FAI staff were privately fuming over how Delaney's personal life was affecting FAI business, but the board remained supportive.

Tony Fitzgerald, now seventy-one, had taken over as President on a four-year term that summer from Paddy McCaul. Other board members knew about the harassment complaint against Fitzgerald from 2012, which had never become public. One says: 'I don't think he was compromised, but if John said black was white, Tony would agree.'

An early example of Fitzgerald's deferential attitude came when he became the first FAI President not to take one of the three FAI directorship positions, alongside Cody and Delaney, on the stadium company board. Instead, Donal Conway, who had become Vice-President, took the role.

Although Delaney was under pressure from the media after a shambolic two weeks, Fitzgerald, who also chaired the FAI Board of Management, gave his Chief Executive the all-clear with a rare public statement:

> Following recent coverage of the cyber-bullying of his partner Emma and the fact that John has publicly apologized if he offended anyone for singing the nationalist song in question, we are happy to bring the matter to a close. The board is more than pleased with the way John Delaney is running the association. He has done an enormous amount for Irish football . . . We recently awarded him a contract extension to 2020 and he is fully deserving of that.

That weekend, Emma English deleted her Twitter account after it was found she had retweeted criticism of Emmet Malone, the journalist who broke the story about Delaney singing the IRA song. One message retweeted by English said that Malone was 'a sneaky wee informing get' and called for him to be 'barred' from the Aviva.

Shortly after this furore, Delaney and English appeared on the front cover of the *Sunday Independent*'s Life magazine Christmas Party edition along with Barry Egan and a group of celebrities. Delaney's presence in the centre of the photograph, smiling while clutching a glass of champagne, over the caption 'The Good Life – after years of austerity, our annual Christmas party is back', caused disgust amongst FAI staff, whose wages had been frozen since the pay cuts of 2012.

One of those in the picture was Oliver Callan, the comedian and mimic behind RTÉ's *Callan's Kicks*. At the party on the roof garden of the Marker hotel in Dublin's docklands, Callan was taken aback by how Delaney spoke to him in what was their first meeting.

'It was kind of a strange atmosphere,' Callan recalls. 'It was just a perfect snapshot of all that was wrong at the time. It was phony Ireland; architecturally ugly building and everyone freezing and pretending to have a great time. Really, they were just there to get their photograph in the paper.'

He continues, 'I was there on my own and we were just chatting away. Then out of nowhere he starts talking about his ex-wife, and he calls her the c-word. That kind of strained my face. I was going, "Oh, ok." He was like, "Oliver, I'm serious. She is an absolute cunt." He went on and on. I had just met this man. How did we start talking about this?'

Delaney then offered Callan corporate tickets for an upcoming match. 'So, in the space of one tiny meeting: ex-wife is a c-word, and come along to the corporate box to watch the match,' says Callan, who believed the disarmingly frank nature of Delaney's opening conversational gambit was part of a strategy. 'What was fascinating was that whatever he was trying to do with the ex-wife story was trying to bring me into the circle of "we all have horrible things and let's share".'

*

Tony Dignam, the FAI's Finance Director, decided he had had enough of Delaney after three years and quit in early 2014. Unhappy with how that looked, Delaney convinced Dignam to stay on as a consultant to the FAI for several months after he had started a new job, so that he could present the FAI's financial accounts at its summer AGM.

Dignam's replacement was Eamon Breen, an accountant who had worked as a finance manager for Dixons Retail. His fellow staff believed Breen was enamoured with the football side of the job, but he was also seen as 'an empire builder'. After he settled in as Finance Director, Breen began to add on responsibilities, becoming Head of IT and taking control of the FAI's human resources and business partnerships. He also took over some operational and ticketing responsibilities.

Finance staff working under Breen raised concerns about the amount of personal expenditure that Delaney was billing the FAI for or putting through his company credit card. Such concerns were dismissed by Breen. Staff were told that personal expenditure by Delaney could be written off against holidays that the CEO was 'owed' because he hadn't used them.

With his added responsibilities, Breen began to travel regularly on away trips with the men's team, not something his predecessor as Finance Director had done. He told more than one FAI employee that he would be interested in taking over the top job at the FAI if Delaney ever moved on.

*

In late May 2015 fourteen people, including senior FIFA officials, were indicted in America for allegedly taking millions of dollars in bribes. The scandal was the death-knell for Sepp Blatter's term as FIFA President. For Delaney, it was time to lord it over the man who had so annoyed him five years previously when he mocked the FAI's thirty-third-team-at-the-World-Cup plea.

On RTÉ radio's *Ray D'Arcy Show*, Delaney said he didn't admire Blatter at all, but gave him credit for being resilient.

'It took a wave of momentum to finally get him to admit to stepping down,' said Delaney. 'He was brilliant at dividing and conquering and getting the Asians and the Africans behind him. I've never seen anyone better at it.

'He met Emma, my partner, in Vienna recently. He stared at her for seven or eight seconds and he said: "I approve of your new girlfriend." I swear to you. I just asked him to move on. "Just move on, please." She is a great girl and I love her very much. It was an extraordinary moment.'

D'Arcy asked if FIFA got a cut of the FAI's sponsorship deal with Three. Delaney patiently explained that wasn't how it worked. FIFA gave all associations an annual payment.

'And what was that €5 million?' D'Arcy asked. 'It sounded to me like we were being a nuisance about the Thierry Henry handball and they said, "Go away and shut up and here's €5 million."'

It was the question Delaney, the FAI and FIFA had avoided answering ever since the *Irish Sun* story a year earlier. When asked about it on RTÉ's *Morning Ireland* earlier that week, Delaney had said there had been an 'arrangement' made over the FAI's complaint but 'it certainly wasn't bestowing patronage to us'.

Now, in a chatty mood with the amiable D'Arcy, Delaney felt willing to elaborate. He said he had used foul language with Blatter because of how he sniggered at the FAI before they came to a deal. 'It was a very good agreement for the FAI and very legitimate agreement for the FAI,' said Delaney. 'I'm bound by confidentiality from putting the figure out there. You've put a figure out there. Fair play to you.'

What was the agreement?

'It was a payment to the association not to proceed with a legal case,' said Delaney. 'They decided to put a confidentiality agreement where I can't talk about the amount involved. You've used a figure, well done to you.'

Back in Abbotstown there was consternation that Delaney had just confirmed the FIFA payment story, despite the FAI being sworn to secrecy. When Delaney returned to base he couldn't understand why two members of his executive team, Sarah O'Shea and Peter Sherrard, were so exercised.

In the middle of global coverage of the FBI investigation into FIFA, the world's media picked up on the astonishing FAI pay-off as an example of the sort of deals that Blatter had made. Both FIFA and the FAI were repeatedly forced to deny that the payment amounted to a bribe.

Delaney agreed to show RTÉ's Tony O'Donoghue the documentation from the deal at his home in Kilmacanogue. After filming the documents and recording an interview with Delaney, O'Donoghue did a piece live to camera from the car park of the nearby Pluck's bar.

O'Donoghue noted that Delaney was vocal in calling for greater transparency from Blatter. He said that the FAI's need to service its Aviva Stadium debt had clearly trumped the need for openness in Delaney's own dealings with FIFA.

As soon as O'Donoghue came off air from the nine o'clock news, he got a call from a furious Delaney, who accused the reporter of calling him a hypocrite. 'I said, "Show me where I used the h-word, John," because I said what I said, and I believe what I said to be true,' O'Donoghue recalls.

The debate spilled over to Berlin, where the Champions League final between Barcelona and Juventus was being held. The German FA President, Wolfgang Niersbach, who was also a member of the FIFA Executive Committee said: 'It's a joke that they [FIFA] paid this money out to stop the Irish taking them in front of court.' Des Casey, an honorary life member of UEFA, in Berlin with his wife as a guest of the European governing body, was doorstepped by reporters at his hotel. 'Everyone is talking about it. People keep asking me if it's true. It's unprecedented in football to seek compensation for a referee's error,' said Casey. 'I regret the damage being done by the current saga and I'm deeply saddened by the events.'

Not even Casey, also an honorary life Vice-President of the FAI, was untouchable. Shortly afterwards, his tickets to the directors' box at the Aviva were withdrawn, even though he was in his mid-eighties and he struggled to walk up the stadium's steps where his new seats were located. 'He felt he could do what he liked,' Casey says. 'Instead of the VIP tickets, I was getting tickets in the crow's nest.'

Amidst international disquiet about the FIFA payment, members of the Oireachtas Sport Committee initially said they would summon Delaney to explain the deal. But after Delaney rang some of the politicians it was announced there would be no such hearing.

Speaking to the *Sunday Times*, Eddie Murray, the FAI's Honorary Treasurer, confirmed that the board backed Delaney. 'You can call him a hustler if you like, but he is doing the business for the association and doing it properly,' he said.

In June 2015 Scotland were in Dublin for a vital qualification match. In the build-up to the match, Scottish FA Chief Executive Stewart Regan was asked about the Henry pay-off and said that Scotland would not have taken a case over a refereeing decision.

For Delaney, the war was still on. Before the game the FAI scrapped 18,000 copies of its match programme, and reprinted them minus references by Delaney to the 'obvious' culture of 'corruption and bribery' in FIFA. Despite the blunder, which cost the FAI over €5,000, the FAI Chief Executive was in bullish form when the Scots arrived on his patch.

The boards of the two associations met for the customary pre-match meal. The Scotland delegation went to the designated hotel, only to find it deserted. They then received a phone call saying the dining venue had been switched to a suite in the Aviva Stadium. 'I went over to shake John's hand and put my hand out and he literally just walked right past me and completely blanked me,' says Regan. 'I thought, "This is going to be an interesting lunch!"'

Normally at such functions the protocol was for the respective associations' presidents and chief executives to sit opposite each other in the middle of the table. Regan discovered that he had been placed in a corner position beside the waiter's trolley, while Delaney, with Emma English sitting on his left and Tony Fitzgerald on his right, faced Alan McRae, the SFA President, at the centre of the table.

'This was the first time I'd ever known in any match I'd ever been to, of a girlfriend or a partner of the CEO attending the official function,' says Regan. 'I spoke to our President [about the seating] and said, "This is outrageous. What the hell is going on? How do you want to play it?" He was a little bit nervous. He didn't want to make a scene.'

Regan sat in the naughty corner through the dinner. Delaney wasn't finished, however.

It was customary for both presidents to make speeches. McRae thanked the FAI for the hospitality, wished them well and presented a memento. Then Delaney, rather than Fitzgerald, stood up to respond for the FAI. Regan says it was 'the most vitriolic speech' he'd ever heard.

'He talked about football people and the need to have people who understood the game involved in running it, people who knew how to behave towards other members of the football family, people who understood what the game was all about,' says Regan. 'He never mentioned me personally, but it was very clear that it was a personal attack on me. His view was obviously coloured by our previous dealings. I had to sit and listen to him talk about behaving professionally and then treating me like this. I literally had to bite my tongue as this was a formal event.'

An uncomfortable silence followed Delaney's speech. Regan decided to walk over to Delaney and offer to shake his hand, telling him 'good luck' for the match.

'He didn't know what to do,' says Regan. 'He was obviously wondering whether he should snub me in front of everybody. He had no option other than to shake my hand. At that point, all my colleagues from the Scottish FA board just gave a very large round of applause. It was my way of saying, "You're not going to make me feel small and I'm the bigger person in this situation." It was a pretty distasteful situation.'

In the run-up to the following month's FAI AGM in Sligo, the media focus was on the appearance of the FIFA €5 million in the FAI accounts for the first time.

On RTÉ's *Morning Ireland*, Claire Byrne introduced a preview of the AGM by saying there appeared to be a 'big black hole' in the FAI's accounts. Tony O'Donoghue said the FAI's accounts were in a 'dangerous' situation. Within hours, RTÉ received a demand for an apology and retraction from the FAI. A High Court writ followed weeks later from solicitor Paddy Goodwin, on behalf of the FAI, seeking damages, including punitive and aggravated awards.

The writ claimed Byrne, O'Donoghue and RTÉ had acted 'maliciously' in broadcasting a report implying that the FAI's accounts, business and finances were 'mismanaged', that 'money had gone missing without explanation', that 'proper books of account had not been kept' and that the FAI was 'insolvent'. It complained that the reports portrayed the FAI as 'not a fit company with which to do business' and one that 'should not be advanced any further credit'.

As RTÉ considered its response, O'Donoghue brought in former FAI board member Brendan Dillon to speak to RTÉ executives about his ongoing concerns about the FAI's finances. O'Donoghue hoped Dillon's insight would help convince RTÉ that this was not a case where they should raise the white flag and apologize. It was not a normal situation for a sports reporter to find himself in.

'RTÉ were very good on this with me,' says O'Donoghue. 'There were many meetings I had to go to with the solicitor's office. My line manager and the Head of News and Current Affairs were involved. We almost had to persuade RTÉ to defend it. If you have to go into the witness box, this could be a two-day or a two-week trial. Then the pressure is on you in a witness box. Nobody wants that. Without sounding too Woodward and Bernstein about it, this was about fair comment and freedom of speech. If RTÉ give in to something like this, then where are we left?'

Looking back at the writ served by the FAI, O'Donoghue finds it eerily on point.

'Maybe between the words "black hole" and "dangerous", they kind of conflated them and said we were saying terrible things about them,' O'Donoghue says. 'But the things they claimed we said were that the accounts are mismanaged, the plaintiff is insolvent or close to insolvency, that monies are being hidden – a whole list of things. It was like a confession.'

8.   The Candidate

As 'Amhrán na bhFiann' blared over the speakers, the actor Colin Farrell, dressed in denim, stood shoulder-to-shoulder with the Ireland players. For the Irish Homeless World Cup team in Amsterdam in September 2015, it was a moment of immense pride to represent their country at an international tournament. Meeting Farrell, a long-time ambassador for the Homeless World Cup Foundation, was a bonus. Farrell, who was filming *Fantastic Beasts and Where to Find Them* in London, listened to the life stories of the Irish players and told them he could have ended up in their position himself. 'There but for the grace of God . . . ,' the actor said.

The Irish team finished tenth out of forty-eight countries in the 2015 Homeless World Cup, a laudable effort which provided a moment of sweet satisfaction for Sean Kavanagh, the editor of the *Big Issue*, who has organized the Irish entry every year since the inaugural tournament in 2003.

After getting word out about organizing a team for the four-a-side tournament in 2003, Kavanagh had expected about fifteen people to turn up for the selection trial. Instead, he was shocked when over a hundred men arrived at the Iveagh Grounds. Stephen Kenny, who was then manager with Bohemians, came down to help train the first Irish Homeless World Cup team.

Inspired by the power of football to get young adults, many of whom had drug-addiction issues, to re-engage with society, Kavanagh decided to set up the Irish Homeless Street Leagues. Every year the best players from these teams are picked to represent Ireland at the international tournament, though players can take part in the event only once. Kavanagh says around 70 per cent of players on the World Cup teams experience positive life changes, such as coming off drugs, getting jobs, repairing relationships or even becoming football coaches.

After the Aviva Stadium opened in 2010, Delaney provided Kavanagh with two premium-level tickets for each home international. These were a great help in attracting sponsorship of the street leagues. The match tickets helped bring some corporate money in for Kavanagh's football projects.

Attending some of these Ireland matches, Kavanagh got to see Delaney in full flight in the premium areas of the Aviva. 'It was like he was the Godfather,' he said. 'Everybody wanted to shake his hand. They are all there to pay homage to the man. People would be waiting until he was free and then would run up to him.'

Through the relationship with the FAI, Kavanagh's projects received annual funding of €10,000 to support the street leagues and to cover the costs of the annual World Cup tournament. By 2015, however, Kavanagh had a number of gripes with the FAI. The association supplied kit for the squad of eight going to the World Cup, but sometimes the shorts were dirty. The team were also required to hand jerseys back after the tournament. Unhappy with this, Kavanagh bought jerseys directly from Toplion, the FAI suppliers, so each of the squad would have a memento.

More worryingly, he had to pester the FAI each year before the agreed grants were paid. In late August 2015, with the tournament in Amsterdam two weeks away, Kavanagh was still short some €5,000 of his FAI funding. He emailed Oisin Jordan, the national co-ordinator of Football for All, on 31 August, seeking the remainder of the grant. If he didn't have it by the end of the week to pay for the Holland excursion, 'nobody will be going anywhere', he warned. The team were due to fly out on 11 September.

Jordan responded promptly to say he had requested the money 'urgently' from the FAI finance department. Five days later, on 4 September, Kavanagh wrote directly to the FAI finance office asking for urgent payment. On the morning of 8 September, three days before he was due to fly out with the team, Kavanagh was desperate. 'We are doing pretty well running our programme on the sparse budget we've got, but what makes it impossible is when monies promised are not delivered on time,' he emailed Jordan.

The FAI man emailed back after first trying to phone Kavanagh.

He had been 'down to the finance manager and director'. The homeless team were 'on the priority list to be paid' but the 'FAI are awaiting a payment that has been delayed and [that] leaves them unable to pay out any money at all'.

Jordan apologized profusely. Kavanagh was 'more than welcome to go to John regarding the situation, but I have been told there won't be money to pay out until next week . . . Your situation has been put forward strongly but it's just a case that there is no funds to pay your funding,' said Jordan. He was sorry about 'how this seems to always pan out each year'.

Kavanagh thanked Jordan for his efforts and his honesty. 'The failure to honour the financial commitment in time says a lot about how we, the homeless street leagues, are perceived within the FAI,' he wrote. 'I shall be releasing a statement within the next twenty-four hours in the hope that someone will step in to make up the shortfall to enable the lads to participate in the Homeless World Cup.'

Kavanagh cc'd John Delaney in the email. He braced himself and clicked 'send'. He went for coffee in The Square shopping centre in Tallaght and had just sat down when he got a phone call from the FAI's finance office.

There had been a terrible mistake, Kavanagh was told. The FAI would courier the cheque around to his home straight away. Within an hour, Kavanagh was back home when a courier arrived on a motorbike with the FAI cheque. The threat to go public had produced an instant result.

After the tournament, Kavanagh was asked to come to Abbotstown to meet Jordan and his line manager. They couldn't understand why Kavanagh had threatened to go public. Nobody did that, he was told. The meeting ended amicably, he believed, but soon Kavanagh and his organization were being frozen out. The FAI stopped sending complimentary tickets for internationals. Then, just before Christmas, an FAI official told him that he should send Delaney a written apology 'for the trouble' he caused.

Kavanagh was indignant. He wrote to Delaney, but not to apologize. He explained that he had run out of options in September and felt he had no choice but contemplate going public. He suggested the only apology should have been from the FAI for failing to deliver a promised grant. Kavanagh ended his correspondence by wishing Delaney a happy Christmas. 'Roll on the Euros,' his letter said.

Kavanagh found he was frozen out by Delaney after that. Invites for launches and press events for the street league and Homeless World Cup team were turned down. Delaney was too busy.

The senior men's team had qualified for Euro 2016, and Delaney knew that this would generate up to €4 million in extra revenue for the FAI. In the meantime, the FAI's finance department was under constant pressure to ensure the association had enough cash to meet its bills. Many creditors, like the Homeless World Cup team, were long-fingered for due payments until the FAI had no other choice but to pay out.

Delaney had struck up a friendship with Newcastle United owner Mike Ashley. The abrasive self-made billionaire had made headlines not only for his business dealings but also for his high-stakes gambling exploits. In 2008 he won £1.3 million betting on 17 black at roulette, the same gamble that James Bond made in *Diamonds are Forever*. In 2011 Ashley reportedly lost £1 million on a night out gambling with Alan Pardew, the Newcastle manager.

After they became acquainted in 2015, Ashley took Delaney to the exclusive Palm Beach casino in the May Fair hotel in London, where Delaney was impressed by the huge amounts wagered by Ashley. Delaney posed for a photograph, smiling as he held one of the casino's £500,000 chips with Ashley behind him.

At the January 2016 FAI board meeting, Delaney told his fellow directors that he had 'good news': Sports Direct had 'offered' the FAI £10 million. Delaney said he was 'keen' to get £5–6 million from the company for sponsorship of the FAI's National Training Centre in Abbotstown 'rather than borrow the full amount'. It was an outlandish amount of money, but the FAI's directors just assumed their CEO was about to pull another financial rabbit out of the hat.

At the same meeting, Delaney reminded board members about a fashion show that Emma English was organizing in April in Citywest hotel to raise funds for the John Giles Foundation and the Capuchin Day Centre for homeless people. FAI sponsors were contacted and encouraged to buy tickets for the event at a cost of between €30 and €50. Junior clubs were asked to advertise the event on their social media pages. Anyone who bought a ticket would have first preference on buying tickets for an upcoming friendly between Barcelona and Celtic in the Aviva Stadium. Delaney had secured sponsorship of €10,000 for the event, he told the board.

In the same month Delaney received criticism from across the political spectrum when he accompanied Alan Kelly, a Labour TD and Minister for the Environment, on a number of photographed visits to junior football clubs and a barber shop in his Tipperary constituency just ahead of a general election in February. Delaney denied allegations that he was actively canvassing for Kelly, but on two local radio interviews he praised Kelly and said it was important for Tipperary people to keep a minister in their constituency.

Kelly, who was supporting Delaney's application for government funding to build a new centre of excellence in Glanmire in rural Cork, was delighted with the controversy and subsequent media attention. 'That's the media coverage you want ahead of an election,' says a source on the Labour TD's campaign.

In February 2016 Delaney told the board that Bank of Ireland was looking for 'further comfort' about the FAI's finances ahead of a planned refinancing of the stadium loan. Delaney said this brought Sports Direct 'into play'. He said the company would provide funding 'via sponsorship of summer schools, academy, purchase of a [corporate] box' and other things. Delaney assured the board that the FAI's legal advice was there was no conflict with the association's kit suppliers as long as any rights granted to Sports Direct were not the same as those already granted to Toplion.

At the board's March meeting, ahead of a friendly against Switzerland, Delaney said the Irish team would be wearing jerseys with special crests commemorating the 100th anniversary of the Easter Rising. Delaney told the board he had been warned that the FAI risked being fined for breaching FIFA rules prohibiting political symbols being displayed on team kits, but he was confident the FAI could defend its position. There was a militaristic feel to the pre-match ceremonies for the game on 25 March, as men wearing 1916

Irish Volunteer uniforms took to the pitch and the 1916 Proclamation of Independence was read out. FIFA would fine the FAI €5,000 for breaching its rules by using the 1916 crest.

The Sports Direct deal was sealed in June 2016. For €6.5 million, Ashley's firm took a fifty-seat box for home matches in the Aviva, became title sponsors of the FAI summer schools programme, and would take on the naming rights for the FAI's national training centre in Abbotstown. (The first two parts of the sponsorship were activated but the training centre was never rebranded.)

The FAI was contracted till 2020 to have its kit supplied by its long-time partner, Toplion, the Irish agents for New Balance and Umbro. The Sports Direct deal included an option agreement for Mike Ashley's company to become exclusive suppliers of FAI kit and retailers for FAI merchandise from August 2020, in return for a further payment of €6.5 million in that year.

The deal also contained a clause that allowed Sports Direct to withdraw from the deal at any point prior to 1 April 2020, and this would mean the FAI would have to repay the initial €6.5 million 'within seven days' of receiving written notice from Sports Direct. Delaney was so desperate to bring money in that he had given Ashley, the high-stakes gambler, a risk-free bet on the FAI.

Details of this extraordinary clause were not given to the board or to Deloitte, the FAI's auditors. The €6.5 million paid in June 2016 was treated as income when it should have been recorded as a loan, given that Ashley could demand repayment at any time up to 2020. For the unwitting board, however, the deal was yet another example of Delaney's genius.

At the fashion-show fundraiser in Citywest hotel on 7 April 2016, a Thursday, there were dozens of empty chairs. Many FAI staff had been instructed to attend and assist. Corporate sponsors had bought some tickets but few attended. Delaney had wanted the FAI's social media to be used to promote the event, but there was resistance from the communications staff. Delaney could not understand why FAI staff had not embraced the charity event being run by his girlfriend as he had asked.

FAI security personnel were brought in to remove the extra chairs around the catwalk. One FAI staffer remembers looking on as Delaney and English kissed passionately while sitting at the front of the catwalk. The staffer decided he would retreat to one of the hotel's bars.

Brian Kennedy was one of a number of musicians to perform a grand opening for the show. The musicians were followed by circus performers doing aerial acrobatics, pyrotechnics and drumming. Four scantily dressed dancers doing a 'Moulin Rouge' version of the can-can were the last of the pre-show warm-up acts.

Amongst those modelling clothes on the catwalk were Alan Kelly, who remained Minister for the Environment post-election, and ex-footballers Ray Houghton and Jason McAteer. Eamon Dunphy was also amongst the models. The football pundit agreed to do the show after Delaney asked him a number of times. 'The reason I did it was not for anything other than the possibility of getting two tickets for Manchester United for friends of mine,' Dunphy says. 'That's the truth and that's how the fucker operated. I ran out of Citywest after the gig was done.'

Afterwards, Delaney reported that €20,000 had been raised for the two beneficiaries. 'A nice round number,' thought one FAI staffer.

At the board's next meeting in May, Delaney told his fellow directors that while the FAI staff were pushing for pay restoration from the 10 per cent cuts of 2012, the FAI could only afford to pay back 3 per cent of salary and pension. The board agreed.

Near the end of the meeting, Tony Fitzgerald asked Delaney and other staff to leave. Fitzgerald told the remaining board members that Delaney had spoken to him about extending his contract for four more years after it expired in 2020. Even though that was four years away, the board took a unanimous vote to agree to the request. Delaney would remain on his present salary until his current contract expired in 2020 but the board was committing to offer him a four-year extension at that time. Delaney was invited back in and told the good news.

*

On the eve of Euro 2016, the FAI announced that Bank of Ireland had taken over its Aviva Stadium mortgage from KKR, the American private equity group, in a deal that involved the FAI's debt being written down from €45 million to €35 million. An FAI statement thanked Denis O'Brien and his firm, Island Capital, for assisting in the refinancing move, but made no mention that the Sports Direct payment of €6.5 million had been key to allowing the deal to happen. The statement said O'Brien would continue to pay a portion of the managerial salaries through to the 2018 World Cup.

The European Championship kicked off in June, with Ireland in a tough group that included Sweden, Belgium and Italy. After a creditable draw against the Swedes, the Irish team's lack of quality was exposed as the superstar-laden Belgians cantered to a 3–0 win.

By the time of Ireland's last group match, Italy had already qualified for the second round by beating both Belgium and Sweden, and fielded a second XI in Lille. With five minutes left, Robbie Brady headed in for a win that would take Ireland past the group stage of a European Championship for the first time. France, the host country, lay in wait. Despite taking a fifth-minute lead from a Brady penalty, Ireland lost 2–1.

Still, it was seen as a reasonably successful tournament for Martin O'Neill. For Delaney, with Emma close by his side at all times, there was no return to the drunken antics of Poland four years previously. However, the eyebrows of staff were raised by the fact that Delaney ensured that at least six seats on the team's chartered flight from Dublin to France were reserved for members of the couple's families. While in France, the FAI hired Freddie Passas, a Frenchman who was married to Emma's sister Clodagh, as an interpreter and aide.

FAI security briefed French stewarding teams to seize banners with anti-Delaney messages. Carl McNamara, who was a liaison officer with Football Supporters Europe, which worked with UEFA on a fans' embassy project at Euro 2016, said the FAI instruction had unintended consequences. The FAI briefed the fans' embassy team that they were particularly on the lookout for a flag with a huge picture of Delaney smiling alongside English over the text 'Miracles can happen – COYBIG [Come on you boys in green]'. Pictures of the fans with the flag had been widely circulated on social media. Delaney was not pleased.

At Ireland's first match, against Sweden in the Stade de France out-side Paris, the stewards, many of whom were low-paid immigrants with little English, tried to seize any Irish flags with writing on them. 'It led to quite a few heated, tense scenes outside [the stadium] as stewards confiscated all flags with writing on them,' says McNamara. 'It didn't matter if it was "Delaney Out" or "Ireland Abú", which obviously the vast amount were, just innocent support banners.'

Delaney personally got involved in policing what fans were saying about him online after the Belgium match. Two days after the defeat and two days before Ireland played Italy, at 3.18 a.m., Delaney emailed Ian Mallon, the FAI's Director of Communications, with the subject 'Shocking post'.

'This is on YBIG site,' wrote Delaney. 'Time for action here, Ian.'

The FAI Chief Executive attached a screenshot from his mobile phone of a discussion on the YBIG forum about whether Martin O'Neill should continue as Ireland manager after the tournament. A poster called Andy wrote that he wanted O'Neill to stay on but 'after his reign is over I'd love to see Chris Hughton in charge. And for John Delaney to be shot.'

It was clearly a throwaway, if nasty, comment, but Mallon con-tacted YBIG to demand the post's removal and for the forum to issue a public apology to Delaney. YBIG were told that the FAI had made a complaint to the police. The post was removed immediately but no apology was issued.

While Russian and English fans were fighting in Marseilles, Irish fans were revelling in being back at a major tournament and were keen to uphold their reputation as well-behaved fans. A number of videos went viral on social media, including one showing Irish fans singing a lullaby to a baby on a train and another showing fans clean-ing up the streets after a drinking session chanting 'Clean up for the boys in green.'

Behind the scenes, though, the FAI's poor service to Irish support-ers meant it was the only one of nineteen associations participating in a scheme of fan 'embassies' at the tournament to lose accreditation. After the Belgium game in Bordeaux, Football Supporters Europe (FSE), which ran the fan embassies in co-operation with UEFA in the cities where matches were played to provide advice and assistance to supporters, wrote to the FAI to terminate its agreement with the association. Daniela Wurbs, CEO of FSE, wrote in an email to Joe McGlue, the FAI's Head of Security and Match Operations, that she had 'no other option than the immediate withdrawal' from the agreement with the FAI 'due to gross violations and the repeated non-fulfilment of the minimum working standards'.

Amongst Wurbs's complaints was that instead of the FAI providing a staff member at a designated information point at the stadium in Bordeaux before the game it had instead used the area as a ticket collection point. The FAI's use of the Fan Embassy Information Point for ticket collection was a 'gross violation' of the project's agreements with host cities, thereby putting the whole scheme 'at risk'. Much to the FAI's annoyance, FSE then turned to volunteers from the YBIG supporters' group to run the Irish Fan Embassies and hotline for the remainder of Ireland's run in the tournament. Wurbs later publicly praised YBIG's 'outstanding' service to fans.

*

In August, during the Olympic Games in Rio de Janeiro, Pat Hickey, the President of the Olympic Council of Ireland (OCI), was arrested in Rio over alleged irregular selling of tickets.

Delaney, as a Vice-President of the OCI and member of its Executive Committee since 2005, was expected to be at the games but did not travel. The police in Rio released footage of Hickey's arrest that showed the naked seventy-one-year-old opening a hotel bedroom door to the police search team before going off to fetch a white bathrobe.

Another Irishman, Kevin Mallon, was also arrested. Mallon was an agent with THG, a company owned by the same Marcus Evans who had worked with the FAI back in 2010. The Olympic organizers had refused to authorize THG to sell Olympic tickets. Brazilian police alleged that Mallon had been in possession of over 800 tickets, at least some of which had been sourced from the OCI.

Delaney was unavailable for comment about the ticketing scandal, even after Brazilian police, under the mistaken belief that he was in Brazil, said they were seeking a warrant to seize his passport. Police had sought to talk to Delaney and other OCI directors after Hickey told them that it was the OCI board that had agreed to hire THG as its official ticket resellers.

On 27 August, a Saturday, Delaney was due to travel to Galway to open the new grounds of Ballymoe FC, but decided not to leave his home in north Wicklow because there was a *Sunday World* photographer outside.

Delaney was due down in Ballymoe at 1 p.m. but the club was told he was delayed. With the press camping out, Delaney eventually called off his visit. Ballymoe proceeded with the unveiling of a plaque that said the facility was 'officially opened on 27 August by John Delaney, CEO FAI', even though Delaney had stayed at home. Assured that the press were not there the following day, Delaney travelled down on the Sunday and the club had the date on the plaque amended to 28 August.

While Delaney was remaining quiet, he was reading everything that was being written about him in relation to the Rio ticketing scandal. His lawyers forced the *Irish Daily Mail* to print an apology conceding that Delaney had 'no role whatsoever' in the OCI's ticketing arrangements.

At an FAI board meeting on 29 August, Delaney said that he had a 'peripheral' role in the OCI. 'Hickey was the decision-maker,' he said. He told the board he would not seek re-election to the OCI and that he had retained two senior counsel to act for him against media organizations that had repeated what the Brazilian police had said.

By the next FAI board meeting, on 3 October, Delaney could tell the members that he had settled some of the legal claims he had initiated over the Olympics reporting. He would tell the board later that year that while his defamation case against thejournal.ie was weak, he was keeping the case alive 'so they don't write anything about us'.

Delaney also told the FAI board that he had held an informal meeting with Niall McGarry, founder of JOE.ie. 'Niall McGarry wanted to give an apology without agreeing settlement,' he said. Delaney told McGarry that his website had not been supportive of the FAI and he should 'go away and reflect on this'. JOE.ie later published a lengthy apology to Delaney over its article, paid him damages and said it accepted the FAI Chief Executive had no role in the OCI's ticketing arrangements.

Delaney finally broke his public silence on the Rio scandal on 22 September, over a month after Hickey's arrest in Brazil. His statement said he was speaking out due to requests from the 'football family' that he clarify his position. He denied any involvement in the OCI's ticketing arrangements. The Brazilian police had never contacted him and had withdrawn the warrant issued against his passport.

★

The position of UEFA President became vacant after Michel Platini, whom Delaney had lauded for his leadership, was suspended for taking a payment of 2 million Swiss Francs (€1.5 million) from Sepp Blatter of FIFA and breaching ethics rules.

The FAI backed Aleksander Čeferin, a forty-eight-year-old Slovenian lawyer, and Čeferin was elected by a comfortable margin. Delaney had already told the FAI board that Čeferin had 'indicated' that he would 'encourage' Delaney to run for a position on UEFA's powerful Executive Committee, known as the ExCo.

Delaney and Čeferin had hit it off on a personal level. Although many association heads privately mocked Delaney for 'bringing his girlfriend to work' and noted how amorous the two were in public, Čeferin had warmed to English. She became friends with Čeferin's wife, Barbara, and it seemed the Slovenian was supportive of Delaney's own ambitions for advancement in UEFA.

While Delaney was planning his assault on Europe, the board was also being informed that, just months into their new banking agreement with Bank of Ireland, a breach of one of the FAI's three banking covenants was 'likely'. The covenants stipulated what level of debt and cash the FAI should have at any one time. Delaney promised that he was working on getting €3.25 million in from Sports Direct for 'future sponsorship'.

Delaney also addressed an issue that threatened to strike at the heart of the way he ran the FAI. Following the OCI ticketing scandal, Shane Ross, the Minister for Sport, had asked Sport Ireland to implement new governance standards for all sporting bodies in receipt of state funds to ensure there were limitations on how long directors could serve on their boards.

'We will fight the term limits,' Delaney told his board, many of whom were then eleven years in post, from the time Delaney became Chief Executive. Delaney emphasized that the FAI had enjoyed improved 'stability' under the current board.

As 2016 ended, the board was told that the FAI had an agreement with Dundalk FC to 'manage the portion of their European prize monies which are still held on their behalf by the FAI'. Dundalk, managed by Stephen Kenny, had become only the second League of Ireland club to qualify for the Europa League group stages, earning some €7 million in prize money from UEFA. The money was to be paid through the FAI, but the association held on to more than €2 million of it. It would only release the money to Dundalk in instalments over 2017 as the club increased the pressure on the FAI to pay up.

There was more bad news: Denis O'Brien had told Delaney he was planning to end his annual payment of €1.3 million towards the cost of the men's international management team. This was despite the FAI announcing just months previously that O'Brien had signed on for at least two more years.

Delaney tried to put a good spin on the development. At a 20 December board meeting he talked of a 'very positive' discussion he had just had with the Malta-based billionaire. He had offered O'Brien honorary 'life presidency' of the FAI, as the board had previously recommended. He proposed that Michael Cody now write to O'Brien to formally propose the honour in recognition of O'Brien's 'significant investment' of some €13 million over the previous eight years. Nothing would come of the 'life presidency' idea until 2018, and in March 2017 Delaney confirmed that there would be no further annual funding from O'Brien.

★

Delaney spent much of the early part of 2017 on the election trail ahead of the April vote by associations on the new ExCo members. National associations across Europe received a specially commissioned thirty-two-page 'John Delaney – An Introduction . . .' brochure promoting 'The Candidate'. The tagline on the black A4 cover was 'Unity is our strength – together we stand strong'. There were nine different photos of Delaney, including two full-pagers. A foreword from Tony Fitzgerald said the FAI board endorsed Delaney's candidacy. He said the FAI CEO excelled 'at creating a stable environment for football administration'.

The booklet listed Delaney's achievements under four main headings: 'The Strategist', 'The Leader', 'The Collaborator' and 'The Achiever'. Delaney described himself as a 'proud Irishman' who would bring the same passion and enthusiasm to the UEFA job, if elected, as Irish supporters were renowned for across Europe. He claimed to have brought 'financial and commercial stability' to the FAI 'despite [the] worst recessionary period in history'.

Delaney's 'vision' would 'drive to broaden and strengthen the scale, type and depth of the relationships between UEFA, its member associations, and key stakeholders and partners'. He promised to 'ensure that UEFA sets the highest standards worldwide for best practice in administration and leads the sporting world in this field'.

Along with the brochure, each association head received a piece of crystal and an Ireland jersey. Delaney flew across Europe to visit many of the national associations personally, often accompanied by Emma English.

This show of confidence belied the fact that, in April 2017, the FAI was facing an immediate financial crisis. It was about to run out of cash.

9.   Strike

On 8 March 2015 Emma Byrne, the Arsenal goalkeeper and captain of the Republic of Ireland Women's Team (WNT), sent an email to the general email account for the Professional Footballers' Association of Ireland (PFAI). The subject heading was 'Representation'.

Byrne's email was passed on to Stephen McGuinness, the PFAI's General Secretary. McGuinness was aware of Byrne as one of the most high-profile Irish women players, but didn't know her personally. A national women's league had been set up by the FAI in 2011 and there had been huge growth in the women's game in Ireland since then, but Byrne was amongst a small number of Irish women playing in professional leagues abroad.

Until that email from Byrne, the PFAI had no dealings with any of the WNT players. Byrne had complained publicly about their conditions in a 2014 interview in the *Sunday Times*, but then rowed back on some of her remarks under pressure from the FAI.

Now, Byrne asked whether the PFAI was affiliated with the FAI. McGuinness wrote back saying that, although the PFAI was located in the FAI building, it was not an affiliate, but a stand-alone organization representing some 300 professionals in the men's game in Ireland.

McGuinness was due to travel to London that April to attend the English PFA's awards ceremony in the Grosvenor House hotel in London. Byrne was going too. At the black-tie event, where Eden Hazard was named the men's player of the season for powering José Mourinho's Chelsea to the Premier League trophy, McGuinness and Byrne met. The head of the PFAI was shocked by what Byrne outlined to him. 'I just couldn't get my head around the conditions they were working in,' says McGuinness. 'The tracksuit thing was just outrageous.'

He was referring to the fact that Ireland's women had to change out of their FAI tracksuits in airport toilets when they returned from training camps or matches and return them to the association. That was the stand-out complaint, but there were other, more fundamental issues. The women weren't being paid, despite each giving up an average of forty work-days to train for games in 2016. A per-diem payment for attending international camps had been withdrawn, and there was no bonus for wins or draws. Players who had to take time off from their full-time jobs for training and matches were not entitled to recover lost earnings. While some players tried to keep on top of their jobs when in camp, the hotels booked by the FAI often had no Wi-Fi. The women felt that training was often sub-standard, and there were no individual strength-and-conditioning programmes for players.

McGuinness offered Byrne advice on how the players could make their case to the FAI, but little progress was made over the following year, with momentum dissipating each time the players left camp and returned to their clubs. While the PFAI represented League of Ireland players, it was not involved in negotiations for the men's national team, who instead employed the services of Ciarán Medlar, a partner with BDO accountants. The PFAI knew that Delaney would not want to set a precedent of the players' association representing one of its national teams and so initially tried to get the players themselves to make the running.

Byrne emailed McGuinness directly on 5 February 2016, saying that the players were losing patience with the FAI and were 'all happy to take whatever actions that are needed to get the attention of John Delaney'.

McGuinness started to meet other women players and to sign them up as PFAI members. A strategy was worked out for senior players to raise their concerns directly with Ruud Dokter, the FAI's Head of High Performance, Peter Sherrard, who was now the FAI's Head of Operations, and Sue Ronan, manager of the women's team. Again, the players felt this got them nowhere.

Relations between the PFAI and the FAI were particularly frosty at the time. Simone Flannery had left the FAI, where she'd worked as an administrator under Fran Gavin in the League of Ireland, to join the PFAI in 2016. Flannery was required to serve one month's 'gardening leave' by the FAI before she was allowed to start work as the PFAI's office manager in a different part of the same building. The PFAI believed that FAI staff were subsequently instructed not to talk with Flannery, even in the women's toilet in Abbotstown. New carpets were laid around Abbotstown, but stopped before they got to the PFAI's offices. FAI staff called the area around the PFAI's offices 'the Gaza strip', such was the tension that some felt over their presence in the building.

On 28 September McGuinness emailed Sherrard in the hope of opening formal discussions with the FAI about the issues raised by the WNT. Sherrard wrote back that evening to say that he had met Áine O'Gorman, one of the senior players on the team, and was happy to continue talks with her. He said it would be against FAI policy to deal with the PFAI on national team issues. 'Playing for Ireland is not the same as a club environment where players choose to play for the honour of representing their country, unlike clubs, where contracts come into play for non-amateur players,' wrote Sherrard.

'When I got that, I went absolutely fucking bananas,' says McGuinness. He walked out to the shared coffee dock down the hall from his office. 'I don't drink tea or coffee,' says McGuinness. 'I was just walking because I was that fumed.'

At the coffee dock, McGuinness bumped into Sherrard, who told him that he hoped he hadn't taken the email 'the wrong way'. The furious PFAI boss said he believed the FAI was trying to 'dictate' who his association could represent.

The PFAI felt it was in a strong position to progress the team's case, given the lack of progress made to that point. 'I honestly thought when I wrote to Sherrard, he'd respond and say, "C'mon, let's go and meet,"' said McGuinness. 'I thought the money was so small, this will be a doddle. Obviously, we didn't realize at the time how bad the financial problems were.'

McGuinness asked Sherrard to get the FAI to reconsider its position. In an email he described the association's refusal to enter talks with the players' chosen representatives as 'insulting and nonsensical'.

Just before Christmas, McGuinness wrote directly to Delaney

asking him to enter talks with the PFAI about the concerns of the women's national team. The letter complained that the policy of not dealing directly with the PFAI was 'discrimination of the most basic and obvious kind', given that the men's team had negotiated pay bonuses through a nominated representative, a reference to the role played by Ciarán Medlar. The letter warned that the 'team will take matters into their own hands' unless the FAI engaged with the PFAI. Delaney responded in writing to say he would bring the issue to the board's attention.

The PFAI left packs of documents outlining the women's grievances at the reception of Abbotstown for each FAI director so they would know the story from the players' perspective.

After a board meeting early in 2017, an FAI director stuck his head into McGuinness's office.

'Delaney said we can't do this,' the director said.

'What do you mean?' McGuinness asked.

'We don't have the money,' the director said. 'We're just not doing it.'

After that, McGuinness started preparing the team for strike action.

'I spent probably three days talking to every player in the squad, convincing them it was the right thing to do,' says McGuinness. 'They needed to be convinced. I've never witnessed fear like it. After every phone call they were getting calls from the FAI. There was huge pressure on them. They were threatened with their international careers. There were all types of stuff thrown at them.'

On 3 March, Delaney's PA, Denise Cassidy, wrote to the PFAI to say that the Chief Executive was 'travelling extensively with UEFA at the moment'. She would bring the requests for a response to his attention as soon as possible.

On 27 March a one-page letter from the women's national team was hand delivered to Delaney's PA. It said that if the FAI didn't meet with the PFAI as the team's representatives then 'we will have no choice but to publicly highlight the complete lack of regard and respect shown to the WNT'. The letter gave notice of the team's plan to 'withdraw our services and availability' for the upcoming international friendly against Slovakia on 10 April.

Dokter, Sherrard and Ronan co-signed a six-page reply the

following day. The letter insisted that the FAI had addressed or was working on all the concerns raised. It also said that the FAI board had decided the association would not negotiate with the PFAI regarding international football because 'it is an entirely different relationship to that between clubs and players on contracts'.

Another FAI letter sent on 31 March urged the players to meet the FAI directly or through a mediator and warned that there was a danger their actions would 'set back the development of the game generally' and 'the development of your own careers'.

Emma Byrne emailed the FAI at 9.50 p.m. Sunday, 2 April, to say the women would agree to mediation only if the PFAI could represent them. 'We are simply not equipped to participate in such important discussions without the appropriate support,' she said.

Senior players in the squad were having second thoughts about going ahead with a planned press conference in Liberty Hall, the Dublin city-centre headquarters of SIPTU, Ireland's biggest trade union, the following Tuesday.

The PFAI had decided to pay for the players' flights and hotel accommodation when they came to Dublin in the week ahead of the Slovakia game. McGuinness believes that was key to ensuring the team stayed united.

'The FAI thought, "As soon as they get in camp, we'll have them,"' McGuinness says. 'We kept them completely out of the FAI's reach. We had them in different hotels. We just knew that if the FAI had got hold of them all together, we felt we were in trouble. They could break them.'

That Tuesday morning, fourteen internationals wore green T-shirts emblazoned with the word 'Respect' as they posed for pictures outside Liberty Hall. It was a powerful image. Inside, Stephanie Roche – whose wonder goal for Peamount United had gone viral globally in 2013 – told the media that the FAI must negotiate with the PFAI as representatives of the women's national team. 'We're footballers; we're here to play football,' she said. 'There's not any of us that are skilled negotiators and to ask us to do that is unfair.'

Byrne, the team captain, said they were 'fighting for the future of women's international football'. She explained that many women who could have been on the team had had to stop playing because of the lack of support from the FAI. 'First of all we are not allowed to keep the kit,' she said. 'So, we turn up to camp in our civvies . . . It's humiliating to have to go into a public toilet and change. No matter what. Give us a tracksuit, it's not that difficult. I'm actually a little embarrassed talking about it.'

In what was the biggest confrontation between players and the FAI since the men threatened to go on strike in the late 1960s over similar issues, the leaders of both organizations were not 'on the pitch'.

Delaney was in Helsinki in Finland for the UEFA congress, where he would learn if his campaign to get on the ExCo had been successful. Meanwhile, McGuinness, who had done so much to orchestrate the WNT's stand against the FAI, was on holiday with his wife and three children in Disneyland, Orlando. The PFAI's Simone Flannery and Ollie Cahill kept the show on the road, while Stuart Gilhooly, the PFAI's external solicitor, became the main spokesman for the team.

Well versed in media interviews as a senior member of the Law Society, Gilhooly dropped a number of eminently quotable phrases into the Liberty Hall press conference. Confirming that the Slovakia match was in doubt if the FAI did not meet the players' demands, Gilhooly said the women's team had been treated like 'fifth-class citizens' and the 'dirt off the FAI's shoe'. He said this was the team's 'Saipan moment'.

The PFAI press conference got a huge reaction on social media and the radio airwaves. Many were shocked that the players had been forced to go public with such meagre demands. There was outrage over the revelation that the players were forced to change out of their FAI tracksuits in toilets.

In what was now a full-scale PR battle, the FAI riposte was underwhelming. It issued a statement expressing disappointment in the team's 'unprecedented ultimatum'. Ruud Dokter was sent out as the FAI's spokesman in radio interviews. His insistence that the board had decided not to negotiate with the PFAI did nothing to win sympathy for the FAI. Few in football were in any doubt that it was Delaney driving the association's stance.

After just three players turned up for the scheduled training camp on Wednesday, 5 April, the FAI crumbled. It invited the players to mediation that evening, 'along with your representatives'.

Later that day, Delaney succeeded in garnering the second-highest number of votes amongst the eleven-strong field running for the eight vacancies on the UEFA ExCo. UEFA announced the results in a press release entitled 'UEFA Congress approves good governance reforms'. It said UEFA had now introduced term limits of twelve years for its ExCo and presidential positions while 'ethics and good governance' would become statutory objectives.

Delaney's election was welcomed by Shane Ross, the Minister for Sport, back in Dublin. 'This is a hugely positive development for Irish sport and for football, which will now have a significant voice at the decision-making end of the European game,' he said.

In the Clarion hotel in Liffey Valley, the initial talks between the FAI and PFAI through mediator Peter McLoone did not make progress. The women let it be known that they were considering an invitation to appear on the *Late Late Show*.

After nine hours of negotiations, the players agreed that they would play the Slovakia game when the FAI agreed to meet most of their demands, including dedicated women's team tracksuits and payments for matches. The PFAI believed the deal cost the FAI double what was sought in 2016.

'Victory,' tweeted Emma Byrne.

Ireland beat Slovakia 1–0, with Stephanie Roche scoring the only goal. Many women and young girls in the crowd held up placards at the match in the Tallaght Stadium. One read: 'Because of you we'll get equal pay when we grow up.'

★

When Ruth Fahy moved with her family from Dublin to live in Galway at the age of eight, the only team she could play for was Salthill Devon under-12s. After turning twelve, the only team available to her was Salthill's senior women's team. The coach let Fahy and future Ireland international Méabh De Búrca train with the senior women from the age of thirteen, and they started playing matches at fourteen.

Fahy would go on to play for Castlebar Celtic and then Galway in the new women's national league. She then travelled around the world, playing football and picking up a Master's in Sports Law in Nottingham. Back in Ireland in 2015, she got a call from the reigning Women's National League champions, Wexford Youths, and jumped at the chance to win trophies. She was a centre-half in Wexford's treble-winning team for the 2015–16 season and got to play in the Women's Champions' League. Fahy was called up to a few Ireland training camps and also played for the Ireland university side.

Working as a trainee solicitor in Dublin, her passion for football was costing her money as she travelled to matches and training. Dabbling in media as well as working in law, Fahy was asked to start writing a player's column for the FAI's Women's National League website. This led to a weekly column in the *Irish Daily Mirror*'s football pull-out and punditry slots with RTÉ television.

In the summer of 2016, Fahy tore the anterior cruciate ligament in her left knee. She was on crutches when she was approached by the FAI, who wanted her to join its legal department on an eighteen-month contract. Fahy, who had been unsuccessful in an earlier application to join the FAI's media department, jumped at the opportunity.

Working for the FAI as a legal administrator, Fahy continued the *Mirror* column she had started a couple of months previously. She felt better able to comment on women's football now she was not an active player. A few weeks after starting in Abbotstown she was advised not to say anything controversial in her column by the FAI. She thought this advice was 'grand'.

When the women's strike happened in April 2017, it stirred up powerful emotions in Fahy. She felt there were embedded inequalities in football, and had experience of coaching in a club where the boys' teams got greater resources than the girls'. 'Those kind of things stuck with me. So, when this was all kicking off, I was getting angry, really angry,' says Fahy.

Fahy believed what the women's team achieved that week was amazing. 'I had done that with the tracksuit,' she says, referring to an overseas training camp she had attended with the senior team. 'You had to wear it on the plane but then you give it back. That was standard. It was so normalized that you forget that it's disgraceful. You're just there to play first of all. You kind of hope someone else is sorting that out, but no one else was until the PFAI came in and made a difference.'

Neil Fullerton, Fahy's editor at the *Mirror*, offered her the chance to write a longer column than usual about the women's achievements. Fahy jumped at the chance. 'It wasn't about the FAI,' she insists. 'It was about this moment and the positive repercussions that it will have going forward for kids coming up. That was the biggest emotion I felt from the whole thing and it was really important. I tried to set aside any anger, or rage, but I just had to write the piece.'

Fahy wrote about how an old coach had recently reminded her that as a twelve-year-old she had written to her local club questioning what pathways were available to young girls looking to progress in football. Sixteen years later, the women's game had developed 'incredibly', but if she was afforded the chance to talk with her twelve-year-old self she would have mixed emotions.

'Nothing the senior Irish WNT said this week shocked me,' wrote Fahy. 'Their grievances were valid and warranted.'

Fahy added that, although there had been change, 'fundamental problems remain', and that when 'those who have the power to make change are dismissive, injustice ensues'.

Although she made sure that the FAI was not mentioned in the article, Fahy expected there to be repercussions over what she had written. She phoned her FAI manager the evening before the article was published to advise her that she was writing about the strike. Fahy was told it was a bad idea. Fahy declined a suggestion that she submit her copy for the FAI's approval before publication.

For Fahy, as a footballer and a professional solicitor, working for the FAI, the only major employer in the football business in Ireland, had been a 'dream job'. She knew her column could bring an end to that dream. Still, Fahy felt the right thing was to use her newspaper platform to celebrate the WNT's fight rather than bite her tongue and preserve her burgeoning FAI career.

Fahy prepared a resignation letter for the FAI and brought it into work the following day, a Friday. In Abbotstown, Fahy and some of her work colleagues were on edge, waiting for the backlash. Nothing happened for an hour or two, but then Fahy was called into her manager's office. She was told to turn off her phone and place it on the table. 'I was asked why had I put my career in jeopardy,' says Fahy. 'I let loose, saying, "This is way too important to me to not write this."'

Her manager asked was it not a better idea to stay in the FAI and try to fix it from the inside. Fahy responded that she didn't have ten or twenty years to do something that wouldn't guarantee success. She regrets that she did not try to argue, as she strongly believes, that her column had not breached her contract of employment. Instead, upset, she simply said she was not sorry for what she had done. She was told she had brought the FAI into gross disrepute with her column and that she was in breach of her employment contract. She was officially suspended, and had to meet an FAI HR Manager within the hour. A colleague could accompany her.

The HR Manager read from a three-page letter saying that Fahy was now suspended and was on 'confidential' leave as part of a disciplinary process, meaning she could not talk about it. Fahy pulled out the resignation letter she had prepared the night before and handed in her notice. The HR Manager took the letter, Fahy recalls, 'and she handed it back to me. She said, "I'm not accepting your notice." I said, "I don't think you can do that."'

The HR Manager left the room for forty-five minutes. Fahy believed the FAI was concerned that if she was allowed to resign then the confidentiality clauses that applied to the disciplinary process might not apply. Eventually, she was told she was suspended. She was allowed to say her goodbyes and collect her things.

That same day, Fahy received an email from a mid-ranking FAI official whose name Fahy has asked us not to reveal. Having previously helped her get media jobs, he was now furious, fearing he would be caught in the internal backlash. He warned that Fahy would be barred from future media work, and that there would be 'no more TV appearances' – a strange claim, given that that was not for the FAI to decide.

Despite that assertion, both the *Mirror* and RTÉ continued to employ Fahy. Six days after she was suspended, Fahy received an email from the FAI to say it had accepted her resignation. The FAI's letter 'reminded' Fahy that the confidentiality clauses of her employment contract continued to apply to her. The letter quoted extensively from the contract's confidentiality section, including section 18.6, which said the requirement for confidentiality about all FAI business, plans and personnel extended beyond the end of her employment. The letter said if Fahy breached her contract, 'in particular section 18.6', then the FAI 'will take legal action' against her. The letter also quoted from the 'Media Related Activities' section of the FAI's employee handbook, which said staff were 'not at any time to make disparaging or critical comments about the FAI'.

Fahy believes the action of the players on the 2017 strike team was a landmark moment for the women's game and that future generations of Irish players will be forever grateful. 'The team left a legacy,' she says. 'Those players like Emma Byrne . . . When you talk to the players here playing now, it's completely different.'

*

When Delaney returned to Abbotstown after the UEFA election, FAI staff were brought into the boardroom to applaud him and shake his hand in congratulations. Peter Sherrard said a few words in recognition of his accomplishment. Delaney said it had been an 'arduous journey'. He thanked his two personal assistants and praised Emma English for her help on the campaign.

At the FAI's 12 April board meeting, much of the criticism for the women's strike was laid at the door of the government and Sport Ireland; it was felt that state funding was being channelled into women's rugby and ladies' GAA but not women's football. The PFAI was accused of hijacking the situation and the media were criticized for inaccurate reporting. At the same meeting, the directors were warned that the FAI was experiencing 'a number of cash income delays'. Payments to creditors were being restricted as a result. There were no questions.

Later in the meeting, Delaney suggested that it was time for the FAI's Finance Committee to be 'retired'. The committee of twelve FAI Council members, led by Eddie Murray, the Honorary

Treasurer, discussed the FAI finances once a quarter. Delaney felt it had become 'redundant'. People were travelling long distances to attend the meetings, which lasted about twenty-five minutes, and many financial issues were not discussed at them because the information had been deemed 'too sensitive'.

Delaney suggested that the FAI introduce a tighter, three-person sub-committee of the board to deal with financial matters, similar to how UEFA's Finance Committee was a sub-committee of the ExCo. However, no change was made. The committee limped on, providing the façade of financial oversight.

By May, Delaney was able to report to the board that the FAI's immediate cash-flow problems had been solved thanks to a €2 million payment from UEFA. He said the FAI also had 'other options', including Dundalk's Europa League prize money, which was transmitted from UEFA to the club via the FAI, and more money from Sports Direct.

The FAI's AGM in Kilkenny passed off quietly, a heavy security presence ensuring the media didn't get close to the delegates. Delaney and English brought with them their new dog, an enormous and very boisterous Hungarian Vizsla called Hudson, which FAI staff were pressed into looking after when its owners were busy.

Murray, the retired garda superintendent who was the FAI's Honorary Treasurer, was in his late seventies and had privately sought to step down from the board, but Cody and Delaney convinced him to go for one more four-year term. He was re-elected unanimously.

*

At the Monday morning management meeting after Delaney's fiftieth birthday party in October, Delaney told his executives that Emma had had a great time in Mount Juliet. A number of FAI staff had worked to set up and run the event. Eamon Breen, the FAI's Finance Director, mentioned that his wife, Nicola, had created the huge Aviva Stadium birthday cake for the party. 'Now you know if you ever need a cake, Nicola is available,' said Breen.

Other management staff didn't know where to look.

As the year went on, Delaney told the board that big football nations were keen to develop better relations with him now he was on the UEFA ExCo and would be offering the FAI friendly fixtures.

His ExCo role also led to Delaney becoming chair of UEFA's Youth and Amateur Football Committee and vice-chair of its Women's Football Committee. Although he had been widely blamed in the media for the debacle of the Irish women's strike, internally he faced no criticism from his board.

Instead, Delaney used the episode to belittle Ian Mallon, the FAI's Director of Communications. At a board meeting in June 2017, Mallon was due to present his communications strategy. Before he came in, Delaney told the board that the presentation needed to show that Mallon had taken previous criticisms on board and that he had fresh ideas. When Mallon entered, Delaney tackled him on what he could have done better over the women's strike. Mallon said that a different approach could have been taken from the outset.

Delaney continued to attack. He said the board needed certainty that inaccurate material in newspapers would be challenged. Other board members rowed in behind Delaney. One asked Mallon why he hadn't given journalists whose coverage of the women's team had been sympathetic 'a skelp'. One director jumped to his feet demanding that Mallon challenge 'inaccurate' press reports.

After Mallon left the room Delaney laid into him again. He said Mallon had 'shown a lack of initiative' by failing to challenge comments made that weekend in the *Irish Independent* by Bernard O'Byrne, his old adversary. O'Byrne had complained about the lack of recognition from the FAI for the twentieth anniversary of the Brian Kerr-led under-17 team that finished third in the world in 1997.

By the end of 2017, Delaney was communicating with his Head of Communications only through lawyers. 'We've tried the Head of Communications from Ryanair [Peter Sherrard] and now a seasoned journalist,' Delaney told the board (Mallon had been hired from Independent Newspapers). 'Neither have worked.'

In a statement issued in February 2018, the FAI said Mallon had resigned his job to take up 'a role with UEFA as National Associations Communications Consultant'. The statement thanked Mallon for his 'immense' contribution to the FAI and wished him well.

Under the terms of a confidential settlement, the FAI would be obliged to pay Mallon €30,000 a year for three years.

Told about what Delaney said about him to the board, Mallon says he believes this was an attempt at 'face-saving' by Delaney over the women's strike: 'I can only suppose that the speaker was trying to give an impression of being in control at a time when the record shows that a lot of senior staff were leaving the organization.'

In 2018, the make-up of the FAI board and the decline of the men's team were at the forefront of John Delaney's mind. The association was facing new rules that would by 2019 require all sports bodies in receipt of state funding to limit directors' terms to nine years. This would entail significant change on the FAI board: by 2019 seven of its eleven directors would have been on the board for more than twelve years. Delaney, the longest serving with eighteen years, would be exempt from the rules because he was Chief Executive.

The governance code for community, voluntary and charitable bodies had existed as best practice since 2012, but sports minister Shane Ross ordered that state funding be linked to adherence with the code in the wake of the Rio ticketing scandal.

Delaney now accepted that the FAI would introduce term limits of a maximum of eight years for directors, thereby more than meeting the state's requirements, but there would be exemptions for current board members to allow them to see out their terms of office. Cody could stay until 2020, when he would be eighty. Murray would remain Treasurer until 2021, when he would be eighty-two. Full compliance with the code would come slowly. 'Stability' would be retained for the next three years, Delaney assured the FAI directors.

On the managerial front things were not so stable. Martin O'Neill's bid to become only the third Ireland manager to qualify for a World Cup finals ended in November 2017 with a crushing 5–1 home defeat to Denmark in the second leg of a qualification playoff.

After the match, O'Neill went for his traditional – and mandatory – post-game interview with RTÉ's Tony O'Donoghue. The soccer correspondent's live interviews with O'Neill had become more entertaining than some of Ireland's matches, as the manager became increasingly tetchy in the face of any perceived criticism.

O'Donoghue asked O'Neill if Ireland had become 'a shambles' after his substitutions and if the result was a 'humiliation'.

'I would say we were well beaten,' a clearly irritated O'Neill shot back.

When O'Donoghue listed off the games in which Ireland had let leads slip away, and the home games they'd failed to win, O'Neill riposted by listing Ireland's impressive away results. He prevented O'Donoghue from interjecting several times. By post-match standards, it was a long and tough interview, but it still didn't look good when O'Neill walked away as O'Donoghue tried to ask a follow-up question.

O'Neill was out of contract after the qualifiers finished. Coming into January 2018 he was being linked to a number of English club jobs, with Stoke City, Everton and Nottingham Forest all showing interest.

At the 14 January meeting of the board, Delaney told his fellow directors that O'Neill had been offered a new contract before Christmas and said he would sign, but he hadn't yet done so. He feared that O'Neill could take a job offer and leave the FAI without a manager. The FAI had been paying O'Neill, as Delaney believed they had an oral contract. O'Neill would have to pay the FAI compensation if he did leave, he said. Delaney told the board that O'Neill's hesitation about signing the new deal was due to his concerns about 'the Irish media', which he believed had been unfairly aggressive.

By 17 January, O'Neill and his coaching team, including Roy Keane, had agreed a new two-year deal under which the FAI would get €500,000 compensation if O'Neill was poached by a club. Delaney said Keane had been a 'big influence' on O'Neill's decision to stay.

Sponsors were beginning to turn away from the association and an O'Neill team that played dour football. Bank of Ireland, the FAI's bankers, did not renew its €150,000-a-year sponsorship deal with the association when it ended in 2018.

Delaney blamed Francesca McDonagh, Bank of Ireland's new Chief Executive, and said the bank only seemed to be interested in rugby. He told the board that a senior official in the bank was related to Rory Best, the Ireland rugby captain.

On top of that, Dundalk FC had been bought by Peak6, an American investment company. To allow the deal to be completed, the FAI had to pay over some €2 million of the club's UEFA prize money that it had held on to for over a year.

Delaney had secured a €175,000 dividend from the Aviva Stadium company in 2017, the first agreed with the IRFU since the joint venture was created. The stadium company and the IRFU agreed to bring forward the renewal of the Aviva naming deal in 2018, and give Aviva a significant discount, well in advance of the 2020 end date of the original deal, largely because they knew the FAI was tight for cash.

The €18 million sponsorship extension, which ran until 2025, gave the FAI a €6 million windfall, with the other €12 million split between the stadium company and the IRFU. However, Delaney then pushed for the stadium company to pay out €2 million of its €6 million naming rights money to its two shareholders. Again, the IRFU agreed, hoping the FAI would at least keep up to date with its monthly €200,000 licence fee obligations to the stadium. The Aviva naming extension deal was worth €7 million in total for the FAI in 2018, but still the association was struggling to pay its way. By the end of 2018 it owed the stadium company €1.2 million.

Delaney worked hard on both FIFA and UEFA to bring forward payments due to the FAI in later years. Although the monies from the footballing federations are supposed to support a variety of football initiatives in member associations, in the FAI's case nearly all these funds were channelled straight into paying off the stadium mortgage or its monthly running costs.

The FIFA Forward 2 development programme, which spreads the wealth FIFA generates from its World Cup every four years, was to deliver $6 million to each of the world body's 211 member associations between 2019 and 2022. A third of that could be taken as a lump sum for various projects, including stadiums, pitches, lighting and training grounds. But Delaney succeeded in getting FIFA's agreement to pay the FAI two-thirds of the FIFA Forward 2 money upfront, with $1.75 million going to the stadium company, $2 million to the stadium mortgagees and $250,000 towards developing the women's game in Ireland.

Delaney did secure other funding for the women's game. After intensive lobbying by Delaney, Shane Ross wrote to Sport Ireland in March 2018 directing it to allocate €195,000 to the FAI's WNT programme, whose costs had ballooned after the deal made to avert the threatened strike in 2017. Sport Ireland had advised Ross against the move, believing that any extra money should be made available for women's international teams across a range of sports. Kieran Mulvey, the chairman of Sports Ireland, feared other sports bodies could take legal action over the 'discrimination' in favour of football.

'When we got our budget, there was a special grant designated for the FAI and that was on the basis that John Delaney lobbied Minister Ross and against our advice and the advice of our officials he gave the grant,' Mulvey says. 'John was a good salesman.'

Delaney had invested some time in building up a relationship with Ross. When the sports minister came looking for match tickets for the 2017 Europa League final between Manchester United and Ajax in Stockholm, Delaney was happy to help out. Ross paid for the tickets.

In June, Delaney attended a children's football tournament at Wayside Celtic, a club in the minister's constituency in south Dublin, where Ross had committed to presenting the winners' medals. Delaney and Ross took turns on a microphone to address the crowd of over a hundred children and their watching parents after the games finished.

'I want to thank the minister for all the funding he gives to Irish sport and in particular Irish soccer,' said Delaney, who then referenced a forthcoming game at the Aviva Stadium, where Denmark were again the opponents. '[The minister] came over to me, just as we came in. Ireland didn't make the World Cup, we know that . . . We are playing a team, Denmark, that did make the World Cup, in October. And we are looking for a bit of revenge. The minister asked me to ask all the kids to come to the Aviva to see the Irish team play Denmark. So well done to you, Minister.'

Delaney had just gifted 300 free tickets to the children and their parents, who were all likely voters in Ross's constituency. A smiling Ross joined in the applause for Delaney. He said, 'Thanks, John,' as the FAI CEO made his way back over towards the minister after the giveaway.

In his own speech, Ross told the crowd he hoped to see them all in the Aviva in the autumn, 'because John Delaney is not like a politician. He keeps his promises!'

*

At the February 2018 board meeting, Delaney assured the board that the FAI was on its way to being debt free by 2020. 'Not too long ago we owed FIFA €4 million, Danske €56 million, UEFA €11 million and Ticketus €6 million,' Delaney said. 'There has been a vast improvement.'

By June, Delaney was promising the board the FAI would 'hit a good profit this year'.

On the eve of the AGM on 18 August, in Cork, the FAI hosted a gala dinner that was attended by both Denis O'Brien, who was about to be made an Honorary Life President of the FAI, and Simon Coveney, the Tánaiste and Cork TD.

'Our legacy from Cork will be the relationships we have built politically with the Tánaiste,' Delaney told the board. Also attending the AGM was David Martin, the President of the Irish Football Association, which runs the game in Northern Ireland. Martin broached the idea of the FAI joining the four UK associations in a joint World Cup 2030 bid. Delaney was instantly interested.

At the pre-AGM meeting on 17 August, Delaney was ever more bullish about the FAI's ability to meet his long-promised goal of being free of the stadium debt by 2020. 'The current economic climate should leave room for us to exceed targets,' he said.

In a state-of-the-union-type address to the board, Delaney promised that the 'next major investment by the FAI would be in the League of Ireland'. He envisioned that the league would be run on a 50/50 basis by the FAI and the clubs. He was tired of getting the blame for 'all that goes wrong' in the league.

While the FAI was now signing up for a potential World Cup bid, Delaney admitted to the directors in September that his administrative staff 'are worked to the bone'. 'We take on projects we don't really have the capacity for,' he said.

Delaney had been busy on the political front, meeting Paschal

Donohoe, now the Minister of Finance, and Sinn Féin leader Mary Lou McDonald. He told the board that McDonald 'thinks the FAI are doing a great job' and that Donohoe had described the association as a 'great organization'. He also said that Shane Ross had spoken to him about his desire to see an all-island Irish team in the future.

The Cork AGM marked the end of Tony Fitzgerald's underwhelming four-year term as FAI President and chairman of the board. His replacement was Donal Conway, an assistant school principal who had retired at sixty in 2014, when he became FAI Vice-President. Conway had been on the FAI board since 2005 and had concentrated on reforming the association's under-age player development systems.

Conway says he felt the office of FAI President, ostensibly the most important role in the association as chairman and Delaney's boss, had been 'completely emasculated' under Fitzgerald. He says Fitzgerald didn't even speak at the formal receptions held with other associations around matches. Conway was determined to claw back some of the position's prestige and power from Delaney, but believed this would be done through 'baby steps'. He insisted on meeting with Delaney and senior staff before board meetings so he could be briefed on operational issues. Getting Delaney to share the limelight proved more difficult. The two sat down with their diaries before Conway received the chain of office to review upcoming public events where the FAI would be represented.

'I even said, "You pick what you want and I'll do the rest,"' says Conway. 'We did exchange diaries for about a month or two and by the end of the second month he wasn't having it, so it didn't continue.'

As for the pre-match formalities, Delaney insisted that the other associations would want to hear from him because he was a member of the UEFA ExCo. A compromise was reached. Both men would make speeches on behalf of the FAI at the pre-match meals.

*

Ireland opened its Nations League campaign on 6 September 2018 with a 4–1 defeat to Ryan Giggs's Wales in Cardiff. The Welsh had nine players in their squad younger than Ireland's youngest player, highlighting the lack of emerging talent in O'Neill's side.

When a leaked WhatsApp voice recording from Ireland full-back Stephen Ward revealed that Roy Keane had verbally abused two players, Harry Arter and Jon Walters – who had retorted by offering to fight the assistant manager – there were calls for Keane to be sacked. Martin O'Neill stood by Keane and said sometimes coaches had to use a bit of 'industrial, heavy-duty language'.

With the team in Poland for a friendly, Delaney asked for a meeting with O'Neill, which Keane also attended, along with the FAI's internal solicitor Rea Walshe, on a phone link from Dublin. Delaney later told the board that after the meeting he had phoned O'Neill 'with a view that Martin should at the press conference later that day let them know who the manager is'.

As the team continued to struggle – Wales beat Ireland in the UEFA Nations League in Dublin and O'Neill's side could then only manage a goalless draw at home to Denmark – the media became increasingly critical of O'Neill. Delaney was also coming in for flak for presiding over a regime that had produced a football team that people were no longer willing to watch.

On 3 November Delaney told the board that the FAI was 'pushing costs out to next year' where it could. He said the national team's poor performances were affecting the finances of the association. When a director suggested boosting advertising for the upcoming Northern Ireland game, Delaney said everyone already knew about the game.

'We have an issue that people do not want to pay to watch this team,' he said.

Delaney had a plan, though – and it involved the return of Mick McCarthy, who had just finished a lengthy spell at Ipswich Town. Delaney told the directors that he had had a highly confidential meeting with Robbie Keane, the retired Ireland striker and record goal-scorer. Delaney said he saw Robbie Keane assisting McCarthy in managing the Irish team. He saw Robbie Keane eventually becoming the Irish manager.

He also said that Stephen Kenny, the Dundalk FC boss, had been offered the manager's job for the Ireland under-21s. Delaney mentioned that he had consulted with John Giles.

Giles says he told the FAI CEO that he had already taken a call from Kenny and that he had advised the Dundalk manager to take the Ireland under-21 job only if he was guaranteed to get the senior job later.

★

On 18 November the FAI board convened for an early morning teleconference. The performance of the senior men's team was the only topic on the agenda. Three days previously, O'Neill's team had been outplayed by Northern Ireland in a 0–0 draw. Delaney said that, given the recent results, performances and 'negativity surrounding the team', it was important to hear what the board was thinking. That was the cue for unanimous criticism of the O'Neill regime, as recorded in the minutes.

Conway, the new President, told the meeting that while he was not a coach, there seemed to be an 'incoherence' in what Martin O'Neill was doing. Eamon Naughton said he usually sold about fifty tickets for each Ireland home game, but he now found it hard to give them away. 'It's a dangerous sign,' he said.

Mick Hanley said he had sat behind two 'football people' at the Northern Ireland game who decided to walk out at half-time because they had had enough. He had never seen it as bad.

Jim McConnell, from Donegal, said he didn't mind media criticism, but they were 'losing the football family'. He would usually sell a hundred tickets, but had only sold one pair for the Northern Ireland game.

Eddie Murray said a man beside him at the Northern Ireland game had pointed out that O'Neill had set the team up 'like he was playing Germany'. Murray had lost faith in O'Neill's coaching team because they had 'lost the plot'.

Niamh O'Donoghue, a former Secretary-General of the Department of Social Protection, had joined the board in the summer of 2017 as part of a merger of the women's football association with the FAI. She was regarded with suspicion by Cody and Delaney, but other directors say she brought competence and the odd searching question.

After being on the board for a number of months, O'Donoghue wrote a critique of the board's operating procedures that she shared with Delaney and other directors. She suggested that rather than directors getting agendas and reports just before the monthly meetings, they should be sent those details some days in advance to allow them to prepare properly. This was strongly resisted by Delaney and Cody, who warned it would result in leaks to journalists.

Regarding O'Neill, O'Donoghue agreed with the board consensus. 'They looked like a tired management team and tired players,' she said. Referring to the WhatsApp row, she believed 'public hearts and public minds have been lost' as it seemed the management team 'condone an unhealthy atmosphere'.

Delaney said he had offered Stephen Kenny the under-21 job again, but Kenny was holding out for the senior role. Delaney believed Kenny could get the position eventually, but he was currently 'missing an international element' to his CV.

Delaney told the board he had met O'Neill the previous night at the Aviva Stadium, where Ireland's rugby team had just recorded its first home victory over the All-Blacks. They had a 'strange conversation' during which each man repeatedly asked the other how he was. Delaney told the board that O'Neill had told him he could 'tough it out'. Delaney mentioned to O'Neill that the poor results were harming the FAI's finances. O'Neill, according to Delaney, had suggested he could take half of his wages and the rest could come in bonuses. Delaney also told the board that O'Neill asked Delaney 'straight out' if he had confidence in him. Delaney said he responded by saying that was a question for the board to answer.

Delaney told the board he was worried that if Ireland beat Denmark in Aarhus in their final Nations League fixture, O'Neill would return home to England and 'leave us stew'. He also felt the Irish rugby team's win against the highest-ranked team in the world would have a negative impact on how the Irish football team was viewed. He felt this was 'unfair', given that the FAI 'had never been better off the pitch'.

Delaney told the board he had lost confidence in O'Neill, citing the performances, the approach by Stoke, the Arter/Walters issue and the case of Declan Rice, who had withdrawn from the senior squad following an approach by England. Delaney said it was 'key' that when O'Neill asked him if he had confidence in him, he had not answered. He did not see O'Neill going voluntarily without a pay-off.

Delaney said Mick McCarthy was 'waiting in the wings' and would 'probably' take Robbie Keane as assistant. Conway said he believed support for Stephen Kenny getting the job would probably be 'short lived'.

The board formally authorized Delaney to enter immediate negotiations with O'Neill. Michael Cody then asked if the board was happy for Delaney to offer the job to Mick McCarthy.

Delaney intervened to say that, 'technically', they should get Ruud Dokter, the FAI's Head of High Performance, to make the decision. Niamh O'Donoghue asked if Dokter had a view on McCarthy. Delaney said he was not sure but he would check that out. He said David Nucifora, the IRFU's Technical Director, was Dokter's counterpart in rugby, and Nucifora was involved in every IRFU managerial appointment. Delaney said it would be good to say that Dokter was involved in McCarthy's appointment.

Delaney said Dokter was keen to have Robbie Keane involved. With Robbie Keane as assistant manager to McCarthy and Kenny as under-21 boss, they would have 'two contenders' to succeed McCarthy as the senior manager. Delaney insisted that he had not spoken to McCarthy yet – and yet he was talking to the board about McCarthy's successor.

The meeting, which started at 10 a.m., was paused when Delaney got a text from Gareth Maher, an FAI press officer who had been with O'Neill. They reconvened at 11.15 a.m. According to Delaney, Maher had reported that O'Neill 'looked unshaven and like a guy who had not slept and was not in the best form'. Delaney felt that O'Neill 'wants us to say we have lost confidence in him so that he can say "feck ye" or "let's negotiate"'.

Although the game was inconsequential, the atmosphere in Aarhus was one of the most fractious and poisonous that Irish fans can remember attending. All the animosity was between the Irish fans. When some supporters started chanting against the CEO, Delaney loyalists tried to drown them out. Several groups of Irish fans almost came to blows.

One of those in attendance was Wayne O'Sullivan, head of the Ballybrack Supporters' Club and one of Delaney's most ardent fans. Delaney had an agreement in place to sell O'Sullivan's club over 1,100 premium-level tickets for each home match at reduced rates. O'Sullivan says they had a 'you scratch my back, I'll scratch yours' relationship.

The toxicity between fans who supported Delaney and those who opposed him spilled out into the open that night. 'I'm not sure any-one could have enjoyed that trip,' O'Sullivan says. 'It wasn't an Ireland away end that night. It was personal and angry. A sad day.'

Word quickly got around the supporters that O'Neill's days were numbered, no matter the result. Emma English went to a pub where a large group of Irish fans had congregated before the game. When one fan went to take a picture of her on the dance floor, he was put in a headlock by another Irish supporter. The would-be photographer was told by his assailant that he had promised Delaney he would 'look out for' English.

The day after a 0–0 draw in Denmark, Delaney and Cody flew to London to meet O'Neill and his legal adviser, Paul Gilroy QC, to reach a deal on terminating O'Neill's contract. Delaney told the board at a teleconferenced meeting on the morning of Friday, 23 November, that it was a good deal as it was less than the cost of O'Neill's €2 million salary. The cost of the settlement with O'Neill and his backroom staff was €1.6 million. FAI records would later show that Roy Keane, who was paid €680,000 in 2018, would receive a further €214,000 in 2019, separate to the €1.6 million pay-off.

The board congratulated Delaney on the result. One said 'it wasn't a mess like the media would have wanted'.

Delaney had by now offered Stephen Kenny the under-21 job with the guarantee he would become senior boss after the Euro 2020 cam-paign finished. He and Dokter were due to meet McCarthy in an hour to offer him the manager's job up to the end of the Euro 2020 campaign. Delaney accepted that it was an 'unusual enough' arrangement, but said it incentivized McCarthy 'to qualify and to teach this young man'.

Delaney said that McCarthy might ask, 'What if I do well at the Euros?' In that case, Delaney told the board, 'We would then try to squeeze Stephen Kenny back a bit.' If Kenny did poorly and McCarthy did well with the seniors, Delaney said, then the public would want them to change the plan.

Dokter, who was in on the meeting, said that Robbie Keane wanted to be the assistant manager but McCarthy would probably bring in Terry Connor, his long-time assistant. Keane was said to have told the FAI that he had the 'connection to the public' which Connor did not and that he would be able to challenge McCarthy because he was not as close to him as Connor.

If the deal worked out, Delaney saw Keane becoming Kenny's assistant manager after 2020, and that would be him 'boxed away'. 'Robbie has a lot of learning to do here,' he said. 'We need to couch the contracts with that in mind.'

Cody said that Robbie Keane was the least important of the three. 'We should try and fit him in as best we can but he is really not that significant.' One director said he knew from following Keane on social media that he had 'a huge opinion of himself and he needs to know his boundaries if he comes on board'. Delaney said McCarthy had already spoken with Robbie Keane and he did not want another 'Martin/Roy Keane situation', so he would not be putting Robbie Keane out to hold press conferences.

McCarthy, who had previously told people privately that he would have taken €500,000 a year, was to be paid €1.2 million per annum, plus a planned 'exit payment' of €1.13 million when he left in August 2020. The board had given Delaney carte blanche to negotiate the deal, and the result was another huge managerial salary on the FAI's books. Ryan Giggs, the Wales boss, was on £400,000 a year. McCarthy was guaranteed at least €3 million from the FAI for managing the team for just over a year and a half. No one on the board questioned the salary level or the unusual seven-figure 'exit fee'.

Ahead of the public announcement of the deal, the FAI board met on 24 November. Delaney said the only complication was Robbie Keane. The former Irish striker had 'overvalued himself', according to Delaney, believing he was worth more than McCarthy. Stephen Kenny, for his part, was refusing to commit to retaining Keane as assistant manager when he took over in 2020. McCarthy would accept Keane as part of his coaching team but 'he was not bothered about having him', Delaney told the board.

Before McCarthy's deal was publicly announced, Delaney would agree a four-year deal with Robbie Keane on a salary rising to €250,000 a year, as a first-team coach – meaning he would remain in contract when Kenny took over. The details of McCarthy and Keane's deals never came before the board for approval. Kenny would be paid €205,000 in 2019 and would move up to €300,000 for 2020 and €540,000 in 2021.

Delaney said that McCarthy had suggested Shay Given for his goalkeeping coach, but Delaney believed this would be 'too complicated'. Alan Kelly, who had been the goalkeeping coach under Trapattoni, was instead brought back into the role.

*

Most pundits had been assuming the FAI faced a binary choice between McCarthy and Kenny. When Delaney announced he had a deal that involved both of them, it was broadly welcomed as a canny, if unusual, move. In the *Irish Times*, Keith Duggan wrote: 'John Delaney is a shrewd operator; the events of the past seven days were a vivid example of a born survivor at his most nimble-minded.'

It helped that Shane Ross, the Minister for Sport, seemed oblivious to any shortcomings in Delaney's running of the FAI. In a gaffe-ridden interview on Newstalk shortly after the McCarthy and Kenny deals were announced, Ross was asked was he aware that many Irish fans were critical of Delaney.

'I don't hear people giving out,' said Ross. 'I read about it in the press all right. There's a lot of criticism about John Delaney. My own experience is that when I go to these local games in the constituency on the ground, I see John Delaney and representatives of the FAI all the time. They're always on the ground doing things, relating to those really important things that young people are doing.' In the same interview Ross called Stephen Kenny 'Shane', and mixed up the names of several Irish footballers.

From appearing stressed in Aarhus, Delaney now seemed to have vim in his step. The great and the good of European football were in Dublin on 2 December for the UEFA draw for the Euro 2020 qualifiers. One UEFA official remarked that they were decamping to 'Delaney-land' for the weekend. Some 650 guests and 350 media were in town and Delaney wanted to ensure there were no potentially embarrassing protests.

An email from Joe McGlue, the FAI's Head of Security, was sent to Delaney and copied to Emma English, setting out the close-protection arrangements for the FAI's celebrity CEO that weekend:

> There will be a very discreet presence by one [security] person in the hotel. You will not notice this person. There will be other security personnel on duty but that's for UEFA stuff. This person is specific to watching you. I will also be around the hotel. Following your meeting and if you are walking to [the] Mansion House [the bodyguard] will be walking behind you – five or six metres. I will be outside the Mansion House for your arrival along with another person (specific for your movements) where we will have a handle on anything outside.

McGlue wrote that he had plans to cover Delaney in the Shelbourne hotel after an event in Dublin Castle. 'If it's a case where you attend the bar for a drink [the bodyguard] will be on site in a discreet manor [sic] until you head to bed.'

Knowing that McGlue and the FAI monitored the YBIG forums, supporter Zeno Kelly had posted some messages indicating that a protest with banners was planned for outside the Convention Centre on the morning of the draw on 2 December. Kelly was actually in America at a wedding at the time, but it put McGlue on alert. He forwarded Kelly's YBIG post to a private email account of a member of the Garda.

In his email to Delaney, McGlue wrote that he did not believe any commercial planes or extra boats up the Liffey were booked for demonstrations. He noted that there was a WhatsApp group with ten to twelve fans set up by Kelly or Tommy Shields, a supporter from Galway. 'Gardaí are trying to hack into it,' wrote McGlue. 'Further update later.' Although there was no solid information about protests, McGlue said there were plans to intercept them if they happened. The Garda would later state there was no attempt to hack any supporters' group.

*

The FAI had budgeted for a €2.5 million profit for 2018, but at a 14 December board meeting Delaney blamed the senior men's team for this target being missed. Instead, he said, the FAI would return a profit of between €750,000 and €1 million. He said that was 'conditional' on the severance of €1.6 million paid to O'Neill and his team being included in the following year's accounts.

A loss of €2.5 million was projected for 2019. To help 'plug the gap', Delaney said he had 'obtained money from Denis O'Brien, UEFA and other sources', but 'cash was tight'. O'Brien had contributed €150,000 more to the FAI, Delaney said, and '€20,000 of that is personal'.

The FAI's blue-chip suppliers had been tapped up to buy corporate premium-ticket packages worth at least €50,000 each. AON, the FAI's insurance company, A&L Goodbody, the FAI's long-time solicitors, and Deloitte, the FAI's auditors, all agreed to buy ten-year tickets in advance of 2020.

Other money had been obtained from 'grassroots' affiliates of the FAI. The Leinster Senior League had bought €25,000 worth of tickets, the Leinster Football Association had spent €100,000, the Schoolboys Football Association bought a corporate box for €50,000. The Tipperary Southern and District League, run by Delaney's friend Tommy Lewis, spent €50,000. All these amateur leagues and associations were effectively bailing out the FAI, buying tickets they couldn't use until late 2020.

Delaney told the board that McCarthy would agree to bring in fewer players for matches and would notify them earlier of their call-ups. Longer notice and reduced squads meant cheaper transport costs for the FAI and reduced players' fees. The board was also told that in the new year, the FAI would hire Cathal Dervan, from the *Irish Sun*, to be 'the voice' of the FAI.

Delaney wanted the FAI to write to Martin O'Neill and Roy Keane to thank them for their service. He said the FAI needed to insert confidentiality clauses in both their termination agreements with sanctions for any breaches. While he had spoken to O'Neill, Roy Keane had not responded to a long voicemail or text messages that Delaney had sent him. He noted that O'Neill watched everything that was said about him, and that after Sky Sports reported critical comments by Matt Doherty, the Wolves and Ireland defender, O'Neill had rung both Sky and Doherty to complain.

As it was the last board meeting of an eventful 2018, one member decided to raise something in the Any Other Business part of the meeting. It wasn't about succession planning for Delaney, as the minutes of the meeting record: 'It had been a great board over the last twelve months . . . The CEO had done a fantastic job and they didn't know where he got the time. As a team, the board were getting better and better.'

Two other board members chimed in to agree. Another said Delaney's ExCo role had not hindered him, indeed it had helped the FAI. Donal Conway expressed amazement at Delaney's work ethic. Conway said he had met Delaney recently at 4.30 a.m. in Dublin airport to fly off for a meeting with Gianni Infantino, the FIFA President. Delaney had worked on the plane going out. When they came back they drove to an event in Tullamore. Delaney worked on the way there too. There had been 'some difficult customers' in Tullamore. He got home around 1 a.m.

'From FIFA President to talking about cutting grass in Tullamore,' remarked Conway. 'Those types of days are pretty frequent. The abuse the CEO has to put up with is draining and I don't know how he does it.'

11. 'No story here'

On 1 March 2019, a Friday, an acrimonious court battle between Denis O'Brien and the *Sunday Business Post* reached its denouement in Dublin's Four Courts. The FAI's Honorary Life President had spent the majority of February sitting in uncomfortable seats in Court 25 eyeballing the jury despite having a multinational phone business, Digicel, to run.

O'Brien and his solicitor, Paul Meagher, believed it was important for the billionaire to show the jury just how important the case was to him by appearing in court every day. O'Brien missed one morning session in that last week, as he had to attend a conference in Barcelona, where he signed a new deal with a Turkish company; but he made it back for the afternoon, slightly out of breath as he took his seat after lunch.

However, on the Friday, with the jury out for two days to consider their verdict after the month-long trial, there was no sign of Ireland's richest man. Late in the afternoon the jury returned its verdict. It was a devastating finding for O'Brien. The jury had rejected six separate claims that a *Business Post* article about large bank debtors who helped 'destroy' Ireland's economy was defamatory of him. The verdict left O'Brien defeated for the first time in a libel action and facing a €1 million legal bill. Ian Kehoe and Tom Lyons, the journalists behind the story, called the result 'a great day for Irish journalism' and said it showed the need to stand up to businessmen who threaten legal action in an attempt to silence investigative reporting.

With those words still ringing in his ears, Mark Tighe returned to the *Sunday Times* office on Friday evening to file his report on the case for that weekend's paper. When he got to his desk, he found an envelope lying on his computer keyboard.

Inside were two documents. The first was a photocopy of a personal cheque made out by John Delaney to the FAI for €100,000. The second was an FAI remittance statement, made out to Delaney, saying he had been repaid €100,000 in June 2017.

The photocopy of the cheque was truncated on one side, so the year of the cheque was unclear. It looked most likely to be April '2018', which would in turn suggest that Delaney had got €100,000 from the FAI in 2017 and repaid it in 2018.

A check on the FAI's published accounts for 2017 showed that no transaction between any director and the association had been declared beyond the normal salary payments.

If the documents were genuine, there could be an innocent explanation. Perhaps the FAI had made a mistaken overpayment to Delaney, and he had repaid it.

Tighe decided the best thing to do was contact the FAI immediately. Cathal Dervan, who was the sports editor of the *Irish Sun*, had recently been recruited as the FAI's Director of Communications. He was not due to start officially until April, but Tighe had heard that Dervan was already advising Delaney on PR matters.

Both the *Irish Sun* and the *Sunday Times* are owned by News UK and Ireland, a company ultimately controlled by Rupert Murdoch. Their offices are in the same building, the Watermarque, in Ringsend, separated by a glass partition wall. Tighe decided to walk into the *Sun*'s office after colleagues confirmed that Dervan was working that Friday evening.

Tighe had never spoken to Dervan before, beyond a brief nod or 'hello'. He knew of him as a keen golfer who sometimes came into the *Sunday Times* office to discuss golf matters with John Burns, the *Sunday Times* associate editor, who was a fellow member of the Dublin journalists' golf society. Dervan had been a high-profile soccer correspondent for decades. He was well known because of his support for Mick McCarthy against Roy Keane during the Saipan controversy, so it seemed to fit that he would join the FAI now, after Keane's departure as assistant manager and McCarthy's return as manager.

Tighe located Dervan, showed him the two documents he had just received, and asked if he could contact Delaney and the FAI for an explanation. Dervan looked at the documents, but said he hadn't yet started with the FAI, so he couldn't help. Tighe went back to his desk.

Ten minutes later Dervan knocked on the *Sunday Times* office door and asked Tighe to come out. In the no-man's land between the two newspapers' offices, Dervan said he had checked it out and insisted 'there is no story here'. He gave the impression he had just spoken with either Delaney or Delaney's solicitor. He told Tighe 'it's not what you think it is', but he couldn't give any further information other than to suggest the documents were somehow related to a family-law matter.

Tighe said there was clearly a question for the FAI to answer, as no €100,000 transaction between Delaney and the FAI had been declared in its published accounts. Dervan insisted there was no story.

Tighe went back to his desk, intrigued by what Dervan had said about a family-law matter. He knew Delaney was separated from his wife, Emer, but he did not understand why that would prevent him explaining what appeared to be a circular €100,000 transaction with the FAI.

Tighe was concerned that the same documents could have been sent to rival newspapers and he did not want to be scooped. Although it was Friday evening and he had a long piece on the O'Brien case to write and file, he decided to chase the Delaney lead a bit further that evening.

He phoned Paddy Goodwin, Delaney's long-time solicitor, and outlined the two documents he had received. The solicitor gave the impression of having been forewarned. Goodwin claimed the documents must have been leaked by his client's ex-wife, and said Delaney would take legal action if Tighe and the *Sunday Times* tried to publish a story based on the documents.

Goodwin cited the in-camera rule that prevents publication of some matters related to family law and other sensitive cases. Tighe insisted that he could not see how a payment between Delaney and the FAI of €100,000 was necessarily a family-law matter, even if the documents had come up in evidence in the divorce case, as implied by Goodwin. Could Delaney not just explain why the payments had been made? Tighe told Goodwin that he was going to submit written queries on the transactions to the FAI. By the end of the conversation, Tighe – who had not felt certain that the documents were authentic – had the firm impression that they were genuine, even if Goodwin was somehow trying to claim they were covered by the in-camera rule.

Tighe's email to the FAI's media department detailed what he knew about the transactions and asked the FAI and Delaney to explain why they had not been declared in the FAI's accounts. Because of the truncated date on the photocopied €100,000 Delaney cheque he was working off, Tighe told the FAI he believed he had evidence of an 'advance' or 'loan' being paid to Delaney in June 2017, and the cheque for repayment from Delaney being lodged in April 2018. He hoped that if he was wrong on the date of the cheque, the FAI would let him know.

The email to the FAI asked four questions.

Can you tell me why there are no records of any directors' loans made to John Delaney in the FAI's accounts for the year ending December 2017 relating to these large loans/advances?

Can Mr Delaney explain why these advances/loans were given?

Was any interest charged on these advances/loans?

Who approved these advances/loans and their terms?

The email said the *Sunday Times* intended to publish a story about the €100,000 transactions that weekend, and the deadline for a response from the FAI was the following day, Saturday, 2 March, at 4 p.m.

The deadline passed with no response from the FAI. Tighe, his editor, Frank Fitzgibbon, and Colin Coyle, Head of News, decided to dig further before publishing a story. Little did they know that Tighe's 1 March email would become vital evidence in court and play a key role in allowing the story of the €100,000 transaction to be published.

In the following week, Tighe fired off another email to the FAI seeking responses to his questions. He spoke with Paul Rowan, the newspaper's soccer correspondent, who passed on some contact numbers of people he thought might be able to assist.

Dervan had by then finished his work with the *Irish Sun*, and was

soon to start in his new role as the FAI's PR Director. As is customary when a journalist leaves a newspaper, a humorous mock-up of his
paper was presented to Dervan as a going-away present. Dervan's
head was photoshopped onto an Ireland player's body, and he was
pulling proudly on the FAI badge on his jersey. The headline said
Dervan was 'answering Ireland's call'. A smaller headline over a picture of Delaney, drunk in Poland at Euro 2012, promised a 'Sunsport
Exposé' with the headline 'Just what has John been up to? See pages
48–49'.

By the following week, Tighe had made contact with an FAI
source who was able to confirm that Delaney had indeed been
involved in a circular €100,000 transaction with the FAI, and suggested this was not widely known about in Abbotstown. The source
also suggested that the story would be 'explosive' for both Delaney
and the FAI, but offered no further information about the reasoning
behind the payment. The source could not help on the exact date on
Delaney's cheque, but Tighe was now satisfied the transactions were
genuine.

Because of concern that the cheque's date was not clear and the
FAI's remittance document spoke about a 'repayment', it was decided
that the story would simply say Delaney had made a 'mysterious'
€100,000 payment to the FAI. The *Sunday Times*'s lawyer frowned
upon the use of the word 'mysterious', which he believed could create
a suspicion of wrongdoing, so the new plan was to simply say the
Sunday Times had established that Delaney had made an 'unexplained'
€100,000 payment to his employer.

The newspaper's editorial team had various theories on what the
payment might have been about, but the uncertainty about the date
of Delaney's cheque meant that it wasn't even clear in which direction the €100,000 had travelled first. The journalists suspected, at the
very least, that Delaney and the FAI were in breach of company law
by not having declared the payments as related party transactions in
the 2017 accounts, which had been audited by Deloitte. The threatened legal action from Goodwin and the failure to explain the
payments made Tighe feel that Delaney was desperate to avoid public
scrutiny.

After almost two weeks of silence, Tighe decided to employ a tried-and-tested tactic to try to prompt Delaney into responding formally before publication.

Working with Hugh Hannigan, News Ireland's legal manager, Tighe wrote a letter to Delaney, citing Section 26 of the 2009 Irish Defamation Act, which says there is a defence of 'fair and reasonable publication' for defendants in defamation cases. For a newspaper to avail of this defence, the article must have been published in good faith, in the public interest, not be excessive, and in all circumstances be considered fair and reasonable to publish. Amongst the factors to be weighed by a court deciding on whether such a defence can be availed of is the extent to which the person or organization being written about was given an opportunity to have their side of events represented.

After outlining the details of the €100,000 transaction that were known at that stage, the letter set out the history of contacts Tighe had had with the FAI and Goodwin:

> I have indicated to the FAI and your representatives that I would like to be informed of and have the opportunity to prominently include your response on these matters in our article. I have made every effort to obtain comment from you in this regard. Despite my several attempts to speak with you for this stated purpose, you and the FAI have refused so far to respond to me.

The letter was sent to Delaney's FAI email address at 5.47 p.m. on Wednesday, 13 March. A hard copy was sent by courier to Abbotstown. The letter invited the FAI boss to respond to the *Sunday Times*'s questions about the €100,000 transactions before a story would be published that Sunday, St Patrick's Day. The final sentence of the letter asked if this was a matter that should be raised with the FAI's President, instead of Delaney, because, as chairman of the FAI board, he was technically the CEO's boss.

There was radio silence until that Friday. Just before lunch, Marian McGee, a solicitor with Sheridan Quinn, sent Tighe an email marked 'urgent'. McGee said that Sheridan Quinn had represented Delaney in his divorce proceedings.

Under the heading 'In the matter of Delaney v Delaney', an attached three-page letter said the information or documentation held by Tighe 'could only have emanated from recent family-law proceedings which our client was involved in with his wife'. The letter accused the journalist of breaching the in-camera rule and said it was preparing to bring the matter before the court to make it aware of the possible issue of contempt. McGee said assurances were being sought from the legal team of Delaney's ex-wife that she wasn't responsible for the leak. After citing case law relating to information that was wrongly used arising from in-camera cases, the letter said that unless Tighe agreed not to disseminate this information, he would be made a defendant in contempt of court proceedings.

After taking legal advice from Hugh Hannigan, Tighe responded by email at 3.19 p.m. denying that he was in possession of any family-law material:

> The questions put to John Delaney have nothing to do with family law matters. In fact, given the content of the questions put to him by me, which, notably, make no reference whatsoever to family law matters, it is extraordinary that you write to me under the heading Delaney v. Delaney and that you threaten to hold me in contempt of court in respect of those proceedings.

Aware that this correspondence could end up before a judge, Tighe outlined the public interest in the prospective story:

> I confirm that this newspaper is not reporting on family law matters involving your client and it has no intention to do so. Instead, my press queries and proposed report relate to our understanding of payments made from and to an organization that has reportedly received in the region of €49.5 million in public funding in the last ten years, namely the FAI. These are not matters that originate or derive from any confidential family law proceedings . . . These payments relate to the FAI and are matters of real and significant public interest and importance.

A reply from Delaney's solicitors arrived in Tighe's inbox at 5 p.m. It demanded the return of any documentation that Tighe's questions had been based on. It repeated the claim that any publication of the contents of the documents was a breach of the in-camera rule and a contempt of court.

In a letter signed and emailed by McGee, Sheridan Quinn again asked for an undertaking not to publish. Failing this, they said, they would be going to the Circuit Court 'at the earliest available opportunity' to bring this 'breach' to the court's attention. It said this application would be made ex-parte, meaning only Delaney's side would be represented at the hearing, but that the court may wish to hear from the newspaper on the matter.

As the courts were now closed for the St Patrick's Day weekend until Tuesday, it was unclear when Delaney's solicitors would be heading to the Circuit Court. After further input from Hannigan, Tighe responded at 6.19 p.m., restating his position that the story did not refer to any family-law matter.

Tighe wrote the story about the €100,000 payment that Friday evening, so that the lawyers would have a copy of it in hand in case Delaney decided to go to court immediately. On Saturday, at 11.54 a.m., six minutes before the deadline Tighe had set for Delaney to respond to his queries, Noel Sheridan, a partner in Sheridan Quinn, wrote on behalf of Delaney. He explained that McGee, author of the previous correspondence from the firm, was 'on vacation'. The email restated Delaney's position that 'the documents referred to in our previous letter could only have emanated from Family Law proceedings':

> It is our intention to bring this matter before the Circuit Family Court as soon as possible and seek the directions of the court in relation to these matters and the application of the in-camera rule. In circumstances in which you have been thus advised, clearly any publication would be entirely in contempt of court. Publication by you would be in the full knowledge of such contempt and the court would be alerted to this intentional breach. We await your undertaking that there will be no publication pending bringing the matter back before the Circuit Family Court in early course.

The newspaper decided not to respond. It appeared that Delaney would be seeking a hearing on Tuesday to hold the newspaper in contempt of court after it published its story.

At 4.30 p.m., Tighe was getting ready to leave the office early, anxious to avoid the St Patrick's Day revellers as he cycled home. His Delaney/FAI story was filed, along with a number of unrelated stories. He was putting on a new blue hoodie, a gift from his wife and children on his birthday the day before, when a call came through to Fitzgibbon that stopped him in his tracks. Hugh Hannigan told Fitzgibbon that he had been speaking with Paddy Goodwin and that Delaney's lawyers might be going for an emergency injunction in the High Court. Hannigan then told Tighe to print off all his notes and correspondence relating to the story.

Hannigan soon had confirmation Delaney was indeed going to the High Court. He asked Fitzgibbon: Would the newspaper fight the legal action?

Fitzgibbon was well aware of Delaney's reputation as someone who thought he could bully media organizations into submission. Hannigan was somewhat pessimistic about the chances of a judge allowing the newspaper to publish. However, Fitzgibbon was determined to fight the injunction attempt as a point of principle. He quickly gave the go-ahead for the *Sunday Times* to defend the action.

Hannigan, a keen runner, was wearing a tracksuit when he arrived at the Watermarque by taxi. Tighe joined the lawyer in the cab and they sped down the quays, reaching the courts complex at 6 p.m. Hurrying out of the car, the pair ran past the closed front doors of the James Gandon-designed Four Courts. The black iron gates at the side entrance, where the G4S security hut was located, were also closed. Tighe rattled the gates and called out 'Hello, can we get in please?' Eventually, a security guard ambled over to unlock the gates. Hannigan and Tighe rushed up the stairs to the second floor, where a suited Delaney and his team of lawyers were in Court 19. The FAI boss glanced at the dishevelled and breathless reporter, then turned away. It was notable that his solicitor was Goodwin, his long-time legal adviser, and not anyone from Sheridan Quinn, the firm that had been sending Tighe legal letters. (Goodwin would tell the judge that he was present because Sheridan Quinn had no one available at the weekend.)

Hannigan was given a copy of Delaney's affidavit and his plenary summons, setting out how the FAI boss was effectively seeking a super-injunction by requesting an order that Delaney's application against the newspaper and Tighe personally should be held in-camera. If Delaney won, this would prevent not only the story's publication but also any reporting of the fact that he had brought the injunction proceedings. Delaney was also seeking damages from Tighe and the newspaper for allegedly breaching his privacy.

Earlier that afternoon, Hannigan had found it hard to secure a barrister late on the Saturday of a bank holiday weekend. Eventually he managed to engage Tom Hogan, a senior counsel who had once represented a website that had previously been sued by Delaney.

Hogan had been driving his children to go shopping in south Dublin when Hannigan had first called that afternoon to check if he would be available. After hearing a sketch of what the case might entail, Hogan agreed that he could come to the Four Courts if Delaney went ahead. He advised Hannigan that Delaney had a good chance of winning.

It was some time later that Hannigan called Hogan back to say the case was going ahead. By that point, Hogan's children were trying on ski gear in a shop in Carrickmines. He told them to get their jackets on. The barrister dropped his kids home and changed into a suit before racing to the Four Courts. On the way in, he called Delaney's lawyers. They were threatening to start the injunction proceedings ex-parte, as the judge was ready. Hogan asked that they not begin without the *Sunday Times* being represented in court. He also had a further quick call with Hannigan after 6 p.m. once the *Sunday Times* solicitor had sight of Delaney's legal papers.

At 6.10 p.m. Tighe dashed back down to the gates to find the security guard to let Hogan in. Introducing himself as they quickly climbed the stairs to Court 19, Tighe outlined to Hogan the background to the story and the attempts he had made since 1 March to get comment from Delaney and the FAI.

Hogan took fifteen minutes to familiarize himself with the papers – a very short amount of time for a senior counsel who was soon to be on his feet arguing the case before a judge. The judicial assistant of the judge asked whether the *Sunday Times* was ready.

Judge Anthony Barr, the emergency-duty High Court judge for that weekend, was keen to get going. Hannigan begged for five more minutes so Hogan could read all the papers.

Hogan asked Tighe was he willing to go into the box and give evidence, if necessary. 'Yes, of course,' Tighe said.

At 6.35 p.m. the hearing kicked off. With Tighe in his hoodie and Hannigan in sports gear, they were glad that at least their dapper-looking senior counsel was dressed for the occasion. The judge made an initial order that there could be no social media posts about the case before he had ruled on Delaney's application.

In his affidavit, Delaney said he had been granted an order of divorce by Judge Patricia Ryan of the Circuit Court on 11 January. As part of those proceedings he had been required to supply documentation on his financial affairs. He said the *Sunday Times* had recently contacted him to ask about a cheque and remittance advice relating to him and the FAI. The documents 'could only have come to [its] attention and/or into its possession in the context of family law proceedings', he alleged.

The FAI Chief Executive said he had been advised not to respond to questions about the €100,000 cheque, as it 'could render me in a position of breaching the in-camera rule'. He claimed the newspaper would suffer no prejudice if ordered not to publish its story.

Delaney's senior counsel was Nuala Jackson, a fearsome advocate who specializes in the rough-and-tumble of family-law cases. Jackson set out Delaney's case that the *Sunday Times* had flagrantly breached the in-camera rule. She said if the newspaper were able to go ahead and publish, then what was to stop any litigant in family-law proceedings from dumping their case files into a newspaper's office for them to rifle through for tasty stories 'willy-nilly'.

Jackson proposed that the family-law system in Ireland could be fundamentally undermined if the in-camera rule was allowed to be breached as the *Sunday Times* proposed.

Delaney could not prove the *Sunday Times*'s story was based on documents from Delaney's divorce case, Jackson acknowledged, but he strongly suspected that that was the situation. She said Delaney could draw a Venn diagram of all those who had copies of either of the two documents that Tighe had referred to in his email. She said the overlapping bit in the middle was his family-law case.

Jackson outlined the questions the *Sunday Times* had set out in Tighe's letter from earlier that week. When she mentioned that the FAI payment of €100,000 to Delaney was in June 2017 and that Delaney's €100,000 cheque was said to be dated April 2018, Caroline McGrath, her junior counsel, moved to correct her. Jackson said, 'That's the way they have it.' For Tighe, this was evidence that his assumption about the date on his truncated photocopy of the €100,000 cheque had been incorrect.

Jackson asked the judge to grant the injunction and remit the case back to the Circuit Court for the following Tuesday, when the judge handling the divorce case could decide if there had been a breach of the in-camera rule. If this request was granted, then it would be difficult for the newspaper to emerge from the family-law courts with permission to publish its story. So this Saturday-night case was all or nothing. If the *Sunday Times* lost then its legal advice was to settle the case quickly and agree not to publish, so the newspaper would not get dragged into a lengthy and costly family-law hearing with little prospect of success.

Hogan, despite his scant preparation time, then delivered a bravura performance in defence of the story and the newspaper's right to publish it. Why had Delaney waited until late on Saturday night on a bank holiday weekend to try to injunct the story if he genuinely believed his in-camera family-law proceedings had been breached, Hogan asked. Delaney had been made aware that the newspaper had details of these payments fifteen days previously.

The judge asked: 'Since March the first?'

Delaney had failed to outline in his affidavit that he had had over two weeks' notice on the story. This delay was significant, Hogan insisted.

He showed the judge the 1 March email from the *Sunday Times* to the FAI press office, in which questions were asked about the cheque and reference was made to an earlier conversation between Tighe and Paddy Goodwin, Delaney's solicitor. Hogan went on to question Delaney's bona fides and described the injunction application as a 'desperate last-ditch tackle' and an 'attempt to abuse the in-camera rule'. He emphasized how the *Sunday Times* story would concentrate solely on payments between the FAI and Delaney.

Highlighting the 'overwhelming' public interest in the case, Hogan emphasized how the FAI had received some €50 million in public funding in the last decade and how an Oireachtas Sport Committee hearing involving the FAI was scheduled for next month. He said the TDs and senators were sure to be interested in this story. The senior counsel pointed out that Delaney had provided no evidence that the documents were from his family-law case. The possibility that documents might have been mentioned in a family-law case did 'not forever more shroud them with the protection of the in-camera rule'.

Barr retired to consider his verdict at 7.47 p.m. He said he would deliver judgment at 8.25 p.m. The parties spilled out of the court and into the corridor to talk. Delaney stalked up and down, talking on his mobile phone.

Tighe consulted with his editors back in Ringsend by phone. Because it was so late in the day, the story could not be given the main 'splash' space on the front page, as it would be too much trouble to redesign the whole page if the Delaney story was killed by an injunction.

The two *Sunday Times* lawyers were pessimistic. They thought the hearing had gone well, but the easiest thing for the judge to do would be to kick the case back to the family-law judge on Tuesday. Tighe warned his colleagues to expect a negative ruling.

In late 2017, Tighe had published a story about a state solicitor using social media accounts to accuse named judges, including Barr, of being overly generous in personal injury cases. The story had been illustrated by a large picture of Barr. Tighe hoped the judge hadn't taken offence.

At 8.38 p.m. Barr returned to deliver his verdict. Instead of immediately giving his ruling, he began reciting the evidence and submissions from both sides. It was only then that the *Sunday Times* team realized it had forgotten to tell the judge that its deadline was 9.45 p.m. There was a real danger that the newspaper could win the case but that the ruling would come too late to get the story into print for the following day.

At 9.20, after forty minutes of recapping the submissions and evidence, Barr finally moved on to his findings. He said that he found that any payments between the FAI and its Chief Executive as outlined by the *Sunday Times* in its questions to Delaney were 'matters of significant public interest'. Delaney's head dropped instantly.

The judge said there were two broad classes of documents from family-law cases. One class included pleadings and reports that obviously emanated from such cases and were protected from disclosure. The judge said a second class involved files released under disclosure requirements, such as cheque stubs and ledgers, which were not clearly family-law files but had the same protection.

Barr said the *Sunday Times* was correct that documents that existed before such cases 'cannot become immunized merely because they were referred to in the course of the family-law proceedings'. The judge added: 'That would carry the in-camera rule too far.'

He found there was no evidence that the newspaper got the documents via the family-law case. Barr said people 'might make such documents available to a journalist either through a desire or under a sense of duty, whether they be a whistleblower or because they perhaps hold a grudge against a person who happens to be in family-law proceedings'. He said they could do this 'independently of those proceedings'.

'It would be going too far for the law to state that, merely because a document was contained in an affidavit of discovery in the course of family-law proceedings, that any disclosure of that material to a journalist or a third party would be a breach of the in-camera rule,' he said.

The judge said he had to balance the importance of this rule with the right of news media to report on issues of significant public interest. 'I'm satisfied that the finances of the FAI, generally, and, in particular, any payment and repayment there may have been by the FAI to its CEO, are matters of significant public interest,' he said. He also ruled that Delaney's fifteen-day delay in taking legal action from when Tighe first made contact with Goodwin and the FAI was 'significant'. He said it weakened Delaney's statement of belief that the material could only come from his family-law case. After refusing the injunction and lifting the temporary reporting restriction, Barr ordered Delaney to pay the costs of the emergency hearing.

The verdict was handed down at 9.25 p.m., twenty minutes before the *Sunday Times*'s print deadline. It allowed just enough time to get the story into print. Tighe had to restrain himself from punching the air. Using Slack, a messaging service used by the *Sunday Times* editorial team, he informed them that they'd won.

Delaney had disappointment etched on his face. Hannigan advised Tighe not to approach Delaney for comment on the verdict or for an explanation of the transaction as he huddled with his lawyers. 'It's a bit raw,' he said.

Hogan offered to drive Hannigan and Tighe back to Ringsend. They had less than fifteen minutes before the paper went to print. As they reversed out of a parking spot outside the Legal Eagle pub adjacent to the Four Courts, Goodwin, Delaney's solicitor, rang Hannigan. The *Sunday Times* had the wrong date for the cheque, he confirmed. Delaney had paid the cheque in before the FAI paid him €100,000.

Hannigan relayed the message. Tighe asked him to call Goodwin back. What was the exact date of the cheque? Hannigan made the call. Goodwin confirmed it was 25 April 2017. Tighe called the office to update the story. Although the purpose of the payments remained unclear, the *Sunday Times* could now report that Delaney had written a €100,000 cheque to the FAI in April 2017, and that the association had remitted the same amount to Delaney's account in June of that year.

Tighe and Hannigan jumped out of the senior counsel's Land Rover Discovery, after giving him hearty thanks for his performance, and raced into the office with minutes to spare. They briefly checked the story, on the bottom of page 1, for errors before it was sent to print.

At 10.05 p.m. Tighe tweeted: 'Just spent the last three hours in the High Court after John Delaney tried to get an emergency injunction to prevent us reporting on FAI and Delaney payments. The judge ruled in our favour! Story in the Sunday Times tomorrow.' He finished it with the least triumphalist smiley face he could find.

*

While the *Sunday Times* team were racing back to the office, Delaney and his lawyer retreated to the Legal Eagle.

Staff at the pub recognized Delaney: he had been a regular there while his family-law case was on in January. As he walked through the restaurant area with his phone at his ear, staff had to usher him back out to the bar area because he had no reservation and it was a busy night.

'We deal with senior counsel and judges every day of the week,' says one staffer. 'While they are in charge over in the courts, over here they are all treated the same no matter what they do.'

For the rest of the night, Delaney would curtly order coffees as his phone stayed stuck to his ear. Delaney was arranging an emergency board meeting of the FAI via teleconference. Goodwin, a former member of the FAI National Council, would be on the call too.

Donal Conway, Noel Fitzroy, Michael Cody, Eddie Murray, Niamh O'Donoghue, Eamon Naughton and John Earley were the other board members on the call, which started at 10.30 p.m. Rea Walshe, the Company Secretary, and Cathal Dervan, the incoming Director of Communications and PR, were also on the call.

Delaney had informed the board in passing of 'bridging' payments he had made in 2017 earlier that month, at a board meeting on 4 March, three days after receiving queries from the *Sunday Times*. He said he had made a payment to cover a cash shortfall some years previously. On the conference call from the pub, Delaney said he'd paid €100,000 to the FAI in April 2017 'to keep cash flow correct'. Delaney said the payment happened after Eamon Breen, the FAI's Finance Director and Head of IT, came into Delaney's office to tell him 'we could be over our limit with the bank'. Delaney had been due to fly out of Ireland that evening on UEFA business, so he decided to leave Breen a personal cheque of €100,000 'to cash the next day'. Delaney then outlined how he was repaid six weeks later.

Delaney felt the FAI should issue a statement that night explaining that 'due to a temporary cash-flow issue he had provided a bridge and that was the only time it was ever done'. Cody, for so long Delaney's right-hand man and the director who snuffed out fires for the CEO, then piped up to confirm that he knew about the transaction at the time. He was 'grateful that we didn't have bouncing cheques'.

Murray, the Honorary Treasurer, who had not been informed of the transactions until that month, was happy to provide absolution. 'It doesn't look good from a financial point of view,' he said. 'But it was more of a favour done by the CEO than anything else. No one lost and no one gained. People will try to make mileage out of it but [the] key is nothing wrong has been done.'

Delaney told the board he felt 'very sore' about the story as he had 'merely done a good act'.

'I personally will have to take a kicking over the next few days but that is just something I will have to get on with as we all will,' he said. He remarked that the 'political process' would have something to say about it.

The next question was not about why Delaney had not told the board about this bailout in 2017, or why the FAI's finances were so bad that the association needed an employee to bail it out. Instead, a director asked where the leak had come from.

Delaney said that it had come from his divorce proceedings. Goodwin then said that that had been the basis of the court application, but that they had no evidence to prove Delaney's allegation that his wife's side had leaked the material. (Delaney's ex-wife's solicitor – who happened to be his former opponent on the FAI board, Brendan Dillon – would later have his own solicitor write a letter of complaint to Delaney, denying that they had leaked anything.)

Another director consoled Delaney. 'It had been a good act and it would be unfair to worry unduly,' the FAI's board minutes recorded. 'What the CEO did just showed he cared too much.'

Conway then asked the first pertinent question: 'Would the issue arise as to who knew what? Is that part of where they are coming from?'

Delaney responded that he did not think this was an issue for the board in 2017, as the money had been paid back 'very quickly'. He said that Cody, Finance Director Eamon Breen and Rea Walshe, the FAI's internal solicitor, knew some or all of the details.

Another director expressed 'huge sympathy' for Delaney, and suspected that the question would arise as to 'how difficult the finances had been'. 'Possibly, there would be a question regarding the competence of the board in relation to the financial issues of the association,' this director predicted.

Sensing danger, Delaney insisted that the board was 'well briefed' by Murray, the now seventy-nine-year-old Honorary Treasurer, and by himself. 'If I wanted to be tough on Eamon Breen, I could ask, "How could Eamon just come into me on such short notice about the cash-flow issue?"' Delaney mused, throwing his soon-to-depart Finance Director firmly under the bus.

Like a politician repeating a stump speech, Delaney insisted, 'As a board we should be united on the fact that the board is kept well informed.'

Conway agreed: 'The board get very detailed board reports and we are entitled to stand very strong as a board.'

Delaney then shifted gear, saying that the incident had strengthened the view he had put forward at the 4 March meeting of the board where he had outlined a desire to move into a newly created position that would involve splitting the responsibilities of the Chief Executive into two jobs.

Another board member, not named in the minutes, acknowledged that there would be media focus on the board's competence and said that the board knew 'how tight cash flow was' two years previously. 'Whilst we may not have been briefed at the time about the loan, [Michael Cody] had been briefed and we were all aware of the precarious situation,' he stated.

With that endorsement from his fellow directors, Delaney was free to proceed as he wished. Conway brought the extraordinary, emergency teleconferenced board meeting to a close with a strict instruction that all incoming media queries were to be routed to Cathal Dervan.

At 11.13 p.m. the FAI issued a press statement saying that Delaney had made a 'short-term bridging loan' to the FAI in 2017 to aid cash flow. The statement said the loan was repaid in full within six weeks, and that this was the only time this had ever happened. The statement added that Delaney had donated his 2018 UEFA salary to the association.

'I am aware of stories circulating around this loan dating back to 2017,' Delaney was quoted in the FAI statement. 'I confirm that I made a once-off bridging loan to the association to aid a very short-term cash-flow issue.'

If the FAI thought that statement would kill the story, it was mistaken.

12.   A Nuclear Position

The day the story on Delaney's €100,000 cheque was published just happened to be one of the biggest media days in the Irish football calendar. The FAI International Awards is a ceremony televised live from the RTÉ studios following a formal drinks reception. It is usually a chance for the association to get good publicity and to have some face-time with the incumbent Minister for Sport.

With journalists looking to get Delaney to comment on the €100,000 payment, the FAI boss decided to take a back entrance into the RTÉ studio. Before the cameras rolled, Delaney cornered Shane Ross and assured him that the €100,000 story would soon be yesterday's news. Ross remembers Delaney telling him he would probably be moving to a new role relating to UEFA.

Major bookmakers began quoting odds on Delaney leaving his position by the end of the year, but saw that as a remote possibility, with odds of 14–1 on offer.

Although Ross was happy to pose for pictures with Delaney and Donal Conway at the awards ceremony, his aides were fearful that the €100,000 story could spell trouble. Earlier, at 12.06 p.m., Carol Hunt, the minister's press adviser, had emailed senior civil servants and Ross's political adviser in the department. 'Some media looking to see if we've any statement on the current FAI/Delaney issue,' she wrote. 'Not for us to comment – but any other advice please let me know.' Within thirty minutes Peter Hogan, a principal officer with responsibility for sports policy, wrote back endorsing Hunt's 'no comment' strategy, particularly, he said, with that evening's FAI awards event at RTÉ in mind.

In the build-up to the awards, much of the media focus had been on how there was little to celebrate in the previous year for the men's international team. In the week before the event, the FAI had broken protocol to announce that Declan Rice, a West Ham United midfielder, had won the Young Player of the Year award, despite the fact that he had switched his allegiance to England after winning three full international caps for Ireland. The Goal of the Year category had its eligibility widened to include goals from all the Irish international teams, because the senior men's team had scored just four goals in all of 2018.

Just before the awards event went live on air, the FAI issued a second, lengthier press release entitled 'Statement on FAI Governance'. The 530-word statement outlined how the FAI had formed a Governance Review Committee in February 2017 which had prompted a number of 'key' reforms in the association. It said as part of its 'continuing governance reviews', the FAI board had decided at its meeting in early March to launch 'a full review' of the association's senior management structures and 'executive governance' through an external consultant. This report was expected by 'early April'. A quote from Delaney said the review would 'future-proof Irish football'.

The statement concluded with Delaney offering a further explanation of the €100,000 transaction from 2017. He said he had 'acted in the best interests of the association at a time when immediate funding was needed'. Delaney said he held regular meetings with the FAI's Director of Finance about financial matters and 'all items arising' from these discussions were conveyed to the monthly FAI board meetings.

'This was the case in 2017 when I acted in good faith for the benefit of the FAI and I will continue to do so,' he said.

This strongly implied that the FAI board had been fully briefed on Delaney's 2017 payment to the association – something that, as it would eventually emerge, was fundamentally untrue. Crucially, it would take the FAI board some time before it would correct this misleading statement.

*

The St Patrick's Day statement from the FAI was the first time Delaney had given a public hint of the plan he had put into motion earlier that month, after being told that the *Sunday Times* was asking questions about his €100,000 payment to his employer.

At the 4 March meeting of the FAI board in Abbotstown, Delaney had for the first time mentioned his bailout of the association to the full board. The 3 p.m. meeting started in its usual manner, with the FAI President formally chairing the meeting. Conway welcomed Cathal Dervan and Alex O'Connell, who were attending for the first time in their new roles of PR Director and incoming Finance Director, respectively. Dervan was not 'officially' starting his FAI role until 1 April, it was noted. Eamon Breen was leaving the role of Finance Director at the end of March after five years with the FAI to take up a job with Carrolls Irish Gifts.

Delaney outlined discussions that the FAI was having with Niall Quinn over reforms to the League of Ireland. Both Delaney and Conway were dismissive of the former player's proposals.

The CEO then moved on to talk about the FAI's joint bid with the English, Welsh, Scottish and Northern Irish football associations to host the 2030 World Cup. While Spain was considering a bid, Delaney said Aleksander Čeferin was 'musing' that there should be only one bid from Europe so that all the UEFA associations could unite behind it.

Croke Park, with its 80,000 capacity, had been earmarked for the opening game of the tournament.

Cody, who had represented the FAI with Conway at talks with the other associations in February, told the board he was disappointed with the attitude of the other associations to the English FA. He described them as 'ill-mannered'.

'It was clear that England and ourselves were the only ones making any attempt at being professional about it,' Cody reported.

Conway also spoke dismissively of the Scottish and Welsh FAs. 'There was a clear axis of influence and ability which was the [English] FA and the FAI,' he said, in a reference to the weight carried by Delaney and the FA's David Gill, both ExCo members. 'That will drive it and if it comes to fruition it will be them who will have driven it.'

In his formal CEO's report to the board, Delaney said there was a 'good strategy' around the Club Ireland ten-year ticket scheme that was replacing the disastrous Vantage ticketing scheme.

He said the FAI had 'now looked at it ourselves and priced accordingly'. He credited the PR company Wilson Hartnell along with

Dervan for the 'good strategy' in marketing the new ten-year tickets, which would cost €5,000 – a full €10,000 less than the equivalent tickets sold by the IRFU.

Delaney also told the board he had met Leonard Brassel, the Irish representative for Sports Direct, to discuss drawing down 'the next €6.5 million due next year'.

After a few points regarding the FAI's finances, Delaney said there were two things he wanted noted in the minutes. He said that most of his UEFA salary, which came to €160,000, had been 'put into the FAI last year'. He then said that 'a few years ago' he had had to 'bridge cash flow for the FAI for a small period of time and was repaid very quickly'.

There is no record in the minutes of any member of the board seeking more details on Delaney's disclosure that he had 'bridged cash flow' at an unspecified time in the past. Delaney did not reveal to the board that the FAI and Dervan had been asked questions about that transaction by the *Sunday Times* on 1 March, just three days previously. The thirty-nine-page written CEO's report that was given to each director contained no reference to Delaney's payment to the FAI, and more than one director has since told the authors of this book that Delaney's disclosure on 4 March went completely over their heads.

Eamon Naughton, a director from Galway, had already been tipped off about the *Sunday Times* queries by a staff member. Before the meeting started, he pulled Conway aside to ask if there was a problem. Conway had just learned of the newspaper's queries at his regular pre-board session with Delaney and Cody. He told Naughton that Delaney would address the issue with the board.

'Was that it?' a confused Naughton asked Conway after the meeting. Conway says he pointed out that Naughton could have asked for clarification at the meeting. He then suggested that, as the issue would be recorded in the board's minutes, Naughton could raise it at the next board meeting.

Item 6 on the 4 March agenda was headed 'Structural Review'. Delaney said this was 'something that was a very important matter to him and the association'. He referred to his 'vast' workload, and then spoke of the scale of the organization. 'When I took over there was a staff of thirty and no Aviva Stadium,' he said. 'We now have 200 staff and I would expect by 2025 that this would be 250. I love the job. I have received bigger salary offers in the past which Michael Cody would know about, but I have stayed because I love working with the association.'

Delaney said there were three elements to the job: the grassroots, 'which is fundamental'; the management of staff; and the international aspect. He said he did not think it was 'sustainable for the future, neither personally nor to the organization', for a single person to look after all three. 'It's been on my mind for the last six months. The UEFA bids are eating into my personal time but I can see what we get back from it.'

Delaney said there was a 'guy called Jonathan Hall' who had worked for the English FA, was a UEFA consultant, and had an executive master's degree in European Sports Administration. 'A really strong CV,' Delaney assured the board.

'I would like him to come into the association and see at the top what is the best use of the CEO's time for the association, going forward,' said Delaney. He said Hall would benchmark the FAI with other associations.

'Effectively, what I want him to do is interview from all sides and look at some form of splitting of the roles,' he said. 'For instance, I would be General Secretary and there could be a new CEO to run the domestic side of the operations. This is for debate, as always.'

Delaney said there would be a 'minimal' financial cost to the FAI if it embraced this proposal. 'We would do a deal.'

Delaney had worked out a tight timeline for implementing the findings of a report that had yet to be commissioned. He said the board would 'review Jonathan's proposal' on the day of the European Championship qualifying game against Georgia in Dublin on 26 March 'to see if this was something we could do'. He said Rea Walshe, Cathal Dervan, Donal Conway and Michael Cody had all been briefed in advance. As with his remarks on the €100,000 payment, the proposal to fundamentally change his role at the FAI was not outlined in his written CEO's report.

The first to respond to Delaney's remarks on the 'structural review' was Eddie Murray, the Honorary Treasurer. Murray said every organization needs to plan for the future. When people need to move on they need to be 'happy with that situation'. He said Delaney's plan 'provides continuity'.

Niamh O'Donoghue, formerly the Secretary General of the Department of Social Protection, agreed with Murray. She said organizations have a life cycle and have to adapt to changing situations. Commissioning a report from Hall, whom she had heard about previously, was 'an excellent idea'.

There was almost a stampede from the other board members to welcome Delaney's proposal and to heap praise on his performance as CEO.

John Earley, the schoolboys representative, said he was only surprised it had taken so long for Delaney to seek this change. 'I see you on a weekly basis and you must be wrecked from it,' he said. 'It's only right you do it for yourself as well as the organization.'

Mick Hanley, a representative from a junior league in Limerick, agreed with Earley. 'How John keeps going I do not know,' he said. 'He couldn't keep going forever. The amount of work is huge, and if he thinks this is best then we should have that Hall man and get him to put forward recommendations.'

'You only have to look at the changes since we came from Merrion Square,' said Jim McConnell, a seventy-three-year-old representative from Donegal with over fifteen years on the FAI board.

Noel Fitzroy, the Vice-President who had been appointed to the board the previous year, said he had often looked in from outside the FAI and wondered at how Delaney got through everything that was expected of him. He too was surprised this move had not happened sooner.

Paraic Treanor, the director from the Dublin junior leagues, said the 'standard response for the last ten years was that if John Delaney was not available [then] we would need three people to replace him'.

Cody, ever Delaney's most loyal lieutenant, painted a bleak picture if Delaney's plan was not pushed through. 'I'm afraid if we don't do this we will lose John, which would be a disaster,' said Cody. 'We should get this guy [Hall] in.'

Eamon Naughton said, 'Bring this lad in. We all know the amount of work you put in. There has to be a cut-off point for you and this may extend your tenure in the organization.'

President Conway was the last to speak. He said he agreed with all the supportive comments.

'There are key projects out there,' he said. 'John Delaney is equipped to play a significant if not leading role in that. This is about using the resources we have to best effect as there is so much about to happen.'

Delaney thanked the board for their comments.

'It won't be a culture shock,' he promised. 'I can mentor the person that is brought in as CEO.'

As was Delaney's habit through the years, he warned the board against leaking. He said a public explanation of the move would be given 'when the decision is made'.

One director questioned if this plan was 'do-able' by 26 March, just over three weeks away.

'Yes,' Delaney said. 'Jonathan Hall believes it is. It is not the hardest report to prepare. With ten working days he can do it. It's something I have put a lot of thought into.'

*

That was 4 March. The next board meeting was set for twelve noon on the 26th. The Hall report was pencilled in to be the only item on the agenda. However, in the wake of Delaney's failed injunction on the St Patrick's Day weekend, the schedule was brought forward.

The 17 March statement, issued before the awards show, did not kill the story as the FAI hoped. *The Times*'s Ireland edition, the sister paper of the *Sunday Times*, reported on Monday, 18 March, that 'a whistleblower' had made contact with a politician with concerns about the FAI's corporate governance. It was reported that this person was now preparing a complaint for the Office of the Director of Corporate Enforcement (ODCE), which has powers to bring criminal prosecutions for breaches of company law.

The *Irish Daily Mail*'s front-page headline screamed 'Why did the FAI need €100k loan from its own CEO?'

The bookmaker Paddy Power stopped taking bets on whether Delaney would still be CEO of the FAI by the end of 2019.

Even though it was a bank holiday Monday and the Department of Sport and Sport Ireland were officially closed, officials from both organizations were in frantic discussions about how to respond to the €100,000 loan story after a plethora of media requests for Shane Ross to comment.

At 7.17 p.m. the FAI issued its third statement in as many days. An unidentified 'spokesman' was quoted as saying that 'The FAI is currently undertaking a full review of its executive governance and senior management structures.' Referring to Delaney's 'bridging loan', the final line of the statement baldly asserted that 'The board of the FAI has been kept fully informed in relation to this matter at all times.'

The following morning, Tuesday, members of the Oireachtas Sport Committee were quoted in several newspapers saying they intended to ask the FAI questions about the payment at the scheduled committee hearing on 10 April.

Just before 8 a.m. the Taoiseach's office contacted the Department of Sport seeking a briefing on the FAI story that could be used as speaking points for other ministers who might be asked about Delaney by journalists.

That morning Shane Ross wrote a formal letter to John Treacy in Sport Ireland expressing 'concern' about the media reports on Delaney's payment to the FAI in 2017. He asked Sport Ireland to seek clarification from the FAI board about the circumstances that brought about the payment, and to update him when it received an explanation.

On receipt of the ministerial letter, Sport Ireland wrote that afternoon to the FAI board seeking 'urgent clarification'. Treacy's letter said the terms and conditions of Sport Ireland's grant approval for the FAI required it to be notified about any 'material deterioration' in the FAI's finances, but no such notification had been made.

The publication of the Sport Ireland letter forced the FAI to issue a statement for a fourth day in a row, confirming that it would prepare a response to Treacy's letter.

In a fifth statement, issued on Wednesday, 20 March, the FAI said it had responded to all of Treacy's queries. The statement also revealed that the FAI had written to the ODCE 'offering clarification on any issues raised by a 2017 bridging loan' made by Delaney.

Much of the newspaper coverage of the story on Thursday, 21 March, focused on the FAI's refusal to say whether Delaney would attend the Oireachtas hearings. It was also reported that the FAI had on Wednesday sent a 'gentle reminder' invitation to members of the Oireachtas Sport Committee to a drinks reception and dinner scheduled for 4 April, six days before the committee hearing on the 10th. The social event was to mark the draw for the upcoming UEFA under-17 European Championship to be hosted in Ireland that summer. Noel Rock, a Fine Gael member of the Oireachtas committee, said that, while the invite had been first extended the previous Friday, it was 'badly judged' and it would be 'inappropriate' for any of the TDs or senators on the Sport Committee to attend.

The newspapers also reported Taoiseach Leo Varadkar's first comments on the Delaney payment. 'It does seem a bit unusual,' Varadkar told journalists. 'A body of that size, given its operations and the funding it receives, I would have thought has banking facilities that would have provided for a loan. I know that Sport Ireland and the Oireachtas Joint Committee will want to ask questions about that.'

In its sixth statement in as many days, the FAI suggested moving the Oireachtas committee hearing forward to 3 April. The statement confirmed that Delaney would be a part of the FAI delegation.

This statement was issued following a board meeting convened at 1 p.m. in the Dublin Airport Authority meeting room as some members of the board prepared to fly out to Gibraltar for that Saturday's Euro 2020 qualifier match. Four board members, Niamh O'Donoghue, Jim McConnell, John Earley and Mick Hanley, participated by teleconference.

Delaney told his fellow directors that he and Dervan 'would have thought the story would have died down by now'.

There was no sign of self-examination from the board. One FAI director instead complained about the media coverage. 'It sounded like a witch hunt,' he said.

A&L Goodbody, the FAI's long-time solicitors, had been asked to advise the FAI on its legal obligations ahead of the Oireachtas hearings. Delaney said they were considering instructing John Rogers, a senior counsel, which suggested Delaney believed he needed to be protected from aggressive questioning at the hearing. Rogers, who had served as Attorney-General in the 1980s, had more recently been the lead barrister for Angela Kerins, a businesswoman who successfully sued the Dáil's Public Accounts Committee for its 'unlawful' questioning of her leadership of the Rehab charity.

Rogers was an old-school senior counsel with far greater experience than most judges. In representing Kerins, an unsympathetic character to many because of her €240,000-a-year-salary as Chief Executive of a charity, Rogers succeeded in obtaining a landmark judgment. The Supreme Court ruled that a Dáil committee can be found to have acted 'unlawfully' if it asked questions beyond its remit. Kerins had claimed the aggressive questioning of her by politicians on the Public Accounts Committee and the negative publicity it generated had driven her towards a suicide bid, and only medical intervention had saved her life. Her legal victory had led to Oireachtas committees receiving legal advice to temper their questions, lest they face a Kerins-type case.

Moving on from the report on legal tactics, Delaney told the board that he had received 'a draft' of the Jonathan Hall report and he said he was 'comfortable with it'.

'It's a communication thing,' Delaney said. 'I am very conscious that before we go into any Dáil committee I should speak publicly.' He proposed doing a press conference on 28 March.

'If I was to move to a new role it might look like the request to attend at the committee had precipitated such a move, but that will die down and the strategy is what is best for the organization,' he said.

Delaney said his preference was to do a press conference alongside Conway, the FAI President, as he felt the situation with the FAI was 'deeply personalized currently'. He said Dervan endorsed this strategy.

One of the directors on the teleconference said it was difficult to hear all the conversations going on. This director requested that any discussion of the Hall report be postponed until the following week at the earliest. Delaney said the report would be circulated later that day.

He 'confirmed' that the implementation of the report 'is still for Tuesday'. 'But people should read it and in a nuclear position we would need to progress immediately,' he said.

Delaney said he felt Varadkar had come across as 'OK' in his comments about the €100,000 payment.

Director Paraic Treanor, who was also an EBS bank manager based in Naas, pointed out that he was 'acting and working under the rules of the Central Bank' and that he had an issue with the St Patrick's Day statement saying that all the board had been briefed at all times about the €100,000 payment in 2017. Treanor said that he wanted it recorded in the minutes that not every board member was aware of the payment. A second director agreed that the whole board had not been informed.

The board then moved swiftly on to discuss the quality of the pitch in Gibraltar.

Delaney warned the board there would be 'stuff' at the match. He said there was a flag with a '*Father Ted* reference in it'. A picture of the flag from supporters had been posted on social media that showed a smiling Delaney wearing a priest's dog collar over a slight adaptation of a famous line from the show: 'The money was just resting in their account.'

He said it would be 'uncomfortable', as it was a small stadium and the press 'are only fifty seats to our left. The Irish supporters would be immediately in front of us.'

Conway said the board needed to be careful as 'we were being hounded' and members needed 'to mind each other'.

The board meeting closed. Delaney, Conway and the rest of those going to the Gibraltar match went to catch the FAI's chartered plane along with Mick McCarthy and his squad.

13.   Escape from the Rock

While the FAI board had been meeting, Noel Rock, a Fine Gael backbench TD who sat on the Oireachtas Sport Committee, went on the *Irish Independent*'s Floating Voter politics podcast. Asked about the €100,000 payment, Rock said he was unhappy that Delaney and the FAI had been unable to give a full explanation of what had happened.

Had the FAI breached its bank overdraft limit? Rock asked. Why were there cash-flow issues in 2017?

'It's time for John Delaney to step aside,' Rock confirmed, when challenged by the interviewer on whether he was calling for a resignation. 'There is such a thing as accountability in public life. I think John Delaney has had his time. He has been paid very, very well for his time and the performance isn't matching up to what we are paying him for. There are clear issues of governance, of competence and of finance within the FAI. Time and time again the issues of competence off the field are overshadowing the issues on the field.'

The backbench TD was quickly rebuked by more senior members of his party. Speaking to reporters that Thursday evening ahead of a Fine Gael national conference to be held on the following Saturday, Tánaiste Simon Coveney said, 'It is far too early to make that decision.' Charlie Flanagan, the Minister of Justice, said talk about Delaney's position was 'entirely premature'.

Brian Kerr, the former Ireland manager, was asked about the €100,000 payment on Virgin Media TV that same evening while working as studio analyst for a Northern Ireland game. 'It's a very strange situation, that an organization whose turnover has been over €50 million a year required €100,000 of a loan in a year where their accounts said they'd almost a million euro in the bank in cash,' Kerr said. 'I wouldn't have thought a hundred thousand went very far. But, you know, some very strange things have happened, some bizarre things have happened around the FAI over the last number of years.'

The *Sunday Times* was meanwhile working on a story that would prompt Delaney and the FAI to deploy their 'nuclear' strategy.

The previous Sunday, while Delaney and the FAI were preparing for its awards ceremony, Mark Tighe was at the Dublin St Patrick's Day parade with his family. His phone was vibrating regularly with messages from people looking to talk about the FAI and Delaney. One message stood out. This person said they had information that showed Delaney's personal expenditures had been 'hidden' in the FAI's accounts over many years.

The contact wanted to meet urgently to discuss this face-to-face. A meeting was arranged for the following day. The person that Tighe met was visibly fearful and distrustful, expressing deep concerns over the possible consequences if it was discovered they had spoken to a journalist about internal FAI affairs. The contact was aware that Delaney was well connected with many journalists and editors.

After receiving assurances regarding anonymity and that Tighe's newspaper had no interest in cosying up to Delaney, the source agreed to talk for ten minutes. What Tighe heard in those few minutes shocked him.

The FAI, the source said, had been covering Delaney's rent, costing up to €3,000 a month, for at least a decade, but this had been a tightly held secret within the FAI. The association had also paid large bills for luxury foreign hotels used by Delaney and Emma English that had no clear connection with FAI business. Tighe was told the FAI company credit card had been used by Delaney with wild abandon, and no attempt had been made to seek reimbursements for regular cash withdrawals. There was expenditure on Delaney's FAI credit card that had no obvious link to FAI work. No documents were provided to back up the source's claims, but Tighe now knew what questions he should be asking.

That week he concentrated on the rental payments lead. Delaney's salary of €360,000 was a huge bone of contention for many Irish football fans. Even FAI staff regarded it as exorbitant. If Tighe could prove the FAI had also paid rent in the region of €36,000 a year for Delaney's accommodation, it would be a significant story.

By Friday, Tighe had confirmed with two independent sources that the rent story was accurate. Delaney had had his rent covered by the FAI while he lived in Malahide in north Dublin and, more recently, in Kilmacanogue in Co. Wicklow. The Wicklow house was a mansion owned by Gráinne Seoige, an Irish TV star, and her ex-husband.

The rumour flying around legal, media and football circles that week was that Delaney's €100,000 'loan' had been an attempt to hide money from his ex-wife. Several people rang Tighe to claim this as fact, but it was false. The truth was more serious for the FAI. The FAI needed the €100,000 because it was so financially stretched that it feared being unable to meet its payroll bill that month. Delaney had fought fiercely to prevent the story's publication because it destroyed the façade of financial stability he had presented to the world.

Following a separate tip-off back in February while covering the Denis O'Brien–*Sunday Business Post* trial, Tighe was also able to establish that Delaney had recently spent €868,000 buying Craffield, a nineteenth-century five-bedroom country house with its own tennis court on eight acres outside Aughrim in Co. Wicklow.

At 12.27 p.m. on Friday, 22 March, Tighe sent questions directly to Delaney's FAI email and cc'd Cathal Dervan. The six questions were composed with the assistance of Hugh Hannigan, the newspaper's legal manager:

1. In relation to the €100,000 payment to the FAI by you in April [2017], we understand this was required to meet the FAI's payroll costs. Do you accept that is the case?

2. We have learned that over the last 10 years the FAI has been paying the rent/letting costs arising from your personal accommodation needs in Dublin & Wicklow. Is this correct?

3. It is our further understanding that payment of these accommodation costs by the FAI was on top of or in addition to payment by the organization of your annual salary. Is this correct?

4. We understand that these rental/letting payments covered by the FAI for you included your rental of a house in Malahide; and your rental in a separate period of a house in Kilmacanogue at a monthly rent of €3,000. Is this correct and if not, please specify what aspect of these rental details is incorrect.

5. Who in the FAI approved the payment of your accommodation costs in addition to your salary, and what was the justification for that?

6. Have you received and do you receive any other perquisites that involved significant expenditure upon you by the FAI?

The email concluded:

I take this opportunity to remind you of the significant public interest and importance in respect of all FAI payments to you, especially in circumstances of the substantial amount of public funding granted to the FAI on an annual basis, totalling nearly €50 million or thereabouts over the last ten years. This was expressly acknowledged by Mr. Justice Anthony Barr in the High Court last Saturday, 16 March 2019, when he said 'I am satisfied that the finances of the FAI and any payment and repayment to its Chief Executive are matters of significant public interest', during your failed attempt to injunct this newspaper from publishing its article.

I look forward to hearing from you as soon as possible and ahead of our publication deadline of 12 p.m. tomorrow (Saturday).

No response was ever received.

*

On the Thursday-afternoon flight to Gibraltar on the FAI's chartered plane, Delaney sat near the back with board members while the players were at the front. Before the flight took off Delaney was absorbed by his phone. After take-off, with the phone away, he was not his usual self.

'I knew something was going on,' says a board member who sat near him. 'He was there and he was quiet. He would normally be throwing things at Michael Cody, messing – stupid stuff.'

After a while, Delaney moved to talk to individual board members, but he seemed distracted.

'I was really concerned for him,' says one person who spoke with him. 'He was drifting in and out of the conversation.'

Once in Gibraltar, Delaney was back on his phone. There was a series of meetings with board members as well as Eamon Breen and Dervan on Thursday and Friday in the team base in the Rock hotel.

Jonathan Hall's report had proposed that Delaney would become the FAI's 'Executive Vice-President', responsible for 'key international and special projects'. Under the plan a new CEO would be recruited, with responsibility for domestic football and governance issues. Delaney, with less work on his plate, would be able to remain on the UEFA ExCo, allowing the FAI to retain its influence 'at the heart of the decision-making in European football'.

One director who was in Gibraltar says there were a number of meetings on Friday morning and afternoon, but it wasn't clear if they were formal board meetings. In one, a mobile phone on speaker setting was used to conference-call the directors in Ireland, but not all of them could hear what was being discussed.

'We were talking about the Jonathan Hall report and how we'd move, but in the middle of it John would be looking at his phone, then John would stand up and walk out,' recalls a director. 'Or he'd be on the phone ringing somebody. He just wasn't there [mentally] and we were looking at each other. I turned to Cathal [Dervan]. What's the story? What's going on? [He said] "Oh, the *Sunday Times* have loads more stuff."'

Then Delaney said he wanted to meet Conway and Cody in his hotel room at 5.30 p.m. Board members believed that Delaney was now seriously considering resigning and were told he was seeking outside advice.

In Delaney's hotel room, with Michael Cody present, Donal Conway began writing up the heads of agreement outlining the financial package for Delaney's new position. The terms of Delaney's new job were set out on the Rock's notepaper in Conway's handwriting.

The title was: 'Heads of Agreement on Contract between the FAI and [John Delaney] in relation to the former CEO's new role in the association as Executive Vice-President'. The new arrangement was to come into effect at midday on the following day.

The hand-written agreement would allow Delaney to stay on €360,000 a year until the end of 2019, when his basic pay would be cut to €100,000 per annum up to the end of 2025. Delaney would be able to earn up to €200,000 in bonuses each year based on a list of agreed objectives.

The agreement would allow Delaney to retain his Abbotstown office, his company car and parking space, his mobile phone and his FAI credit card. He would be provided with two free VIP tickets and two committee box tickets for home matches, and ten non-VIP tickets would be made available to him for purchase. The agreement guaranteed Delaney free travel with the official party for all away internationals, and he would retain his personal assistant.

Cody and Delaney told Conway that the FAI would also have to honour financial commitments it had made to Delaney in 2014. Conway was unsure what the other two men were referring to.

'Michael struggled to remember what it was,' says Conway. 'John seemed to know. He wanted it reflected in the [new] contract. I said, "Are they contracts?" I said, "John, I don't know anything about this." '

Delaney insisted the 2014 deals were written contracts. He was referring to two side agreements that he had made with Cody and Eddie Murray in 2014 that guaranteed him an extra €3 million in bonus payments from the FAI if he saw out the term of his CEO contract to the end of 2020. Conway, the FAI President and a board member since 2005, had been unaware of the existence of these 'golden handcuffs' deals until this meeting in Delaney's hotel room in Gibraltar, and was still unsure what the terms were. But he agreed to add a phrase into Delaney's new terms of employment specifying that it would 'reflect two previous agreements' made 'in respect of bonus and pension arrangements'.

Conway recalls that he was thinking this 'would all have to be looked at'. He recalls suggesting that they wait to finish the agreement until they were back in Ireland so he could see these 2014 bonus agreements. He says Delaney insisted that the deal had to be signed off there in Gibraltar and that Cody and Conway had the authority to make the deal.

Conway says he challenged Delaney, whom he had served with for over fourteen years on the FAI board. Was he going to hear something in the future that rendered Delaney unfit for the role or made his position untenable?

'I am asking you straight up,' Conway said. 'We have worked together a long time.'

Conway recalls that Delaney said: 'No way. On my daughter's life, you are not going to hear that.'

Conway signed the agreement.

*

On Friday evening, the directors gathered in the hotel lobby before a planned walk to a restaurant for the customary meal with the Gibraltar FA. With Delaney busy on the phone, there was confusion over whether the Irish delegation should go.

'Are we going to the dinner or what the hell?' one director asked Breen.

'There's a lot happening,' Breen said.

Eventually Conway, now dressed in his suit, arrived in the lobby. 'We have a serious fucking problem,' he told Eamon Naughton, referring to what he had just learned about Delaney's 2014 bonus deals. The delegation decided they shouldn't keep the Gibraltar FA waiting, so they headed for the restaurant.

Over the course of the evening, the FAI President filled in the other directors as best he could on what he had learned about Delaney's golden handcuffs deal of 2014.

Michael Cody, who, along with Eddie Murray, was the only board member involved in agreeing the deals, had kept the signed paperwork from the 2014 agreements in his Foxrock home for safekeeping. Conway told Cody to bring the documents to him on Monday so he could brief the board at their next meeting before the home game against Georgia on Tuesday.

Delaney was at the meal but was constantly on his phone. One of the people he called was Declan Conroy, a long-time adviser on media and other issues at the FAI. Conroy was now working as the lead on the FAI's Euro 2020 hosting project. Delaney asked Conroy whether he should stay or go. His trusted adviser told him the game was up and he should leave.

After the meal the directors returned to the hotel. Delaney, having decided not to take Conroy's advice, persuaded them to call an emergency teleconference board meeting at 10 p.m., Irish time, to formally progress his move to Executive Vice-President.

Eamon Breen, the outgoing Finance Director, and Cathal Dervan were on the call with the directors in Gibraltar to board colleagues back in Ireland. Staffers Rea Walshe and Alex O'Connell were on the call as well.

Conway opened the meeting by thanking the whole board for being available.

He summarized the recommendations of the Hall report. Hall proposed that conflict between the two senior positions of CEO and Executive Vice-President (EVP) could be avoided by having clearly defined responsibilities for each. Delaney, in the new position of EVP, would be responsible for FIFA and UEFA matters, his 'non-transferable' ExCo role with UEFA, FAI tournament bidding projects, international relations including 'the Irish diaspora around the world, including the United States', the John Giles Foundation, the Aviva Stadium director role, the FAI's centenary project for 2021, and other special projects as agreed with the board and new CEO. Significantly, as part of the move, Delaney would no longer be a director on the FAI's board.

The new role was to be called Executive Vice-President because UEFA rules stipulated that only Chief Executives, Presidents and Vice-Presidents from national associations were eligible to serve on its Executive Committee.

'I would like to progress the matter promptly,' Conway told the board. 'Therefore, by the end of the meeting I would like to have sign-off on the report so that the CEO would move into a new role within the association.'

The FAI President asked for board approval to give himself and Cody authority to appoint a new interim CEO from within while the process of recruiting a full-time replacement for Delaney was in process.

Delaney then outlined how he was willing to move to this new position for the greater good of the FAI. 'This has been a difficult period for me,' he said. 'It is hard for me to say that I am willing to step aside as CEO in this way. However, I believe that the board can retain my skills as Executive Vice-President.' He promised to 'bring the board through everything': the ODCE inquiry, the Sport Ireland queries and the media reports.

Unsurprisingly, given that he had conceived, designed and tailored it, Delaney said he 'accepted' the Hall report. He believed the board should now move to appoint an interim CEO. He claimed this move would bring an end to the growing media and regulatory concerns over the FAI.

'I will agree my [new] position with the President and Honorary Secretary [Cody] which will take the heat off and resolve current issues,' Delaney said. He asked the board to authorize Conway and Cody to agree the terms and conditions of his new position in Gibraltar, not mentioning that the agreement had been made earlier. The instant change in roles for Delaney was a deviation from Hall's blueprint, which proposed that Delaney remain in his current role until a new permanent CEO could be recruited.

Conway then asked the other board members to respond.

The first director to do so said it was 'a pity' Delaney was 'deciding to go now'.

A second director said 'I am delighted that John is still very much involved with the association and that is the main thing. I wish him the best of luck.'

A third director spoke with a 'heavy heart'. 'I accept that the proposal is best for the CEO and best for the association,' he said. 'It would ease the pressure off him personally.'

Referencing the media and upcoming Oireachtas hearing, a fourth director expressed concern that 'the board will be asked' why Delaney was stepping into the new role immediately, contrary to the timeline proposed by Hall.

Conway accepted that there was a recommended timeline in the report, but said these dates could change. He said acceptance of the report would be followed by an announcement. They would begin a recruitment process for a new CEO in April and there would be a 'symbolic handover' at the FAI AGM in Trim in July.

The fourth director said the point was that the Hall report advocated a 'good amount' of preparation for creating the two new roles. Job specifications, division of responsibilities and remuneration packages would all have to be worked out and agreed by the board.

'The report envisaged the CEO being in situ until that was all ready to go, and what we are doing now was different to what was being recommended and [this] needs to be agreed,' the director said, according to the minutes of the meeting.

Delaney pressed on, saying that Conway and Cody would agree a new 'package' for his position of Executive Vice-President in the morning, even though the deal had already been drawn up.

Another director, supporting Delaney's request for urgency, said 'events had overtaken the timeline' in Hall's report.

Delaney said if the FAI were to get someone in to benchmark his new salary package it would take longer, but asking Conway and Cody to agree the package with him and put an interim CEO in place 'would not be a huge additional financial burden'.

Another director who came on the line had not had a chance to read the report but agreed with those members who wanted to proceed as Delaney and Conway wished.

Delaney predicted that all the newspaper headlines on Sunday would focus on him 'stepping down'.

Another director, saying, 'I think this is a bit fast to be quite honest but can understand,' asked how the FAI would announce the move.

Delaney said a press release would be issued just after the Gibraltar game, which was scheduled to finish at around 6.50 p.m. Irish time. 'I want to reiterate that as a board we stand together and go down together,' Delaney warned. 'The association is my life. I know by taking myself 90 per cent out of it, that will take the heat off. But I am not walking out the door. I have done nothing wrong here. I have been criticized for helping the FAI. This is quick and it will have surprised people, but within a week or two it will have died down.'

Rea Walshe then read out an email from Fergus O'Dowd, the Fine Gael chairman of the Oireachtas Sport Committee, which said he wanted the FAI meeting to go ahead as planned on 10 April, rejecting the FAI request to come in sooner. The committee planned to have Sport Ireland in first to give evidence on its inquiries into the FAI.

Delaney then called for the board to agree making a public statement the following day, having adopted the Hall report.

A director asked Delaney would he still attend the Oireachtas hearing.

'Yes, I would prefer to,' replied Delaney. 'If events overtake, I will see.' He was planning to meet solicitors on Monday. 'We don't know what the committee will want but we can certainly give them a copy of the Hall report in advance,' he said.

A director said the proposed changes to the timeframe of Delaney's move to Executive Vice-President should be incorporated into the report before it was sent to the committee.

When Rea Walshe referenced the ongoing engagement with the ODCE over the €100,000 payment, Paraic Treanor said he 'presumed' there had been compliance with his request at the previous day's meeting to have it minuted that not all board members knew about the payment.

Conway then said he wanted the proposition that he had put to the board at the outset to be agreed: they would adopt the Jonathan Hall report with proposed amendments to allow Delaney to move to the new role immediately.

Despite the reservations expressed by some directors, the board passed the resolution unanimously. One board member later explained: 'We were into damage limitation. The thing was a frenzy. The feeling was, "Yeah, just go ahead and move him out and do it quick. At least he will be off the board then."'

Delaney then asked Dervan to 'outline the state of play' in relation to the media.

'The *Sunday Times*, the *Independent* and the *Sunday Business Post* were all asking questions based on the Oireachtas committee, whistle-blowers or the divorce case,' Dervan told the board. 'Some of the allegations were libellous, some unfair and some personal.'

Dervan said that a plan had been formulated earlier that Friday.

'We will wait until the game is finished, and at 9 p.m. Irish time we would be in the air,' said Dervan. 'Just after we would release this [Executive Vice-President move] as a statement with quotes from the President, John and from the report itself. What that would do is take the focus away from this . . . and gets the stories into the Sunday newspapers. The newspapers would not have time to dig into it. It would negate any of the above stories.'

Dervan assured the board that this FAI statement would be such big news it would force the Sunday newspapers to alter their planned coverage. 'It gets us back into the game,' he said. 'It would be a nil-all draw but currently we are down.'

Referring to the *Sunday Times*'s questions about his rental payments, Delaney said he wanted Alex O'Connell, the newly installed Director of Finance, 'to identify if there was any Revenue liability for the association'.

He also said the FAI actually owed him 'a substantial sum of money' in relation to the rent arrangements. 'There were rental payments in my contract that the association had to pay. I want to ascertain whether or not the association had any [tax] liability.'

The board agreed that O'Connell would examine Delaney's personal rent agreements with the FAI for any tax liabilities. Many of the directors who participated in the meeting, including Conway, would later say this was the first they had learned about the FAI paying Delaney's rent for a period in excess of a decade. Nobody, according to the minutes, took this opportunity to demand more details or to suggest that the issue should be clarified before creating a new executive position for Delaney.

Instead, the FAI President warned his fellow directors against leaking. 'What was discussed here was confidential,' Conway cautioned. 'I am not accusing anyone, but I feel obliged to say it.'

Board members asked what would be in the press release going out after the following day's match.

'It is difficult, after fourteen years, giving up what I have gotten,' said Delaney. 'The press statement would outline that the board had an independent report commissioned and given current events brought it forward. It will have quotes and confirm that the FAI is happy to engage with all government agencies.'

Conway told the board that a revision to the draft press release was made earlier that day inserting a commencement date of February 2017 for the FAI's governance reviews – a reference to a process led by Rea Walshe to ensure the association complied with new government standards. The statement would say this latest development was part of an ongoing process. Conway hoped this would ensure that Delaney's move was not seen as 'just fire-fighting'.

He asked did directors 'have any doubts, problems, etcetera about where we are?'

A director asked if the FAI President would be able to announce the identity of the interim CEO in the statement. Conway said he hoped so. He and Cody just had to agree on the person.

With that, Conway closed the meeting.

*

Conway would later say that Delaney appeared almost manic over that weekend. He told his fellow directors Delaney seemed unable to keep a coherent conversation going or retain his attention span. Conway feared for Delaney's health.

Before the game, Delaney phoned both Kieran Mulvey, chairman of Sport Ireland, and Shane Ross, the Minister for Sport, to let them know he was moving to a new executive position in the FAI.

Ross was sitting in his car with his wife in Skerries, about to go into the home of James Hamilton, the former Director of Public Prosecutions, who was having a birthday party, when he got the call. The brief conversation left him with the impression that Delaney was moving to a job in UEFA.

Mulvey was sitting down to watch the match in his home when Delaney called.

'John always spoke rapidly,' Mulvey recalls. 'I got the sense he was excited. He was pleased to get out. There was a resolution to his Chief Executive problem. He wasn't leaving the ship and he had a new role that they could justify and UEFA were onboard. I didn't analyse it. Once I heard he wasn't staying as Chief Executive I felt, wrongly as the case may be, "That's a lot of targeting gone. What are the press going to write about now?" Sure, it only continued and led to more.'

John Treacy, the Sport Ireland Chief Executive, did not receive a call. 'I wouldn't have been on John Delaney's quick-dial, let's put it like that,' he says.

★

Before the game started, journalists spied Delaney in the sports hall under the main stand of Gibraltar's 5,000-capacity Victoria Stadium, a mobile phone held against his ear and a glass of red wine in his other hand.

During the game, journalists seated a few metres away saw Delaney regularly on his phone, with Conway sitting beside him. One of the contacts that came up on his screen was Barry Egan, the *Sunday Independent*'s show-business journalist and creator of the *John the Baptist* documentary.

As the game started at 5 p.m. Irish time, Mark Tighe got word that the FAI was concerned that the *Sunday Business Post* was running a story on a company called Pillarview. Tighe had written about the company in 2017 after it had taken over some €600,000 of debts owed by JMPHE, a development company run by Delaney and three business partners. He decided to call Tom Finnan, a director of Pillarview, who was also a garda and the Treasurer of the Garda Representative Association. Finnan held a senior position in St Michael's, the Tipperary club where Delaney was Honorary Life President. He had been a key witness for the prosecution in the dramatic Mr Moonlight trial earlier that year – a case that involved a married Tipperary farmer killing the boyfriend of his former lover. Finnan gave evidence about his role in the search for the victim's body.

When Tighe had last spoken to Finnan in 2017, the Pillarview director claimed not to know that his company had taken on debts linked to Delaney's business. Pillarview's most recent filings showed that Karl Heffernan, the FAI's Commercial Manager from 2015 to 2018, was now Pillarview's point of contact for business matters.

When Tighe called Finnan, he was surprised the garda answered, given the Ireland match was on TV. Although Finnan was listed as a director and joint owner of Pillarview with the Companies Registration Office at that point, he insisted he had resigned as director earlier in the year. (Pillarview's annual accounts, filed in November 2019, would list Finnan as a director.)

'I went on to different things,' Finnan said. 'I'm no longer involved.'

'Why is that, Tom?'

'No secret, but it's none of your business,' Finnan responded, before fervently expressing his loyalty to Delaney.

'Do you know what John Delaney does for football in Ireland?' Finnan said, clearly aggravated. 'Maybe you could write on that instead of trying to castigate him all the time. He is immense for the grassroots football. He would be a massive loss to football. You keep going about your business and wait till you see the way football would be run in this country.'

Finnan declined to give any explanation as to what Pillarview was doing and how it was involved with Delaney.

'I've no business except for my own personal finances,' he insisted. He claimed the story written by Tighe in 2017 was 'incorrect in every way'. Asked to be more specific, Finnan said it was 'all' wrong. He abruptly ended the call.

There wasn't enough time to work up a story on Pillarview for the following day's paper. Tighe made further calls to check details of the Delaney rental payments story and he was happy it was sound.

At this point, the rumours that Delaney might be resigning were gathering pace in both Ireland and Gibraltar, with the Executive Vice-President twist still a closely guarded secret. Frank Fitzgibbon, the *Sunday Times*'s editor, decided to make the rent story his page-one lead even if Delaney resigned from the FAI.

The game against Gibraltar on its artificial pitch was dire. Fans in the ground chanted 'cheerio' at Delaney as the wind swirled in the tiny stadium, sandwiched between the massive Rock and Gibraltar's airport. Although no planes were supposed to take off during the match, an EasyJet flight that had been delayed was cleared to go a minute after the game kicked off. The orange and white livery of the passenger jet could be seen on TV coverage as it took off behind Darren Randolph's goal, the thundering sound temporarily drowning out the crowd noise. Some fans would later say this was the high-light of the game.

Ireland squeaked a 1–0 victory over Gibraltar, one of the min-nows of world football whose squad contained a policeman, a customs officer and several full-time students. Before the game ended, a group of Irish supporters unfurled a flag calling for Delaney to be sacked. Others raised a banner that said 'John Delaney – Godfather of Greed'.

The final whistle sounded at 6.50 p.m. Irish time. At 7.29 p.m., RTÉ put out a news alert through its app and website that said Dela-ney was to 'step down' as CEO and assume a new role within the FAI. The FAI had leaked the story to RTÉ shortly ahead of the offi-cial announcement.

The press release was emailed by the FAI at 7.34 p.m. By any nor-mal standards it was an extraordinary statement. Coming in at just over 1,900 words long, it was the result of a lot of work by Delaney, Conway and Dervan.

The headline information was that Delaney was stepping aside into a new position of Executive Vice-President, and Rea Walshe would be interim CEO while the association went through the pro-cess of recruiting a new Chief Executive. Walshe, who had been due to start in her new role of Chief Operations Officer on 1 April, now became the first female CEO of the FAI, even if only on a temporary basis. The statement claimed the move was based on the recommen-dations of the Jonathan Hall report that had been 'commissioned in February'.

The press release contained a long Delaney quote speaking about how it was his 'absolute pleasure and privilege' to have served the FAI as CEO.

He listed the FAI's growth in staff numbers and the association's move to Abbotstown amongst his achievements. He claimed to have improved the League of Ireland 'significantly' and said bringing women's football into the FAI had corrected past mistakes. He said the grassroots of football were stronger than ever before.

There was only one reference to the growing controversy about his leadership of the FAI:

This past fortnight has been very difficult for me on a personal and professional level and I would like to thank the board and my work colleagues across the FAI for their support. In recent days I have received many messages of support from the family of football, from many of the 2,000 clubs I have visited in my role as CEO and from the world of politics and sport which I am grateful for.

Conway was quoted, saying that the board had commissioned the Hall report as, together with Delaney, they had 'for some time' recognized the need to update the FAI's management structures. He said Delaney had the board's 'full backing' in moving to his new position immediately.

'He has transformed how we operate as an association,' the quote continued. 'This new role will allow John to utilize his vast experience and connections in the world of football and will best serve the FAI as we look to the future. John's life has been devoted to Irish football and he will bring the same energy, vitality and inspiration to this new role.'

When Conway saw the press release, he was furious. He had seen a draft earlier and insisted on a number of changes to his own quote, wishing to tone down his praise for Delaney and to remove the references to Delaney as 'John'. He tackled Dervan over why his own version of his testimonial for Delaney had not been used.

'John insisted,' Dervan replied.

★

The John Delaney who boarded the FAI's chartered plane from Gibraltar to Dublin that Saturday night was unrecognizable as the careworn one who had flown in on the previous Thursday evening.

'He was a totally different John going back on the plane,' a source recalls. 'He was high as a kite. Everything is sorted. We'll move on. He thought he was sorted.'

14. New Balls, Please

When she was elected as a TD for Kildare North for the first time in a 2005 by-election, Catherine Murphy promised to be 'a thorn in the side' of the government. An independent TD who started in the Labour Party, Murphy has since gained national prominence for being a co-founder of the Social Democrats and for being a thorn in the side of Denis O'Brien.

The Kildare TD has a personal interest in how football is run in Ireland. Her son Alan played for Leixlip United, an amateur side, from under-age up to the over-35s team, so Murphy was intimately familiar with the challenges faced by small clubs and the politics involved in grassroots football.

In 2016 she joined the Oireachtas Committee on Transport, Tourism and Sport. In January 2017 John Delaney faced the committee, while seated beside Philip Browne and Páraic Duffy, the relatively low-profile bosses of the IRFU and the GAA, respectively. The format of the hearing suited Delaney perfectly. The three sports executives were asked to make their speeches before the committee members asked their questions in sequence. The executives could give one long answer, concentrating on the easy subjects, after hearing all the questions.

Delaney was able to short-circuit his time before the committee. He told them that he had a prior appointment that afternoon in Abbotstown, where he would unveil a plaque to Milo Corcoran, his late FAI board ally, so he had to leave early.

While the hearing was entitled 'Sport in Ireland: Challenges, Strategies and Governance', few of the Oireachtas members focused on governance. Kevin O'Keeffe, a Cork Fianna Fáil TD with a sometimes impenetrable accent, asked Delaney if he was happy that FIFA planned to expand the number of teams at World Cups to forty-eight from thirty-two.

He was. It increased Ireland's chances of qualifying.

Peter Fitzpatrick, a Fine Gael TD and former Louth GAA football team boss, asked Delaney how the FAI was helping to combat obesity. Frank Feighan, a Fine Gael senator, spoke about how he had travelled to Euro '88 with other fans on a double-decker bus. He asked Delaney about setting up fan embassies and for his views on players with dual nationalities.

Murphy's questions to Delaney were more probing. Why had the Genesis report's recommendation of appointing two independent directors not been implemented? Why was the €5 million FIFA payment for the Thierry Henry handball not apparent in the FAI's accounts? Why were there no questions asked at the FAI AGMs?

Delaney was clearly irked at her questions. He said Alistair Gray, the author of the Genesis report, had told the FAI he was happy with its implementation of its recommendations. He said the Oireachtas committee had decided in 2015 that the FIFA €5 million was 'not to be discussed in this house', but it had been explained by the FAI in a detailed statement anyway. Murphy was probably misled by media reports about the FAI, he suggested. He accepted that questions at the AGM must be submitted in advance, but there were hundreds of other meetings where questions were asked 'in the other 364 days'.

With that, Brendan Griffin, the chairman of the committee, thanked Delaney for his time. The FAI CEO quickly gathered up his documents. While the hearing turned its focus to the GAA and IRFU, Delaney took the opportunity to shake hands with the committee members before leaving. As he came to Murphy, he whispered, 'What have you got against Irish football?'

Murphy had no time to react. She was scheduled to be the first committee member to question the GAA.

'There was a lot of criticism afterwards from people in sports that the questions weren't focused,' Murphy recalls. 'I felt a lot of the criticism was justified. There was a degree of fawning, but I think he was clearly put out by my questions.'

When Shane Ross, the Minister for Sport, attended the committee weeks later, on 1 February 2017, Murphy asked him about the FAI's failure to appoint independent directors some thirteen years after they were recommended by Genesis. The minister said any sport body with a large public following in receipt of public funds should have independent directors. Asked if he would use the state's funding to apply pressure on the FAI to implement this reform, Ross weakly said he would 'consider it'.

Murphy's next encounter with Delaney was on 23 February 2019, when Delaney was the guest of honour at Leixlip United's fiftieth-anniversary celebration. Before the event, a senior member of the club joked with Murphy that she was not to 'upset' Delaney, as the club hoped he would announce some FAI funding for the club. Delaney duly bestowed a €5,000 grant on Leixlip. Like many clubs around the country, over a year later and Leixlip was still awaiting its promised grant owing to the FAI's financial issues.

Murphy was impressed with how Delaney worked the room. Delaney personally thanked her for her contribution to the club down the years. Members of the club who were ardent critics of Delaney before meeting him were won over by his charm, she said. 'He got into all the photographs taken,' said Murphy. 'I was probably the only person in the room that was trying to avoid getting into a photograph with him.'

Unhappy with how the 2017 hearing had unfolded, Murphy had decided to push for the Oireachtas committee to invite the FAI to attend a hearing alone to discuss its governance issues. The committee agreed to invite the FAI to do so before Christmas 2018. The association accepted and was originally due to see them in January 2019 and then March, but it postponed twice. The rescheduled hearing was set for 10 April.

'The €100,000 story in March completely changed the dynamic,' says Murphy. 'Now there was so much more to question them about.'

Delaney's move to Executive Vice-President did not have the effect of 'taking the heat off', as he had promised the board. Instead, the news of his move to a new position, coupled with the revelation that the FAI had been paying his rent for many years, led to heightened criticism of the association.

SIPTU, the trade union representing some sixty FAI staff, issued a statement on 24 March that said its members were 'incensed' after learning that Delaney had his rent covered by the FAI while its FAI members, who were on an average wage of €33,000, took pay cuts in 2012. When questioned about the controversy by RTÉ that Sunday, Leo Varadkar insisted that Delaney and the FAI still had questions to answer about its finances and its use of public money. Noel Rock called on the whole FAI board to resign because they had backed a 'farce reshuffle'. The TD said the state should consider suspending its funding for the association.

The FAI board were desperate for a break, but with the Ireland team returning to Dublin from Gibraltar for their qualifier against Georgia, the story continued to gain momentum. There were rumours on social media that fans were planning to protest against Delaney and the FAI by throwing tennis balls onto the pitch during the Georgia game. When Mick McCarthy was asked about it in the pre-match press conference he said he hoped it did not happen. He joked that he would take a tennis racket to the match, just in case.

Niall Quinn, who was amongst the first people to be linked to the now vacant FAI CEO job, then gave a scathing assessment of the new FAI management structure. Speaking on Virgin Media TV, Quinn said there was no way he would apply for the job as it was now set up.

'It reads as half-a-CEO role and anyone going in there will have a huge shadow over them because the departing CEO hasn't departed at all and it would make life very, very difficult,' Quinn said. 'It's a little bit of a charade, given the scrutiny that was in place over the last week. The rush of the appointment, the unanimous decision of the board to tell us all late on a Saturday night in the middle of some serious scrutiny on the CEO at that time, that this was great for the association and it was a great move and everyone should back it. We are not buying it, I'm not buying it.'

The night before the Georgia game, the FAI hosted a customary pre-match dinner for the visiting FA. The meal was hosted in a private room in the Guinness Storehouse with about half of the FAI's board in attendance. Donal Conway made a speech welcoming the Georgians. Delaney kept coming and going, seemingly preoccupied with his phone.

Before the meal, Cody had shown Conway the contracts setting out the two 'golden handcuffs' deals that he and Murray had made with Delaney in 2014.

Jim McConnell, a seventy-four-year-old director from Donegal with fifteen years' service on the board, did not usually attend the pre-match meals if they were held the night before a game, because it meant he had to be away from home for almost two days. However, he had decided that he would not continue on the board after the AGM in July, so he made the journey from Donegal. As the board members talked together in the Storehouse there was a growing consensus that they needed to bring in external accountants to examine the FAI's books.

McConnell, who ran a drinks distribution business, had felt pushed into agreeing to implement the Hall report. He had been unable to fully hear the board discussions through his teleconference connection.

The rental arrangement had come as a shock to board members. Most directors thought the FAI had agreed to cover the first six months of Delaney's rent in 2005 when he was confirmed as CEO. Delaney at that time was looking for a permanent Dublin residence. Directors were adamant that they had not known the practice had continued up until the end of 2016.

In a private conversation with Delaney in the Storehouse, McConnell said that he would vote to appoint independent auditors to review the FAI's books. Delaney told McConnell that he could be owed up to €3 million if he was forced out. This was apparently a reference to his golden handcuffs deals, which McConnell was unaware of. McConnell insisted: 'John, this has to be done. I don't care. We are going for an independent audit.'

The board met in full at the Intercontinental hotel in Ballsbridge at noon on Tuesday, 26 March, the day of the Georgia game. Delaney attended for the first time purely as an FAI staff member. He had formally resigned as an FAI director that morning after Alex O'Connell completed the necessary paperwork. The board wasn't expecting Delaney, but shortly before the meeting started, Cody and Rea Walshe said Delaney wanted to be heard. The board consented. It would give them a chance to ask Delaney some questions.

Conway opened the meeting by saying that Delaney and Rea

Walshe would shortly be asked to leave so the board could discuss their remuneration packages.

An emotional Delaney assured the board that other associations had 'gone through similar issues'. He planned to travel on UEFA business as normal later that week to chair its Youth and Amateur Football Committee, and had upcoming meetings with the other associations involved in the 2030 World Cup bid.

The events of the previous week had been 'very unfair to me', Delaney said. He blamed Eamon Breen for telling him that the €100,000 loan in 2017 did not have to be disclosed in the FAI's accounts. He said 'senior people' had been informed of the loan at the time, so the non-disclosure in the FAI's accounts was 'the only issue'.

The rental payments were part of his contract, he said, but he had recently been paying the rent himself. He claimed that Mark O'Leary, a long-departed FAI Finance Director, had discussed this issue with the FAI auditors, Deloitte, back in 2004 or 2005. He also claimed he was 'broadly €100,000 in credit' with the FAI.

He asked for some time to deal with the ODCE, who were working at a frenetic pace. He said he would be happy to be part of an FAI delegation that could meet Sport Ireland. He wanted to show them the accounts, which, he said, would prove the 2017 €100,000 payment was not part of an effort to hide money from his ex-wife.

'I feel very hard done by,' said Delaney. 'I could be better defended as I cannot defend myself.'

McConnell then asked Delaney why the board had not been told about the €100,000 loan sooner. Delaney insisted that he had informed 'senior people' and he had been advised it did not need to be disclosed.

Delaney said if the board was asked about the loan at an upcoming FAI Council meeting, the 'correct answer' was to say 'it was a good thing to do'. He said people should be told there was a view to 'let it be' so as 'to avoid any bad publicity'.

Conway then asked Delaney to leave the room and he did so, scowling. The rest of the board were mindful that his ally Cody was still present, but still they felt a shift in the dynamic after Delaney departed.

Conway then briefed the board on the details of Delaney's new contract, and on the 2014 bonus agreements: one for €2 million dated 1 January 2014, and a second for €1 million signed on 31 January in the same year. The arrangements effectively tied the FAI into paying Delaney €3 million for completing the term of his contract up to the end of 2020.

The deals had been agreed by Delaney with two of the FAI board's senior officers, Eddie Murray and Michael Cody. The President at the time, Paddy McCaul, with whom Delaney had a frosty relationship, was not party to the agreement. The board were told in 2014 that Delaney's term had been extended for seven years but they were not informed of the two side deals. Murray and Cody had effectively committed the FAI to boosting Delaney's pay by €35,710 for every month he worked, or €428,520 for every year – thus more than doubling his €360,000 basic salary over seven years. The bonuses were due to be paid in instalments after 2021. A clause in the €2 million bonus deal stipulated that if Delaney was sacked he would 'immediately' be due a sum of €23,810 for each month worked after 1 January 2014. If Delaney had left of his own will the money was still due but could be paid in instalments over ten years.

Murray insisted later that they had not presented the deals to the rest of the board due to concerns that there would be leaks to the media.

The dumbfounded board noted that neither the rent payments nor the golden handcuffs deals had been declared in the FAI's audited accounts. The board resolved that Delaney would not be asked to attend board meetings in future, but would be called in as required.

Conway had asked Declan Conroy to help deal with the media onslaught, but Conroy refused. He did not want to risk damaging his Euro 2020 hosting project. Instead he offered the names of five PR people who might be able to assist the FAI and Dervan.

Board members expressed concern about Dervan's lack of experience, given he had ceased working as a journalist only a few weeks previously. The directors decided that he would be instructed to release press statements only on the instruction of Conway or Rea Walshe.

Dervan was then invited in. He presented a timeline as to how the €100,000 loan story first came on the FAI's radar and how the story had developed in the media. The board asked Dervan to prepare a daily report on media stories about the FAI.

The former *Irish Sun* sports editor went through a list of questions that the FAI had been sent by journalists. Who approved the new management structure and why was it done so quickly? How long were the directors on the board? Was the €100,000 needed to pay wages?

Asked by a board member if more was to 'come out', Dervan said he had been told that 'Mark Tighe might be holding something else'.

Rea Walshe said she would instruct the HR manager, Janice Dunwoody, to 'get the whistleblower policy out to staff in a sensitive manner'.

It was noted that Catherine Murphy had spoken about cutbacks made to the FAI's Emerging Talent Programme on RTÉ radio. 'Somebody who knows their way around fairly well is talking to Catherine,' a director said.

One director expressed concern that at the upcoming Oireachtas hearing Delaney would try to shift the blame onto the board.

At this point, Jim McConnell pushed for the release of a press statement to say the board had instructed that a forensic review of its accounts be undertaken. Conway said he wanted a PR company to give advice first. Murray pushed for a 'holding statement' as he feared the FAI was being overtaken by events. Niamh O'Donoghue supported this, as she felt it important to reassure stakeholders and restore public confidence by assuring them that an external review of the FAI's books would take place.

It was noted that one media poll had showed that 70 per cent of respondents believed the FAI board should be removed. The directors noted there was huge emphasis on what they were doing. 'The tide has turned against the board,' one said.

Both O'Donoghue and McConnell said they had felt 'bounced' or 'rushed' into agreeing to transfer Delaney into his new position at the previous Friday night's board meeting, which they both had joined by phone.

As the board meeting went on, Delaney remained outside. At one point he was joined by his sister Jane. One board member spoke to her on his way to the men's room. She asked what was going on.

'We don't know where we are,' the board member told her. 'We are into legal, into the ODCE. We are into serious stuff here.'

Conway spoke to Delaney when he stepped out of the board meeting. Delaney told him he had just come off the phone with Kieran Mulvey, the chairman of Sport Ireland.

Delaney tried to impress on the FAI President that he was getting 'huge numbers of messages of support'. When Conway raised the issue of 'brand damage' and the effect the ongoing controversy was having on sponsors, Delaney offered to show the FAI President messages of support he said he had received from Robert Finnegan, the boss of Three Ireland, Stephen Wheeler, the Managing Director of SSE Airtricity, and Zoran Laković, UEFA's Head of National Associations. There was no suggestion of nervousness on their parts, Delaney insisted. (Conway did not take Delaney up on the offer, and it is not clear whether the messages of support existed.)

As the first meeting of an FAI board without John Delaney since 1999 dragged on, Conway later stepped out to use the toilet and was surprised to find Delaney still waiting outside. Delaney demanded to know when he would be allowed back in. Conway told him to 'go home', as the directors had important work to do.

Back in the board meeting, the directors discussed Sport Ireland's upcoming Oireachtas appearance. Donal Conway noted there was 'an axis' of Denis O'Brien connections between Mulvey and Delaney. Mulvey was O'Brien's nominated director on the board of Independent News and Media (INM).

Conway recalled that Delaney had seemed erratic and incoherent while they were in Gibraltar. He said this would be a factor in how the board dealt with him.

Mick Hanley, the seventy-four-year-old representative from Limerick, defended Delaney. 'We are all human beings, things affect us in different ways,' he mused.

At this stage the board began discussing whether Delaney had committed misconduct. Eamon Naughton said he had heard enough to satisfy him. 'John should be put on gardening leave,' he said. 'The sooner we get the investigation done the better.' (Within twenty-four hours, an intermediary would tell Naughton that Delaney was disappointed that the FAI director had 'let him down' at the board meeting.)

The directors said they needed legal advice on whether they could move against Delaney, and asked could they ensure that Delaney did not find out that they had sought that advice. Rea Walshe told the board she would get the advice and ensure it was done confidentially.

A warning was given that the FAI did not at that point have the budget for an upcoming under-21 match due to be played away in Armenia in November. Alex O'Connell, the Finance Director, said there might be enough money if 'we manage the overdraft and use advance funds'.

Only the previous week, on 19 March, Donal Conway had assured Sport Ireland that the FAI was 'in a strong financial position'. Now the board discussed whether the FAI could be considered a going concern. The board concluded it was, because of the 'support networks' of Bank of Ireland, UEFA's TV money, and sponsorship deals that could be drawn down early.

Bank of Ireland was said to believe that Delaney's €100,000 loan could have caused a breach of the FAI's banking covenants, but it was understood that senior bank officials were 'relaxed' because the loan had been repaid after such a short period of time.

Deloitte had by this stage informed the board that the rent on Delaney's houses had to be regarded as an employee benefit, but no benefit-in-kind tax had been paid by the FAI since 2013. In order to be 'whiter than white', this would have to be disclosed to the tax authorities.

A crisis sub-committee, consisting of Donal Conway, Eamon Naughton, Michael Cody, Eddie Murray and Niamh O'Donoghue, was formed to deal with the developing situation. It was noted that Delaney knew this was coming and was 'not happy'.

The board also voted to appoint the accountancy firm Mazars as external consultants to investigate what had been happening with the FAI's finances and why Deloitte, its long-time auditors, had not previously flagged the €100,000 payment, the rent arrangement or the golden handcuffs deals. The board noted it had committed in correspondence with the ODCE to investigate its financial processes and 'it was only a matter of time' before an external agency 'appointed someone' to do the same.

Niamh O'Donoghue then said she was 'strongly opposed' to Delaney remaining on the Aviva Stadium board. 'It does not appear to tally up with the role,' she said.

Conway initially defended Delaney. He said the Executive Vice-President was involved in organizing high-profile club games at the stadium.

O'Donoghue countered that Conway should look at the situation in reverse. The FAI's future Chief Executive would have 'no say on the main asset of the FAI' under the management structure they had just rushed through.

O'Connell, who was by now bitterly regretting not trying to block the Hall report, backed O'Donoghue up. He said Delaney's new remit should have been limited to UEFA and FIFA matters, along with other special projects.

Cody, who was on the Aviva board with Delaney, stood up for his man and warned that the association would be 'losing our punching power with the IRFU' without Delaney.

'John gets away with things in relation to the stadium that I wouldn't,' Cody said. 'I understand where Niamh is coming from but I feel the FAI's needs are better served by him being on that board rather than not. John will say that he was exhausted from his old role and this new role won't diminish him in the eyes of the stadium directors.'

The board agreed that this issue would be reviewed in 2021, when it would be the FAI's turn to chair the stadium board. From talking about putting Delaney on gardening leave, they were now contemplating him being around for another two years at least.

The meeting closed and the directors prepared to go to the first Ireland home game in almost fifteen years where Delaney would not be the FAI CEO.

*

Mellon's, a busy grocery shop on the South Lotts Road near the Aviva Stadium, had got wind of the mooted tennis-ball protest and advertised on its sandwich board that it had tennis balls for sale.

Before the match, Delaney posed for selfies with fans in the premium seats. He also approached a number of senior administrators from 'the grassroots' to tell them that public messages of support for him would be appreciated. Some agreed to help, although one or two openly told Delaney that they had concerns about the €100,000 loan and would not issue any statements of support.

Emma English, Delaney's fiancée and girlfriend of the last five years, had broken up with him acrimoniously the previous December. The split was not public knowledge, but FAI staff and directors were well aware of the development. With Delaney under huge pressure, his mother, Joan, who was recovering from surgery, asked English to attend the match to support her son. English agreed.

At the stadium, English and Delaney were seen talking animatedly in a corridor outside the FAI's President's suite. A source at the match says she gave him eye drops for his bloodshot eyes as they spoke heatedly. The pair barely exchanged a word for the rest of the evening, but they were pictured smiling and clapping together in the President's box seats just before the game kicked off. Pictures of the erstwhile couple featured on almost all of the next day's front pages. English exhorted Conway to stand shoulder to shoulder with Delaney at the match, but he declined.

Delaney told directors at the match that he had 'done the FAI a service' by standing beside English and getting photographed as though it was business as usual.

'Twisted stuff,' says one director. 'I don't know how he figured that was of benefit to the FAI.'

After thirty-two minutes of the match, Ireland won a free-kick on the edge of the Georgia box. By the time Conor Hourihane had placed the ball and the Georgians set up a defensive wall, the clock ticked into the thirty-third minute – at which point tennis balls started raining down on the pitch from all sides. Though it's not known who instigated the protest, the choice of the thirty-third minute was widely regarded as a reference to Delaney's demand to FIFA in 2010 that Ireland be allowed into the World Cup as the thirty-third team because of Thierry Henry's handball.

It was an extraordinary moment. Despite decades of discontent over how the FAI was run, never before had protests spilled onto the pitch, and Ireland fans prided themselves on being the polar opposite of troublemakers. Many of those who had heard about the mooted demonstration had thought it would be another damp squib, like a 'Delaney out' sky-writing protest that was announced in advance of the Scotland game in 2015 but never got off the ground after gardaí had a word with the pilot who was due to perform the fly past. Delaney and the FAI had previously gone to extraordinary lengths to drown out or prevent protests in the stadium. Now, in the middle of a vital qualifier, the Aviva Stadium pitch was littered with tennis balls.

With its oblique reference to something that had happened nine years earlier, the tennis-ball protest was seen as a reaction against not only the bizarre €100,000 payment, the rental costs or the sideways move to Executive Vice-President, but the whole web of absurdity that Delaney had spun around Irish football. The retired professionals working as TV pundits would later furiously debate whether the protest interrupting play was justified or not.

It took the players and stewards two minutes to clean up all the tennis balls. The fans, meanwhile, angrily sang 'They always cheat, they always lie, fuck Delaney and the FAI.' When play resumed, Hourihane lashed the free kick into the Georgian net. It would be the only goal of the game and capped off three of the most surreal minutes in the history of Irish football. Maybe the crowd should throw balls onto the pitch more often, joked TV commentators.

For Zeno Kelly, who had protested for years against Delaney's regime, it was a landmark moment, and it caught him completely by surprise. Although he travelled to every Ireland away game, Kelly was watching the Georgia game on TV because the FAI had banned him from attending home matches over posts he made on the online YBIG forum. He was moved to see so many fans registering their disgust in a way that could not be ignored.

'I was watching it on a screen not too far from the stadium and I just thought, "Brilliant!"'

15.   Scarlet for You

In the run up to its much-anticipated appearance before the Oireachtas Committee on Transport, Tourism and Sport, the FAI hired Q4, one of Ireland's premier public relations companies. Working with Grant Thornton accountants, A&L Goodbody solicitors and the PR company, the FAI held a number of practice sessions at which the directors and senior staff role-played taking questions from TDs.

Delaney declined to get involved with the group preparation, but shortly before the hearing he asked that Jackie Gallagher, one of Q4's directors, come out to him for one-to-one sessions. On the eve of the hearing, Donal Conway and Rea Walshe were in Abbotstown finalizing Conway's opening address to the committee when Delaney arrived in at 9.30 p.m. He placed the opening statement he intended to make to the Oireachtas committee on Conway's desk and intimated that, having taken legal advice, he would not be answering questions from the politicians. The FAI President was stunned. The strategy was for Conway to 'take point' and lead the delegation. It did not involve Delaney making a statement. When he read through the draft statement later, in Delaney's absence, Conway was even more disturbed. He felt the statement was not fair or completely accurate, as it blamed the FAI's finance department for the €100,000 payment debacle. Despite repeated calls that night, Conway could not get Delaney to answer his phone.

The nine-person FAI delegation and their advisers gathered early on the morning of Wednesday, 10 April, in a room on the ground floor of Buswells hotel, a regular staging post for politicians, lobbyists and anyone else with business in Leinster House across the road. As the FAI delegation ordered breakfast, Delaney arrived with Aidan Eames, his new personal solicitor. Eames was the solicitor who had instructed John Rogers SC in Angela Kerins's successful challenge to the Dáil's Public Accounts Committee. He was also acting for Denis O'Brien in a high-profile case in which the billionaire was suing a lobbying firm for allegedly circulating a negative dossier about his business dealings.

Working with Conway, Eames agreed to edit back some of Delaney's statement. Although Delaney ordered a fry-up he barely touched it, but drank cup after cup of coffee. The fact that Delaney would not be answering any questions about the €100,000 transaction, nor indeed about anything that related to his fifteen years as CEO, dropped like a bombshell for the rest of the delegation.

Although they appeared a united group as they crossed the street in front of a line of press photographers and TV cameramen, some members of the FAI delegation were reeling. 'It was unbelievable,' recalls one. 'We were all going in with one arm as long as the other, except for John who has his legal man with him.'

Delaney's garrulous entrance made him stand out from the rest of the group. The FAI Executive Vice-President looked like he was in the middle of an election campaign as he shared jokes and backslapped with politicians – all while wearing his UEFA coat.

Fergus O'Dowd, the committee chairman, asked the twenty journalists in attendance, from football writers to political correspondents, to wait outside the committee room until the FAI delegation took their seats. Delaney hailed the journalists: 'All right, lads.' Without breaking stride, he strode through the press pack and down the corridor to take his chair in the circular, windowless basement committee room.

*

There was a high sense of expectation. Delaney had become a target of ridicule for many, with his unwieldy new title, but TDs and senators were well aware that Delaney retained strong support around the country. Loyal supporters in amateur football leagues across Ireland's four provinces had issued statements at the end of March lauding Delaney and calling for him to be given the opportunity to continue in his new role. Pat O'Sullivan, the owner of Limerick FC, and Lee Power, the Waterford FC owner, publicly backed Delaney with effusive statements. Gerry Gorman, secretary of the North East Football

League, praised Delaney's support of the 'grassroots' and attacked what he said was a 'relentless, imbalanced negative campaign that has been orchestrated by sections of the media'. He claimed there had been disproportionate coverage of the 'moronic' tennis-ball protest that he said emanated from '.001%' of the 40,000 people in attendance at the match. The letter was disowned by some clubs in Gorman's league who complained about a lack of consultation.

In the days leading up to the committee hearing, Delaney had tried to operate as he had as Chief Executive. On 30 March, he attended a ground in Limerick that was being renamed after the FAI board member Mick Hanley, who idolized Delaney. Those who engraved the black marble plaque commemorating the event did not even try to capture Delaney's new title. 'Unveiled by John Delaney. FAI,' it simply said.

The ceremony was attended by two government TDs, who, along with Hanley, were happy to pose for pictures with Delaney. One of the TDs was Patrick O'Donovan, a junior minister, who had previously been in the Department of Sport under Shane Ross. He joked in his speech that Delaney was 'always a great man to bring out the cheque book'.

'There's a lot of clubs here tonight, John, now and I'm sure that you won't let them down,' O'Donovan said.

On 3 April, the TDs and senators of the Oireachtas committee had grilled Sport Ireland about the FAI. John Treacy, Sport Ireland's Chief Executive, said the association had failed to adequately answer the questions it had posed about the €100,000 payment. Asked by senator Pádraig Ó Céidigh whether there had been any red flags on the FAI, Treacy said: 'The FAI was regularly short of cash and dealing with liquidity issues' and was 'always' looking for early payment of part of its annual Sport Ireland grant of €2.9 million. Pressed by Imelda Munster, a Sinn Féin TD from Louth, on whether he had confidence in the FAI board, Treacy demurred. 'Well, I'm not saying "yes".' Treacy said he was 'surprised' not to have been consulted on the FAI's creation of a new position for Delaney.

On 8 April the FAI board had admitted that it did not know about the 2017 loan and that the statements issued by the press office on 17 and 18 March were wrong. That same day, Delaney and Conway had attended a photo-shoot in the Aviva Stadium to promote stadium tours. When the conversation turned to the €100,000 payment, Conway recalls, Delaney tried to assert that Conway had advised him not to tell anyone about it.

'John, don't try that on me,' Conway replied. 'I don't care what forum we go to. That is not true. So, don't try that with me.'

The day before the FAI's appearance before the Oireachtas committee, Sport Ireland announced the suspension of all funding for the FAI pending further investigations. The Sport Ireland move dominated the front pages on the morning the FAI came in to be questioned in Leinster House on 10 April. A story broken online by the *Irish Independent* the previous evening about Noel Rock, the first TD to call for Delaney to resign, was also causing waves. Based on leaked text messages sent to Delaney's phone some years previously, the *Independent* reported that Rock had sought Delaney's help in securing match tickets and that he promised to 'push back' against plans to call the FAI in before the Oireachtas Sport Committee. Rock was damaged. He claimed not to remember the 'push back' exchange and said he paid full price for the tickets that Delaney had supplied. The story served as a warning shot to other politicians who might take on the FAI man.

Inside the committee room, Delaney appeared relaxed. He had been through Oireachtas hearings before and emerged unscathed. He smiled and winked at Frank Feighan, the Fine Gael senator who chaired the cross-party Oireachtas Ireland supporters' club.

Donal Conway, for perhaps the first time in his presidency, was in the central position of a FAI delegation involving Delaney. Delaney sat to his immediate left, with Paraic Treanor on Delaney's other flank. To Conway's right sat Rea Walshe, and then Eddie Murray, who was suffering from a cold. Ruud Dokter, the FAI's technical head, and Fran Gavin, its Head of Competitions, sat at a lower level in front of the five and would be largely ignored by the politicians. Behind the main five sat Alex O'Connell, the newly installed Finance Director, who was also suffering with a heavy cold, and Cathal Dervan. Directly behind Delaney sat Aidan Eames, his solicitor, a visible warning to the politicians that they overstepped the mark with Delaney at their peril.

The press seats were full, and some 45,000 users logged on to the Oireachtas website to livestream the hearing, up to twenty times the normal viewing figures.

Catherine Murphy had heard from dozens of football people who had questions for Delaney and the FAI. Solicitors, accountants and journalists fed her tips on FAI governance and finances. Murphy timed her arrival to avoid having to make small talk with Delaney.

Donal Conway's opening speech outlined how Grant Thornton was assisting the FAI in a review of its financial records and Mazars had been appointed to carry out an investigation into 'all matters'. He also made a statement about the €100,000 transaction that, unlike the rest of his speech, had not been supplied to the committee in advance. The committee broke for three minutes to read the statement before allowing Conway to read it into the record.

Conway outlined how, after Delaney gave the FAI his €100,000 cheque in April 2017, it was decided to cash it after the FAI received an email from 'one particular creditor' seeking payment. Delaney was repaid two months later without any interest or other charges.

After Conway was finished, Delaney said he had a prepared statement. O'Dowd criticized Delaney for not supplying this in advance, as was normal protocol. After suspending the hearing for twenty minutes to allow the politicians to 'digest' this statement, O'Dowd allowed Delaney to proceed.

Delaney said he was 'truly saddened' by the suspension of Sport Ireland's funding for the FAI. He said he had 'urged' a speedy response to the questions raised about the €100,000 loan by Sport Ireland. He had already met Grant Thornton and would meet Mazars when asked.

'On Tuesday, 25 April 2017, we had an internal finance meeting at the FAI,' Delaney said. 'This meeting was attended by our Director of Finance, Mr Eamon Breen, our Financial Controller Ms Yvonne Tsang, and me as the CEO. At this meeting I was advised that if all cheques and FAI bank transfers issued to third parties at that time were presented for payment that the FAI would exceed its overdraft limit of €1.5 million on its bank accounts, which were held with Bank of Ireland.

'I expressed concern and surprise at the meeting as to how the FAI could have arrived at this position. I recall thinking at the time that if I had been approached even a few days earlier I may have been able to better address the issue.'

He said that as there were only a 'few hours' to prevent the FAI bank overdraft limit from being exceeded, 'as a precautionary measure and to assist the FAI' he wrote a personal cheque for €100,000 to the association. He said Breen was given the cheque before Delaney travelled on UEFA business first to London and then to Geneva. He informed both Cody and Tony Fitzgerald, the then President, of his actions. While in Geneva, Breen called him to say the cheque was needed and he agreed it should be lodged. He was to be repaid when funds came in, and that happened on 16 June 2017.

'I did not receive any interest payment and I would never have expected it,' said Delaney. 'I was only acting to assist the FAI and for the benefit of Irish football.'

Delaney claimed he asked Breen if the FAI had any reporting obligations arising from the €100,000 payment but did not say if a response was given. The transaction did not arise at FAI board meetings at the time, he said.

He said he informed the FAI board of the transaction on 4 March, after a query from the *Sunday Times*. He initiated court proceedings against the newspaper on 16 March, 'at my own cost' because he believed 'at the time' that the information came from documentation filed in the family courts. Delaney said he regretted the 'embarrassment' the controversy had caused FAI staff and football volunteers around the country. He repeated his pledge to co-operate with the investigations underway. Then, despite opening his statement by saying he had 'urged' speedy responses to questions, Delaney said that based on his legal advice he would not be making any further comment on the €100,000 transaction or answering any questions about his time as Chief Executive.

'Given that some members of this committee have made highly prejudicial public pronouncements about me personally prior to my attendance here today, and in light of the recent Supreme Court ruling in the Kerins case, I ask that the committee respects this position,' he said. Delaney said he would be happy to answer questions about his new role.

Catherine Murphy was first up. She asked Delaney what Eamon Breen had said when Delaney asked him if there were disclosure obligations around the €100,000 loan.

'I made it clear in my statement that I cannot add any further to it at this stage given the various investigations that are taking place,' Delaney replied.

To use a football expression, he was parking the bus in front of the goal. Initially, the tactic worked, as the politicians instead peppered Conway with questions. At times Eames would whisper advice into Delaney's ear and then Delaney would whisper to Conway.

Conway was questioned about the state of the FAI's finances, who had issued the inaccurate press statements, how the Hall report came into being, why it was so rushed and whether the 'particular creditor' that sought payment in 2017 was in fact Dundalk FC looking for its UEFA money. In a variety of ways, Conway declined to provide answers to the questions.

Delaney remained mute, drinking copious amounts of water. As Conway grappled with a question on whether Delaney had a pension in place with his new position, Delaney finally piped up.

'Chairman, may I have a comfort break?' he asked O'Dowd.

The Fine Gael TD asked if Delaney wanted the committee to adjourn.

'No, just me, or if anyone else wants to?'

With that, Delaney stood to leave as the hearing continued. Passing Paul Rowan, who was sitting with journalists on the seat nearest the door, Delaney loudly said 'Hiya, Paul' as he went for his comfort break.

Ruth Coppinger, a left-wing Solidarity TD from west Dublin whose sister Reg Coppinger used to work in the FAI licensing department, was the first to try to get Delaney to answer some questions after he returned. She asked did Delaney not believe he had a duty to the public, who paid to go to Ireland matches, to answer questions.

'I have read my statement as it is,' Delaney said.

John O'Mahony, a Fine Gael senator, said he understood that Delaney had previously been quoted saying he would not rest until two independent directors were appointed, as advised by Genesis. This temporarily drew Delaney out of his shell. The quote was incorrect.

'I never said there would be two independent directors,' said Delaney.

The committee broke for lunch at 1.45 p.m. All around Leinster House, TDs were expressing concern about Delaney's stance and the presence of Aidan Eames at the committee hearing. Politicians had never before seen a witness to an Oireachtas committee bring their personal lawyer into a hearing. A referendum that would have enabled Oireachtas committees to be given strong investigatory powers, like their US counterparts, had been narrowly defeated in 2011. The Kerins ruling had a chilling effect, with Oireachtas committees repeatedly warned they must follow legal advice not to become confrontational in their questions.

'Is everyone going to follow Delaney's lead and lawyer-up and plead the fifth [the right to silence] after this?' a worried chairman from another Oireachtas committee remarked.

The Sport Committee members and watching journalists were frustrated at the lack of answers coming from the FAI. Several TDs asked journalists, 'How are we doing?' Not good, they were told.

Eddie Murray, who had been the FAI's Honorary Treasurer for fifteen years, had not been asked a question, despite the focus on the FAI's finances. More than one journalist pointed this out.

As Murray went to the men's toilet, Michael Healy-Rae, the cap-wearing independent TD, had a word with him. Healy-Rae warned Murray that it was going around on social media that the TDs had to 'get Murray'. The former garda thanked the Kerry TD for the heads-up.

He might have been forewarned, but Murray was not able for the questions. Noel Rock was straight in after the lunch break to ask him if he felt 'undermined' by not being informed about the €100,000 loan for nearly two years.

Bristling, Murray said it was 'possible' that he should have been informed, but he would not consider himself undermined.

As Rock asked further questions, it was clear that Murray was struggling to hear. He had to ask for Rock to repeat himself a number of times. He turned around to consult with Alex O'Connell regarding the more technical questions on FAI finances.

After Rock, Michael Healy-Rae finally had his turn to ask a question after waiting more than three hours. In his unmistakable Kerry lilt, Healy-Rae proceeded to deliver a three-minute paean to Delaney.

'The only thing Mr Delaney could be accused of is being passionately committed to his job and to the survival of what I would call the business and that all he was trying to do was good,' said Healy-Rae, as Delaney grinned back at him. The TD said he could 'not for the life of me' see how the three reports being carried out would not come out positively for Delaney, who was 'definitely' the best qualified person to carry out his new job dealing with UEFA and FIFA.

'I want to remember what Mr Delaney has done for the association throughout the country. In every club from the grassroots up, locally and nationally – and on the international scene – Mr Delaney's personal reputation is, in my humble opinion, second to none,' said Healy-Rae.

The Kerry TD promised Delaney 'the mother of all welcomes' when he came down to Castleisland AFC to open its new grounds at the end of April because 'his reputation and his respectability will precede him'.

This tribute to Delaney was met with derision from Coppinger, who called Healy-Rae 'a joke'. She pointed out that he had not even asked a question.

Next up was Jonathan O'Brien, a Cork Sinn Féin TD who was also a member of a group of Cork City fans that had helped rescue the League of Ireland club from liquidation.

'How many bank accounts does the FAI currently have?' he asked Murray.

'Just the one,' Murray responded immediately.

There were heads shaking around the room. Fergus O'Dowd said he thought it was twenty-five, as had been reported in the *Sunday Times* the previous month. Murray sought to consult with Alex O'Connell.

One of the directors watching from home instantly recognized that Murray had just committed a major faux pas. He shouted at the television in frustration.

It took some time for O'Connell and Murray to clarify that the FAI had not one but twenty-four bank accounts.

Pressed by Catherine Murphy, Murray accepted that it was 'unsatisfactory' that he was not told about the €100,000 loan until it hit the media. That the FAI needed a bailout from its CEO was 'totally unsatisfactory', he said.

'It strikes me that the board is very passive,' Murphy told Murray. 'That is part of the reason the Genesis report indicated that there was a need to have independent people on the board to challenge it from time to time. The board must have been very passive if something like this went entirely unnoticed.'

The retired garda objected. 'It is definitely a challenging board,' he insisted.

Noel Rock pointed out that the PDF of the Jonathan Hall report that had been sent to the committee had a creation date and time embedded in its metadata. That showed it was created at 5.10 p.m. on 23 March, during Ireland's match in Gibraltar and a day after the board supposedly signed off on the report. The FAI was unable to respond, as Rock was out of time.

The politicians became increasingly critical of what they saw as stonewalling from the FAI. Robert Troy, a Fianna Fáil TD, accused Conway of trying to 'hide behind' Grant Thornton and Mazars. 'The perception outside here is that the board is a cartel and that it is closing ranks and is not being honest and open with the public,' said Troy.

Conway insisted that while he had been on the FAI board for fifteen years, every two years he had faced re-election. He said four of the ten FAI directors had joined in the last three or four years.

Asked if proper corporate governance had been carried out by the FAI board since 2005, Conway said: 'I am happy with the work of the board during my time as a member.'

Pressed on whether the board would step down if that was a pre-requisite to the restoration of Sport Ireland funding, Conway said: 'We will not jeopardize Sport Ireland funding. We will take whatever actions we have to take.'

Imelda Munster pressed Conway on what sort of engagement the FAI had had with the ODCE. Conway said his advice was not to address this issue at all.

Faced with this defensive approach by the FAI, Munster took a different tack from the other committee members. She decided to start chiding them.

'It is clear that the organization has suffered from the fallout since this story broke concerning Mr Delaney,' Munster said. 'Its funding has now been pulled. People right across the state are watching this and I am sure they are, as the saying goes, "scarlet for you" when they hear the answers forthcoming.'

She asked Conway whether he had sought Delaney's resignation since the story had broken. 'No,' said Conway. Delaney had not offered his resignation either.

Munster asked Delaney directly whether he had considered his position.

Delaney would only say, 'I have read my statement to the committee already.'

'It's just a question,' the TD pointed out.

'I have read my statement,' he repeated three times as Munster pressed.

'The former CEO of the FAI, Mr John Delaney, has behaved disgracefully today,' Munster said. 'He came in with a last-minute statement. He knows the procedures for this committee. He has furnished us with a statement but is refusing to answer any questions on that statement. He is also refusing to answer questions that are ongoing in respect of his time as CEO. What has been going on here has been an absolute disgrace and farcical.'

Delaney bristled. 'I note Deputy Munster's comments,' he said.

Kevin O'Keeffe, a Fianna Fáil TD who had bought World Cup final tickets from Delaney and who was the only committee member to attend the FAI's function to celebrate the UEFA under-17 draw the previous week, said Delaney had been portrayed as 'the Trump of the FAI'.

'He has grassroots support, but somebody in Dublin is out for his neck and is gunning for him, as are people in some parts of the media,' said O'Keeffe.

O'Keeffe asked Delaney if he had taken his eye off the ball in recent years due to his UEFA ExCo role. Suddenly, Delaney found his tongue. He pointed out that he had met O'Keeffe last summer as they handed out €1 million in grants to Cork clubs during the FAI's AGM, but it was 'impossible' to keep doing his CEO job and the UEFA role while trying to have some time with his children.

'I have a sixteen-year-old daughter who might not see me for a month,' he said. 'That is the human side of what I have been trying to do in the past couple of years.' Delaney directed Fran Gavin to answer part of O'Keeffe's question on the League of Ireland.

Conway recalls sensing Delaney physically warming to O'Keeffe's mildly supportive questioning. Eames passed his client a note to remind him that Conway was in charge.

Pádraig Ó Céidigh, an independent senator who has run regional airlines, questioned the FAI's ability to continue as a going concern. 'It seems this €100,000 was vital to keeping the organization afloat,' he said. 'If the organization is down to €100,000 with €50 million of a turnover, I would be worried.'

Murray insisted that he never had any concerns about the FAI's viability, because it returned a surplus every year. Ó Céidigh questioned if Murray understood the difference between returning a surplus and having cash.

When Robert Troy tried to ask Cathal Dervan who signed off on the misleading statements issued after the *Sunday Times* story on St Patrick's Day, the FAI's Director of Communications said he had not been expecting questions. He said he would be happy to respond once he got back to his desk in Abbotstown. The question was never answered.

Fergus O'Dowd, who had repeatedly reminded his fellow politicians that they could not legally press the FAI for answers they did not want to give, called for the FAI board to consider 'regime change'.

He said this would be for the good of all the children involved in the sport.

Near the end of the seven-hour hearing, Coppinger was scathing about the FAI's lack of transparency. 'Mr Delaney is here physically, so he has covered himself in that way, but it is *Hamlet* without the prince because he has not answered any of the questions that people outside this room would have wanted to be answered,' she said. 'I hope journalists and the general public take note of how toothless the parliament has become because of legal threats.'

After the hearing, the Taoiseach criticized Delaney's refusal to answer questions. 'The public, taxpayers, football fans would have liked to have seen those questions answered.'

One sport official who had been keeping a close eye on the hearing says: 'John Delaney walked into that committee meeting still the man in control of the FAI. He came out a dead man walking.'

*

Immediately after the hearing, the FAI delegation retreated to Buswells for cups of tea, coffee and stronger stuff. Murray was furious with Delaney, but he did not confront him. He was deeply embarrassed by his gaffe in saying the FAI had just one bank account. He told his colleagues he had been thinking there was just one bank account from which he was required to sign cheques.

Delaney was in great form in Buswells. Conway couldn't believe it. He left the hotel and went for a drink with an FAI staff member near his home in north Dublin. Conway told the colleague that Delaney thought the hearing was 'a good day'. 'What relationship to reality does that suggest?' Conway asked.

Murray later told the *Sunday Times*: 'I felt I made an idiot of myself on television . . . I tried to do the right thing most of the time but occasionally you get caught up in something you should have been more careful about. I might take people too much at face value.'

That evening, Murray resolved to end his fifteen-year tenure on the FAI board. The octogenarian can still be seen regularly volunteering at Monaghan football grounds, occasionally working a pitchfork into the ground in an effort to get a rain-sodden pitch into shape.

Before the Oireachtas hearing, Rea Walshe had asked Murray if he wanted to avail of independent legal advice. Murray accepted the offer and attended a consultation in Dublin on the eve of the hearing. The solicitor checked back in with him by phone that night and texted him during the hearing. After he resigned from the board, Murray received a legal bill of €3,500 from the solicitor. The FAI's insurance covered some €2,500. This left Murray with an unexpected bill of €1,000 to cap his fifteen years of voluntary service on the FAI board.

16. Endgame

Mobile phone reception in the Leinster House basement, where the committee rooms are based, is patchy. While Tighe and Rowan were covering the FAI hearing in Committee Room 4, Frank Fitzgibbon, the *Sunday Times*'s editor in Ireland, was trying to get through to Tighe. Fitzgibbon had commissioned a radio advert to promote the paper's coverage of the FAI's evolving crisis and he wanted to know how far he could push the script. Tighe had told him he had an FAI story, but was working on getting a better one.

The story that he had ready to go would reveal that the FAI had taken Emma English and some of her family on the official team flight to France for Euro 2016. The FAI had also hired English's brother-in-law Freddie Passas as an assistant for the team. It wasn't enough to hang a radio campaign on. Radio advertising based around a news story is a tricky business. Even if a newspaper has a great story 'in the bag', there is always the possibility a rival could break it before Sunday comes. However, with the Oireachtas hearing on that week and the suspension of state funding, the *Sunday Times* would be giving the FAI crisis extensive coverage no matter what happened after the advert was commissioned and the radio slots booked.

By the time Tighe emerged from the seven-hour hearing it was too late to temper the radio advert. Fitzgibbon had authorized the script to be voiced by Newstalk DJ Tom Dunne, with the ad to run over RTÉ and Communicorp stations that weekend.

'Last month the *Sunday Times* revealed that in 2017 John Delaney had written a cheque for €100,000 to his employer at the FAI, precipitating the biggest crisis in the association's history. For the latest revelations in the biggest sports story of the year, don't miss the *Sunday Times*.'

The pressure to deliver was on now. Tighe had been hoping that a source who had access to internal FAI documents would meet him, but the source was extremely nervous.

In the committee room, just after Delaney concluded his opening statement, Tighe's phone buzzed. It was an encrypted message. The source had re-established contact after weeks of silence and was now amongst those watching on Oireachtas TV or through the live stream.

One of the details given by Delaney was wrong, the message claimed, but the source would not talk further. Over the next day the source remained in contact but would not commit to meeting for fear of being identified. Tighe offered the source the strongest assurance he could that he would never reveal their identity. Ultimately, the source agreed to meet. The rendezvous was set for that Friday afternoon.

In a car park outside a toy shop, Tighe was handed six months of John Delaney's FAI credit-card statements and copies of other internal FAI records. Tighe knew the source's background, and was satisfied that the documents were genuine. Tighe jumped in a taxi. He had less than twenty-four hours to go through the treasure trove of material he had just obtained to see if there was a story there.

Looking through the documents in the taxi heading to the *Sunday Times* office, Tighe noted there were frequent cash withdrawals on Delaney's credit card alongside expenditure in duty-free shops and regular spending in Pluck's, a pub in Kilmacanogue, near Delaney's home. One hotel bill from the Ritz-Carlton Central Park in New York, paid by the FAI, came to over €8,500; a bill from another Ritz-Carlton, in Dubai, was charged directly on the credit card to the tune of €4,500. Amongst the documents were records showing the FAI had paid €60,000 to Susan Keegan, Delaney's ex-girlfriend, between 2013 and 2014.

Tighe told his editor he had an FAI story that would live up to the billing of the radio adverts. Before he went through the documents in detail he wanted to contact the FAI and Delaney to give them as long as possible to respond to questions before the following day's print deadline.

In an email sent at 15.32, Tighe told Cathal Dervan that the *Sunday*

Times had established details of 'a number of unusual payments by the FAI and we would like the FAI and/or Mr John Delaney to comment on them'.

There were a series of questions:

1. In late 2013/early 2014 the FAI made payments totalling €60,000 to Susan Keegan for 'professional services'. Ms Keegan, with an address in Kent in England, was John Delaney's girlfriend just before or even during this period.

    Can the FAI explain why this payment was made and what professional services Ms Keegan supplied to the FAI?

2. The Sunday Times has established that John Delaney, while CEO, frequently withdrew cash sums of between €100 and €250 from ATMs using his FAI credit card. The sums for one year exceed €2,000.

    This seems to be a highly irregular practice as we have established that no receipts or explanations for this spending of cash were provided to the FAI.

    Can the FAI explain why it allows such a practice with its resources? Under what circumstances are staff allowed to withdraw cash using FAI credit cards? Were all these cash withdrawals approved by the FAI?

3. We have also established that John Delaney had a practice of charging spending in shops such as Cath Kidston furniture shop, Thomas Pink menswear, Kurt Geiger clothing, and airport duty free to the FAI credit card.
    a) Can the FAI say whether it approved of such spending?
    b) Did John Delaney ever reimburse these credit card charges?

4. There are also numerous restaurant charges, including charges to Pluck's restaurant in Kilmacanogue. Was John Delaney entitled to charge the FAI for spending in this restaurant near his home or did he subsequently pay this money back?

5. The Sunday Times has also established that the FAI paid for expensive hotels used by John Delaney. These included an €8,514 bill for the Ritz Carlton in New York in December 2015 and over €4,500 for the Ritz Carlton in Dubai in December 2016.

Were these hotel stays necessary for FAI business or were they personal holidays for Mr Delaney?

We are writing about this for Sunday. If the FAI or Mr Delaney wish to issue any answers they can do so by 12 noon tomorrow.

Five minutes later, at 15.37, Dervan responded. It was a short email: 'No comment, Mark.'

The *Sunday Times* contacted an Irish reporter based in Kent to see if he would help on the Susan Keegan aspect of the story. He agreed to knock on the door of the address listed in internal FAI records for Keegan. If Keegan would talk about her knowledge of the FAI payments then this would be the lead story, even ahead of the credit-card expenditure. The Kent-based reporter came back later that evening. He had gone to the address and 'a nice English woman' answered the door. She had lived there for ten years and had never heard of Susan Keegan.

Tighe was still convinced the document referring to the payments was accurate, but he decided that while his story would report that €60,000 in FAI payments were made for 'professional services', they could not name Keegan as she had not been given a chance to respond.

By now, Tighe had entered all the credit-card charges into a spreadsheet. In a six-month period over the second half of 2016, Delaney had spent €40,000 on his FAI card. This included over forty cash withdrawals amounting to over €6,000, with the money extracted in sums of between €100 and €250.

*

Delaney's decision to give the Oireachtas Sport Committee the silent treatment had made some of his solid supporters think again. Board members who had watched online were disgusted that Eddie Murray had been publicly humiliated, and most blamed Delaney for putting him in that position.

'Eddie was a sitting duck,' says one board member. 'He is still hurting about that. He felt he let himself down and let everybody down.'

Aside from the fallout from Delaney's performance before the Oireachtas committee, the board and the new interim CEO were grappling with an unexpected financial blow arising from the FAI's commercial deal with Sports Direct. In late March, the board was told that Sports Direct wanted its €6.5 million sponsorship money back. The fact that the Mike Ashley-run company could seek the return of this money under the terms of its contract with the FAI caused consternation. The board initially laughed off the suggestion.

'I remember being at matches and seeing Sports Direct [advertising] going around the stadium,' says one director. 'I saw their brand at the summer camps. That was fine. The next thing is Rea [Walshe] said, "Sports Direct want their €6.5 million back." I started laughing. I said, "Go tell them to run and jump."'

The terms of the deal meant the €6.5 million should have been booked as a liability that could be called in by Sports Direct at any stage up to 1 April 2020. Rea Walshe, as interim CEO, was looking at a huge new hole in the FAI's finances. The increasingly overwhelmed FAI board were told the reason Sports Direct wanted its money back was because of the company's own financial issues.

Genuine sponsors were also getting jumpy. DMG Media, the owners of the *Irish Daily Mail*, the title sponsors of the FAI Cup for the last four years, had been due to launch a rebranding of the competition under its new Extra.ie website title at a cup draw on 20 March. At the last minute, it requested a delay of the rebranding launch, in the wake of the revelations about Delaney's €100,000 payment. The FAI agreed to use only its own branding at the draw.

DMG told the FAI that it was 'disappointed' about how it was being treated as a sponsor. The newspaper company then requested a photo-call with Mick McCarthy in the Aviva Stadium on 25 March, the day before the Georgia game, to launch the rebranding of the Extra.ie FAI Cup. However, in the wake of the Delaney rent story and his move to Executive Vice-President, this launch was cancelled hours before it was due to happen.

SSE Airtricity, New Balance, Diageo and Aviva let the FAI know they were unhappy with the impact the crisis was having on their brands. Talks with Three about extending its sponsorship for another two years were suspended, as were discussions with potential new sponsors such as Cadbury, Glanbia, Avantcard, Mick's Garage and BioActiv Therapy.

Deloitte was due to start its audit of the FAI's 2018 accounts on 29 March. At an initial meeting with the FAI, the accountants decided that the conditions to carry out its work were not in place. In early April, Deloitte sent the FAI a notice that it believed proper books of account had not been kept by the association and said this would have to be reported to the Companies Registration Office.

Something had to give.

Several directors complained privately to Michael Cody that they were grappling with the ramifications of deals and transactions he had been aware of, but which were never made known to the rest of the board.

'The view of the board is you may need to step away from this,' a fellow director told Cody in a one-to-one. 'There are certain things that we weren't aware of and you were. Just give us a bit of space.'

Conway sought advice from A&L Goodbody about Cody and Murray's positions on the board's crisis sub-committee. He was told the two were 'conflicted' and should step off the committee, given that one of the things now under investigation was Delaney's golden handcuffs deals that the two had agreed in 2014 without telling the rest of the board.

Murray was happy to resign from the board. Cody also decided to resign his directorship while insisting he had done nothing wrong. With his most loyal ally gone, Delaney was fatally exposed.

By that Friday, two days after the Oireachtas committee hearing, the FAI's board resolved that they wanted Delaney gone as soon as possible. A call was put through to Tom Jordan, the HR consultant with previous in internal FAI conflict resolution. Jordan was asked to contact Delaney with one question: Would he meet to discuss a deal? Delaney agreed to meet.

On the evening of Friday, 12 April, Conway and Eamon Naughton were sitting together in a room at the FAI's offices in Abbotstown. Naughton had been out at a club-licensing meeting with UEFA that week. He had received no direction from the European body about how the FAI should deal with Delaney, but his involvement in the negotiations gave some the impression that UEFA was pushing to get an exit deal done with the association's Executive Vice-President.

Delaney was sitting in another room with a friend, known only as Frank to the FAI board. This was Frank Martin, a Director of Asset Management with Hines Ireland, the local branch of the international real estate management company. Martin was there purely in a private capacity to assist Delaney. Jordan shuttled between the two rooms.

By now the board were aware of the *Sunday Times*'s queries, received that afternoon, about the €60,000 payments to Keegan and the expenditure on Delaney's FAI credit card. The queries caused 'panic', according to one source who was there.

At this stage, Conway was expressing enormous regret over agreeing to allow Delaney to move into the Executive Vice-President role. Although the FAI had briefed the media that Delaney would be paid about a third of his CEO salary in his new position, the agreement made with Conway and Cody was that Delaney would continue to get his €360,000-a-year CEO salary until the end of the year, before transitioning onto the lower pay rate. He would still have the ability to earn up to €300,000 a year with bonuses. The legal advice to the FAI was that because of the terms of the golden handcuffs deals there was a potential liability of up to €3.5 million if Delaney's position was terminated.

As Jordan's over-and-back negotiations stretched into the night, Delaney's sister Jane arrived in Abbotstown at around 4 a.m., at a critical point. Delaney had started the discussions demanding an exit package of some €3 million. While he had come down, the amount he was seeking was still far higher than what Conway and Naughton were willing to countenance.

Jane Delaney became emotional as she spoke with the FAI directors, who outlined how serious the situation was for both Delaney and the FAI. She was told the 'media frenzy' would continue as long as her brother stayed with the association. She angrily confronted Conway about the leaks from the FAI.

As dawn broke the four men and Jordan finally came together in what was nominally Mick McCarthy's office beside the FAI boardroom. Delaney refused to sit, and angrily accused Conway of showing him 'no respect' for all that he had achieved and of being on a 'power trip'.

By 7 a.m., Delaney had signed a proposed settlement agreement that would pay him a gross figure of €450,000 to terminate 'all previous contracts between the parties'. This was to be paid in nine monthly instalments of €30,000 up to December 2019. The final €180,000 would be paid in a lump sum by 24 January 2020.

Under the terms of the settlement, Delaney had to vacate his office by 30 April, less than three weeks away. He would be allowed to keep his phone and his telephone number permanently, but the FAI would cease paying for it on 30 June. He would also be allowed to keep his iPad and retain use of his company car until the end of 2019, with the insurance and tax paid for by the FAI. The agreement's terms had to remain 'strictly confidential'.

Delaney insisted that Conway and Naughton sign the deal too, but they refused. The board had to sign off on it first, they explained. In the final face-to-face meeting, the two directors challenged Delaney on the latest query to arrive on their desk from the *Sunday Times*: whether or not the FAI had ever paid money to Susan Keegan? 'Absolutely not,' Delaney responded.

With the marathon negotiations concluded, Jordan headed straight to the airport to begin a family holiday to China. Naughton drove home to Galway. While he was still on the road, Conway phoned him. They had a problem.

After returning home for breakfast and a short rest, Conway had got the FAI's young Finance Director, Alex O'Connell, to come in to Abbotstown on his day off to check the FAI Sage financial system for any payments to Keegan. O'Connell quickly confirmed that there were a number of payments to Keegan recorded in the FAI's books. O'Connell found records of the €60,000 payments in Keegan's name from 2013 and 2014 that the *Sunday Times* had asked about. He also established that there were records showing the FAI had made earlier payments to Keegan totalling €35,000. Some of the payments were said to settle an invoice for arranging a pair of Ireland friendly matches against England.

When the board convened in a teleconference that Saturday afternoon, there were strong objections to paying Delaney anything, given what they were now learning about payments to Keegan. A fuming Niamh O'Donoghue led the opposition to the deal, which the two negotiators now felt had not been agreed in good faith.

Conway was nervous about leaks – a subject on which Delaney's sister had challenged him – and said he wasn't happy discussing everything over a conference call. He wanted the board gathered together either in Abbotstown or off-site to consider the proposed Delaney settlement and the latest legal advice from A&L Goodbody, which was urging caution. The solicitors warned the FAI against committing to a deal before the full facts had been uncovered by Mazars, Grant Thornton and the state investigations.

Conway explained that, legally, 'sacking John was not a runner'. He said that 'the deal is the deal'. They could consider suspending Delaney at a meeting on Monday in 'a secure environment'.

Naughton, speaking from Galway, agreed and told the board how the negotiations had dragged on for twelve hours, up to 7 a.m. Naughton said Delaney had 'misled' them and they should wait for legal advice on the proposed settlement.

The board adjourned, but Delaney, believing his deal would be accepted, had jumped the gun. That afternoon Radio Kerry reported that Tralee man John O'Regan, a veteran member of the FAI Council who had been on TV and radio during the week defending Delaney, had received a text from Delaney saying that he would be leaving the FAI 'today'. The story was quickly picked up by RTÉ and Newstalk. Board members believed Delaney was not-too-subtly trying to push them into accepting the deal.

That evening, a 'Delaney out' banner was unfurled at a match between Cork City and St Patrick's Athletic, one of many protests at League of Ireland games that weekend. Videos showed gardaí and Cork City stewards wading into the crowd. Jonathan O'Brien, the Sinn Féin TD who had grilled the FAI earlier in the week in the Oireachtas hearing, was the only person ejected from the ground. The club later apologized to him.

In Tallaght, where Shamrock Rovers were playing Waterford,

Rovers fans taunted the opposition over its links with Delaney, chanting, 'John Delaney, he's one of your own'.

Reporting in *The Times*, Ciarán Kennedy wrote: 'The away section, perhaps taking a leaf out of the FAI executive vice-president's book, didn't manage to muster up a response.'

*

The *Sunday Times* publishes online just after midnight on Saturdays. At 11.12 p.m. John Burns, the newspaper's associate editor, tweeted an image of the front-page headline: 'Delaney racked up €40,000 spending on FAI credit card'.

As well as reporting details of Delaney's extravagant FAI credit-card expenditure, the story also stated that the association had paid €60,000 to a 'third party' under the heading 'professional fees', and that the FAI would not comment.

The *Sunday Times* stories prompted Shane Ross, the Minister for Sport, to make a statement, his first detailed comments in the three weeks since he asked Sport Ireland to investigate the circumstances of the €100,000 payment. Ross said he had 'ongoing concerns' about the FAI's corporate governance. He warned that the FAI might be ineligible for sports capital grants if it did not reform its governance and become a body in 'good standing'.

With government pressure coming to bear, the FAI board was forced to issue a Sunday-afternoon statement. In a lengthy press release it promised it was taking 'urgent steps' to address the concerns that had been raised.

The emergency board meetings were coming thick and fast. The next one was in the Boeing Suite at the Carlton hotel near Dublin airport on Monday, 15 April. Delaney had arranged such meetings before to terminate the managerial tenures of Brian Kerr, Steve Staunton, Giovanni Trapattoni and Martin O'Neill, but now he was the one up for the chop.

There was a row over who had tipped off the media, as the freelance football reporter John Fallon turned up outside the hotel, soon followed by a gaggle of reporters and photographers. The sub-committee of Conway, O'Donoghue and Naughton had earlier met the FAI's solicitors concerning Delaney's position. The Executive Vice-President was entitled to six weeks' notice pay and a maximum of ten weeks' holiday pay if he was sacked. There was a danger that Delaney could sue the association for the €3 million bonuses that had been agreed with him in 2014.

Conway asked the board to approve a resolution to either suspend Delaney or 'allow' him to step aside voluntarily pending an investigation. The sub-committee would meet Delaney if this was agreed.

The charge sheet against Delaney listed four areas for investigation:

1. Failed to manage the finances of the association.
2. Failed to control his personal expenses.
3. Failed to use his FAI credit card properly.
4. Made payments from Association funds which were not proper payments in the ordinary course of business – payments to Susan Keegan, 50th birthday party, €100,000 payment to [solicitor] Paddy Goodwin.

The list was 'not exhaustive'.

After a phone conversation with Delaney, the sub-committee rejoined the other board members at 11.59 a.m.

Delaney had been invited to meet the sub-committee at 1 p.m. Conway suggested that the board agree to tell Sport Ireland that they would all step down from the FAI board once 'a new structure and way forward' could be outlined. He said this was necessary to restore public confidence in the FAI. For the first time, the FAI board then agreed that independent directors would be a fundamental requirement on any future FAI board.

The meeting broke up so that the sub-committee could meet Delaney, who by then had arrived at the Carlton, walking silently through the waiting posse of journalists and photographers outside. In the hotel, Delaney was again joined by Frank Martin and his solicitor Aidan Eames. Delaney was told that the FAI delegation of Conway, O'Donoghue and Naughton preferred not to have any lawyers in the room. If Delaney wanted his solicitor present, then the FAI would have to bring in A&L Goodbody. The meeting proceeded without lawyers, but Delaney left the room several times to consult with Eames.

'John was shocked,' says one director. 'This was the endgame. The three choices were: be sacked, go voluntarily on gardening leave, or the FAI put you on gardening leave.'

Delaney was resistant to all three. It was only when the FAI side made to leave that he chose the softest option, a voluntary suspension. Delaney then demanded that he be allowed to write part of the press release that would announce the development. He wanted references made to his achievements, but the FAI directors were firm on this: no way.

Delaney agreed to a suspension on full pay, at his CEO-level salary of €30,000 a month. This was conditional on him co-operating with the Mazars investigation. He had to return his FAI credit card and all electronic devices by the following day. He was barred from attending Abbotstown or from contacting any FAI staff, sponsors, supporters 'or other stakeholders'. The FAI had three different lawyers review its press statement before it was issued just in time for the six o'clock news. It announced that Delaney had stepped aside. The statement also confirmed the departures of Cody and Murray from the board and wished them well.

Delaney had left the Carlton at 4.40 p.m., again staying silent in the face of journalists' questions. Outside the hotel, Bobby Ward, an FAI security official who regularly acted as Delaney's driver, picked up the suspended FAI executive in an FAI car and drove off. Philip Quinn, of the *Irish Daily Mail*, tweeted: 'At his lowest career moment, he availed of the trappings of privilege.'

The board members left the hotel, some doing their best to avoid the gaze of journalists and the lenses of the photographers. As he was driven away, Noel Fitzroy, the FAI's Vice-President, covered his head with a jacket.

*

On 12 April, three days before Delaney went on gardening leave, Richard Howard, a partner with Deloitte, the FAI's auditors for twenty-three years, had submitted an H4 form to the Companies Registration Office. This was a rare occurrence: only four such forms had been filed in the previous eighteen months. Deloitte reported the FAI for an ongoing breach of company law in failing to keep proper books of account – a possible criminal offence. Howard made the report after being notified of Delaney's €100,000 bridging loan, his golden handcuffs deals and the Sports Direct 'sponsorship' of €6.5 million, which now had to be repaid under a provision of the deal that had not been disclosed to Deloitte.

News of the filing of the Deloitte H4 report emerged on the morning of 16 April, as Shane Ross, the Minister for Sport, and Sport Ireland were preparing to answer questions before the Oireachtas Sport Committee. At the hearing, Ross announced that the entire board of the FAI had just informed him that they would step down at the AGM on 27 July. Ross welcomed this as 'the beginning of the end for the old FAI'. John Treacy, the Sport Ireland Chief Executive, told the committee that the FAI had accepted his request to allow Sport Ireland to appoint an external firm to audit the association. He promised this investigation would be 'forensic'.

A day after the committee hearing, Revenue wrote to the FAI informing the association that it had been selected for a tax audit. The letter said the investigation 'may cause a degree of inconvenience for you'.

The FAI was now subject to four separate investigations: from the Office of the Director of Corporate Enforcement (ODCE), its own internal Mazars inquiry, the Sport Ireland audit and now the Revenue audit.

The ODCE would require the FAI to provide tens of thousands of internal records to an investigation team led by seconded garda detectives. It wasn't just paperwork the investigators sought. A warrant issued by the ODCE would lead to the FAI handing over CCTV footage to the corporate watchdog from the 'executive corridor' in Abbotstown.

*

On Sunday, 21 April, the *Sunday Times* published details of the FAI's payments worth €60,000 in the name of Susan Keegan, Delaney's ex-girlfriend.

Paul Rowan had decided to visit for himself the address in Kent that was on FAI records for Keegan. It turned out that the first journalist had mistakenly gone to the wrong address. The correct house belonged to Susan Keegan's sister and brother-in-law. They got in touch with Keegan, who agreed to issue a statement through her sister in which she denied receiving any monies from the FAI or Delaney.

The *Sunday Times* story that weekend reported that it had seen an email that Delaney had sent to his finance department in February 2014, directing payment of €15,000 to Keegan and claiming that Michael Cody and Eddie Murray had approved it. Both former directors told the newspaper that they had no recollection of authorizing any payment to Susan Keegan.

On RTÉ radio that Sunday, Kieran Mulvey complained that, despite putting Sport Ireland's audit of the FAI out to tender, no accountancy firm had put in a bid. 'Isn't that saying something?' Mulvey asked. 'At this stage, most firms don't want to put themselves into this scenario for reputational and other reasons.'

Eventually, an accountancy firm from outside the Republic of Ireland answered Mulvey's call. KOSI Corporation, based in Newry, took on the job of sifting through the FAI's books.

Thirty years on from Ireland's debut in a major football tournament, it was Niall Quinn, the former striker and businessman, who got the old Euro '88 team back together with a golfing event in the K Club.

There were a lot of costs involved in organizing the event in the former Ryder Cup venue, including flying in Jack Charlton and some of his former players. Quinn secured sponsorship from bookies Paddy Power, and from Goodbody Stockbrokers, where an acquaintance of Quinn's, Roy Barrett, was Chief Executive.

The date was set for 24 September 2018. Not only did the majority of the 1988 team attend, along with Charlton and Mick McCarthy, but other players from throughout Charlton's reign as Irish boss, including the 1990 and 1994 World Cups, came to reminisce, play golf and raise money for the family of Liam Miller, the former Irish international who had died of cancer earlier that year at the age of thirty-six.

At the reception after the golf, Gary Owens, the captain of the K Club, made a speech to welcome Charlton and the former Irish internationals. Owens, an insurance executive who had played amateur football into his mid-thirties, had been the favourite to become Chief Executive of the FAI in 2003 before Fran Rooney pipped him at the post. Amongst the guests was John Delaney, although that wasn't the original plan. The scandals of 2019 were still in the future, but relations between Quinn and Delaney were strained.

'At one stage John wasn't even invited,' Owens says. 'Niall didn't want to invite him. I don't know how he did it, but eventually Niall says, "he's coming". The next thing was, "Where are we going to put him?" I think they put him down the back somewhere. He wasn't at the top table. I don't think he was happy.'

At the top table, Quinn was filling in the former Ireland captain Andy Townsend about how shambolic the regime at the FAI had become. Like so many events involving Irish football, there was more going on than was apparent on the surface, in both what would become the old FAI and what emerged as its replacement.

The golf event took place in what turned out to be the last weeks of Martin O'Neill's time as Ireland manager. Owens says he believes that was the night that Delaney offered Mick McCarthy the Ireland job. It was also the night McCarthy took on board the idea of Robbie Keane being his future assistant. Robbie Keane never played for Jack Charlton, but he was Irish footballing royalty, and he was present at the K Club with his wife, Claudine. Keane wanted a role as assistant manager if McCarthy became the next Ireland manager, as was being widely speculated at the time. McCarthy later described how Keane was 'nipping in my ear, asking, "Would you consider me?"'

Meanwhile, Owens, Barrett and Quinn were having a discussion that would lead to them taking over from Delaney at the top table of Irish football.

'We all have a passion for football,' Owens says. 'We're nattering around the table, "Jaysus, it's in a terrible state." That night we started talking. "We're all successful in our own right, how can we get involved and help sort it out?" A few months later, it all started to evolve. The information started to come out. The *Sunday Times* report started all of that. The shit hit the fan.'

*

Although none of the investigations launched into the FAI in April 2019 would conclude rapidly, a review of the FAI's governance and management structures was due on 21 June. The FAI agreed to the governance review by a committee of five, including two FAI appointees and three from Sport Ireland. To feed into this review, Shane Ross decided to host a Football Stakeholders' Forum. Some 200 people from Irish football gathered in the Mansion House on 31 May.

Many believed the event was little more than a publicity stunt by the minister, but it turned into a cathartic event as the voices of several people who had been marginalized in the Delaney era were finally heard. Brendan Menton, the former FAI General Secretary outmanoeuvred by Delaney in 2002, women's international Stephanie

Roche and Stephen McGuinness of the PFAI were amongst the speakers. The FAI was represented by board member Niamh O'Donoghue and acting CEO Rea Walshe, though neither spoke publicly. Paul Cooke, the former Waterford United delegate, was also in attendance. Cooke, a chartered accountant and long-time Delaney opponent, had just joined the FAI's crisis board sub-committee following an invitation from Donal Conway.

Each table of six or seven guests at the Mansion House had a civil servant on hand to record any suggestions for reforms. Soon the historic circular room was abuzz.

From the stage, Quinn spoke about his work with the 'Visionary Group', which included his K-Club friends Barrett and Owens. Quinn had plans to revamp the League of Ireland, and the group had produced a document setting out wider proposals to reform Irish football. The document was highly aspirational, but low on details.

Quinn said the FAI crisis was a 'great opportunity for change'. He drew a round of applause when he stated that the FAI's priority should be ending the 'culture of fear' amongst staff. Quinn said he hoped that the governance review would lead to his group being called in to help. It didn't, at least not immediately.

The review, endorsed by Sport Ireland, was published on 21 June and made seventy-eight recommendations. The most drastic of these was to reconfigure the FAI's board so it would contain four independent directors, one of whom would be chairperson.

The review also proposed that the FAI President, who is elected by delegates from the various FAI constituencies, would be a normal director on the board and would also chair a new Football Management Committee dealing only with football matters. The new CEO would not be on the board, and the membership of the FAI Council would be expanded to seventy-nine, with positions for the PFAI and supporters' groups for the first time.

*

In early June, at the request of the FAI, Noel Mooney of UEFA had replaced Rea Walshe as interim CEO on a six-month secondment. An old speech came back to haunt Mooney. 'The FAI is one of our most progressive and well-run federations,' the man from UEFA had told the FAI AGM in 2017. 'It really is a super federation and you can be proud of yourselves, the board and all the members here.'

Shane Ross viewed Mooney as an 'FAI loyalist' and refused to meet him. Elsewhere, however, there was a significant thaw.

A meeting in April with Stephen McGuinness of the PFAI had been arranged under Delaney's instructions with an agenda to get the PFAI out of Abbotstown. Instead, Walshe told McGuinness she wanted to improve relations with the players' union. Relations with the PFAI further improved under Mooney, who lifted a ban on the players' union participating in a weekly FAI five-a-side. Dozens of dissident Ireland supporters were also unblocked from the FAI's official Twitter account. Mooney sent a letter to Zeno Kelly, welcoming him back to the Aviva.

Mooney also reached out to another arch-opponent of Delaney, Stewart Regan, who had left his job as Chief Executive of the Scottish Football Association in 2018, inviting him to review the FAI's five-year strategic plan. Regan found the mess that Delaney had created 'staggering'. 'There was a complete lack of process, a complete lack of effective governance and no controls in place for managing financial performance or risk.'

At the FAI's AGM in Trim on 27 July, a dozen security guards wearing earpieces – as counted by wary journalists in attendance – was one unwelcome throwback to the Delaney era. The remnants of another – the old FAI board – resigned. Donal Conway, however, was re-elected unopposed as President, with just five votes against and one abstention. Conway had regained some respect by leading the reform process, while also trying to stop the association going offside with UEFA and FIFA. He promised to guide the FAI through its crisis and step down the following summer.

Ross opposed Conway's decision to run again, but a not-so-subtle game was at play. Before the AGM a joint letter by Fatma Samoura, FIFA Secretary General, and Theodore Theodoridis, the General Secretary of UEFA, was sent to the FAI warning that it risked suspension from international football if there was undue government interference in the FAI's internal affairs.

Ross took heed of the warnings but maintained his opposition to the re-election of Conway and John Earley, the head of the schoolboys' association and the only other member of the old FAI board elected to the new one in 2019. Earley, who had resigned from the old board in June in protest at what he saw as the diminution of his constituency's representation under the proposed new structures, pointed out that the governance review endorsed by Sport Ireland had said that up to two of the old FAI board could remain on the new one to help with the transition.

Six new board members were elected. Paul Cooke became FAI Vice-President after defeating Gerry McAnaney, from the Defence Forces, in an election – a procedure now back in vogue. Also elected were Martin Heraghty, from Sligo Rovers, Joe O'Brien, from the colleges, Dave Moran, from the Leinster Senior League, Dick Shakespeare, from UCD, and John Finnegan, from the Munster Senior League.

There were many questions from the floor, but the board had few answers, given that it had no 2018 accounts available and both the Mazars and KOSI investigations were ongoing. The AGM would reconvene later that year when the accounts were ready.

The FAI had apprised UEFA of its emerging financial plight as it sought financial support to keep it solvent. At a meeting in Nyon in Switzerland that May between the FAI and Josef Koller, UEFA's Finance Director, Theodoridis came in to hear about the Irish association's likely debts of €55 million.

Theodoridis told Koller that UEFA, which had regularly given the FAI advance payments from TV deals, had 'been taken for a ride' by the Delaney regime.

*

Grappling with a growing financial crisis involved finally getting Delaney off the books.

The association had been paying him €30,000 a month since he went on gardening leave in April. More than one of the new board wanted him sacked, but the legal advice was that if he was dismissed, a likely High Court challenge by Delaney could mean the FAI would have to continue to pay his salary while a costly and protracted employment-law case was fought through the courts.

Paul Meagher, a solicitor who was best known for his defamation work for his long-time friend Denis O'Brien, was brought in to negotiate on the FAI's behalf with Delaney's solicitor Aidan Eames. Meagher, a keen football fan who specializes in employment law, declared his link with O'Brien. The board briefed him to negotiate a deal whereby Delaney would resign with a pay-off lower than €500,000, and not the €3 million he may have been entitled to under the 2014 'golden handcuffs' deals.

In the offices of RBK Accountants in Clonskeagh, south Dublin, fractious talks between Delaney and the FAI were mediated by Bryan Phelan, an accountant and businessman. Late on the night of Saturday, 28 September, the deal was finally done. The FAI had rejected requests from Delaney for two tickets to future Ireland home games and the continued use of a top-of-the-range Ford car. There was a renewed stand-off over Delaney's demand that a statement announcing his resignation would contain a list of his 'achievements'. Delaney eventually signed off on a curt statement which noted that during his tenure as CEO the FAI had become partners in the new Aviva Stadium and that he had been elected to UEFA's ExCo in 2017.

The total package was worth €462,000 to Delaney. It was a similar value to the package that Delaney had agreed in April but which the old board had refused to ratify. There was a public backlash over the pay-out, but the board insisted that it was the prudent thing to do.

*

KOSI Corporation's report on the FAI's finances, which ran to 103 pages, was delivered to Sport Ireland on 24 November. The directors of the state agency were given less than an hour to read the report before they had to hand back their copies. After taking legal advice, John Treacy decided the report could not be published and instead referred the findings to the Garda. Noel Mooney, as the FAI's interim CEO, described the referral as a 'punch in the stomach' for the association.

The KOSI report – which has yet to be published at the time of writing, but which has been seen by the authors – is a damning indictment of the latter half of the John Delaney era at the FAI.

KOSI noted that in 2018 a UEFA circular, issued to all member associations, had identified ten principles of good corporate governance and management rules. The rules had been approved by UEFA's ExCo, of which Delaney was a member. Associations were encouraged to fully adopt the ten principles.

KOSI found the FAI had clearly not adhered to eight of them.

The first UEFA recommendation was that associations have 'a clear, transparent business strategy' that was reviewable on a regular basis with measurable objectives. KOSI found that, while the FAI experienced sustained cash-flow challenges, the financial information going to the board was limited, and was tainted with 'optimism bias'. Even the limited information that reached the board should have been enough 'to cause concern and unease at a continuing negative state of affairs', but 'rather than challenging and contesting, the board was too passive, taking its lead from the FCEO [former CEO, i.e. Delaney], rather than holding the executive to account for its actions'. The reasons for the lack of challenge within the FAI were a 'concentration of power accompanied by a feeling of reliance and dependency as well as a lack of information, insufficient financial competence, complacency and fear for career prospects'.

UEFA recommended term limits or age limits for its members' boards to avoid excessive power being concentrated in individuals, and advised associations to provide for free elections and proper definitions of roles. KOSI found that, contrary to this recommendation, the 'FCEO was central to all key decisions made by the FAI'. Delaney was the 'key influencer on the board' and was able to 'navigate the machinery of governance of the FAI in a way that negated the checks and balances to his requests and actions'.

An example of this was when he asked the board to delegate responsibility for his personal employment terms to Eddie Murray and Michael Cody in late 2013. KOSI found Delaney relied on those two, without the collective authority of the board, for approval of actions and transactions at different times 'which should not have been given' and which 'should have been communicated to the wider board'.

Instead of prioritizing 'sound ethical values' and good governance, as recommended by UEFA, KOSI found that the FAI's financial governance was undermined at several levels.

'Despite the association's ongoing difficulties there were examples of extravagant expenditure and an absence of financial control,' it said. 'The evidence is of ex-post analysis of expenditure rather than ex-ante control. Finance staff were left chasing the reasons for expenditure after it was incurred rather than being in a position to challenge its basis beforehand.'

The FAI's Finance Committee, which operated as a sub-committee of the FAI's board, did not have formal terms of reference. KOSI concluded that this committee 'relied on interpretations provided by the former Finance Director [Eamon Breen] and the FCEO'.

Finance decisions on current and future matters were not made by the committee. When in 2018 the FAI was in breach of its banking covenants with Bank of Ireland and there was a proposal to draw down future operational funding to meet loan obligations and other urgent current demands, KOSI said there was 'an absence of a record of concerns raised at how this reflected on the future stability of the FAI'.

The FAI's Audit Committee also had no terms of reference. KOSI found the FAI's finance team, consisting of six people with no credit-control personnel, was too small for a business with 200 staff and a €50 million turnover.

KOSI concluded that the FAI did not have an internal audit and compliance function. There was no Remuneration Committee either; salaries across the executive level were set 'on an ad hoc basis' and were 'not balanced with a definition of role, responsibilities and performance expectations'.

Regarding the John Giles Foundation, KOSI found financial statements were prepared for a thirty-six-month period up to the end of 2016, but no accounts were prepared for 2017 or 2018. It noted that the foundation was 'not a registered entity or charity', so there was no requirement to make its accounts public. The foundation was managed by FAI staff.

KOSI analysed the FAI's September 2008 deal with Con Martin Jnr. It noted that the FAI held no signed copy of the contract with Martin. Instead, the FAI had an unsigned contract that showed the FAI agreeing to pay Martin for the use of his 'concepts' of the John Giles Foundation, the Walk of Dreams and the idea of collective purchases of football gear. KOSI found that Martin was paid €543,000 under the contract: €200,000 up front in 2008, €300,000 through sixty-two instalments from March 2011 to May 2016 and a 'settlement payment' of €43,000 on 24 May 2018. The report cast serious doubt on the value of Martin's 'concepts'. It recommended that the foundation become a separate entity from the FAI, with its own banking arrangements. The FAI has told KOSI that it is consulting with the Foundation's trustees about its future and that it intends to publish its accounts.

★

The KOSI report found that Delaney's first contract of employment as Chief Executive was dated 22 November 2005, over seven months after he was given the job.

Less than a year later, on 27 October 2006, Delaney was given a 32 per cent increase in his salary, bringing it from €290,000 to €382,800. His apartment payments were increased by 70 per cent. This contract was signed by Delaney, Cody and David Blood, the FAI President at the time.

Delaney was given another 5 per cent increase in salary in December 2007, and the letter confirming this was signed by Cody. In January 2009, following the outbreak of the global financial crisis, Cody wrote to the FAI's finance department to say that Delaney was not exercising his right to a 3 per cent consumer price index salary increase. In May 2010, Delaney was given a 5.5 per cent increase in salary, bringing his annual pay up to its peak of some €431,000. This agreement was signed by Delaney, Blood and Cody.

KOSI found that in November 2013, Delaney sought and was given board permission to discuss his situation with Cody and Murray. On 1 January 2014, amendments to Delaney's 2006 employment agreement were made. Delaney had already reduced his salary to some €360,000 in 2012, when FAI staff had to take cuts. The 2014 deal kept Delaney's salary at the same level but increased his rental payments by 22 per cent. The rent payments were supposed to cease by the end of 2014 but went on for two more years at up to €39,000 a year.

In lieu of pension contributions by the FAI, it was agreed that if Delaney remained employed by the FAI up to the end of 2020, he would be paid €2 million in instalments up to 2030. Extraordinarily, if Delaney left the job early for any reason, the FAI would have to pay him €23,810 for every month he had worked since 1 January 2014. The deal was signed by Delaney, Cody and Murray. KOSI noted that this liability was not accounted for in the FAI's audited accounts.

A further deal, signed on 31 January 2014, gave Delaney another €1 million for completing a seven-year period of work up to the end of 2020. Like the earlier deal, if Delaney's term was terminated early, either voluntarily or against his will, the FAI would have to pay him €11,900 for every month he had worked after 1 January 2014. The two deals meant Delaney was guaranteed to get an extra €3 million in bonus payments for completing his term of employment.

Contrary to the FAI's own rules, the deals were not declared either to the full board or in the accounts. There was no evidence that the FAI Finance Director in 2014, Tony Dignam, was aware of the terms of the two deals. KOSI pointed out that the FAI 'was on a pay freeze between 2012 and 2016', when Cody and Murray agreed the deals.

On the FAI's procurement practices, KOSI found that in 2015, in response to queries from Sport Ireland, Eamon Breen claimed that the FAI continuously reviewed the market and requested tenders where appropriate for high-spend areas such as travel, accommodation and catering. KOSI said it found no evidence to support this claim and that no procurement protocols were identified in the FAI until 20 March 2018.

The FAI had no procurement policy, no rules for tendering and no contract-register, and it was unable to demonstrate value for money in large-expenditure deals. There was a Risk Committee, but it did not meet in either 2018 or 2019.

KOSI found that €260,000 had been paid by the FAI between 2015 and 2018 for a public relations agency that was coded 'Professional fees – CEO department' in the FAI's accounts. KOSI said no contract was held by the FAI for this relationship, though 'a contract is believed to exist'.

The PR company, not named by KOSI, was Keith Bishop Associates PR, a UK business run by one of Mike Ashley's closest advisers. Bishop, to whom Delaney turned for help during the 2015 controversy over his singing of a republican ballad, had been a regular contact for Delaney in his dealings with Ashley down the years.

*

KOSI's analysis of Delaney's 2020 deadline for making the FAI debt free is devastating.

The FAI's books show that in 2010 the association had a €50 million loan from Danske bank and a €6 million overdraft. Despite payments of €34.8 million by the FAI over the next ten years and a €12.5 million write-off of debt, the FAI still owed some €29 million on the stadium debt, which is now held by Bank of Ireland.

Between 2010 and 2019 the FAI paid €24.4 million in interest and penalties to the institutions that owned the debt. Just under €9.5 million was paid in capital repayments.

In December 2013, the Danske loan and overdraft were bought by KKR in a deal that involved a €12.5 million write-off of the FAI's debt. KKR received a €1.115 million arrangement fee, and charged 6.2 per cent interest to the FAI, which worked out at €7,296 a day. The FAI immediately began to accrue penalty interest with KKR in 2014 which amounted to €3.67 million by the time the FAI managed to transfer the loan to Bank of Ireland in 2016. Delaney's 'vision' of being debt free by 2020, KOSI found, 'did not reconcile with the debt agreements which included at times interest-only loan repayments, excessive penalty and debt restructuring costs and high interest rate agreements'.

*

Regarding Delaney's one-time girlfriend Susan Keegan, KOSI established that there were five payments, totalling €95,000, made by the FAI in the name of Keegan from Christmas Eve 2012 to 6 February 2014.

The 2012 payment was a €10,000 cheque made out to Keegan, with a signature on the back that was 'purportedly' Keegan's. A €25,000 bank transfer on 22 January 2013, which referenced Keegan in the FAI's accounts, went to John Delaney's bank account. KOSI found an email showing that the instruction to pay came from Delaney.

The FAI had retained an invoice from November 2012 for the €35,000 worth of 'services' provided by Keegan. The document's metadata showed that a copy of Microsoft Office registered to JDelaney@FAI.ie was used to create the invoice document.

The three other transactions in Keegan's name on the FAI system were a €10,000 bank transfer made to an Ulster Bank account in Swords in August 2013, a €35,000 bank transfer made in January 2014 to an EBS account, and a €15,000 payment in February 2014 that went to Delaney's bank account. KOSI noted that current FAI management 'have not been able to advise on the purpose of the payments'.

The investigation looked at the FAI's involvement with defamation actions taken on Delaney's behalf in 2016 after the Rio ticketing scandal resulted in coverage of the Brazilian police's attempts to interview Delaney. A total of €416,822 in invoices was billed to the FAI from the legal actions taken by Delaney. The FAI paid €339,462 of these bills.

KOSI found that Delaney received five settlements from the legal actions, with the smallest being €7,500 and the largest €120,000. The auditors found no evidence that any part of the €267,500 total settlements that were advanced to Delaney were returned to the FAI to offset the bills it incurred supporting the legal complaints. It also said no request by the FAI to Delaney for repayment of all or part of the €267,500 payments was identified.

KOSI also found that three 'personal legal expenses' had been paid by the FAI on Delaney's behalf outside of the Rio cases, to a combined value of €200,000.

The auditors also revealed the bizarre case of Delaney's own Vantage Club purchase. On 15 July 2009, Delaney signed a contract with the FAI to buy ten Vantage tickets at a price of €12,000 each. The €120,000 cost was to be paid in monthly instalments of €1,000 for ten years.

Two years later, Michael Cody signed off on an agreement allowing Delaney to cancel eight of his Vantage tickets with immediate effect while two of them were to continue for a further year.

Delaney already owed €19,200 on the eight tickets when Cody gave an instruction to the FAI finance department that a credit be raised in Delaney's favour for €16,800 on 19 July 2011 on the basis that the refund 'represents fair value to the association given the number of matches played since the inception of John's payments two years ago'. Cody's instruction reduced the price of Delaney's eight tickets from €19,200 to €2,400 – so the cost to him was €150 a year per ticket instead of the retail price of €1,200 a year.

The FAI paid €164,000 to airports and travel companies, costs that appeared to be for the personal benefit of Delaney, between 2015 and 2018.

In relation to Delaney's fiftieth birthday party at Mount Juliet, KOSI found that the FAI had made payments totalling €69,198.04. (Mazars would later locate additional party-related costs, and its draft report would put the FAI's overall spend in excess of €80,000.) An invoice of €26,293 from Mount Juliet, that was paid by the FAI, had been addressed to Emma English. The invoice on the FAI file contained a hand-written note from Eamon Breen advising that the payment was to be 'offset against CEO account, chq [cheque] provided by CEO to reimburse'.

KOSI also conducted a review of Delaney's expenditure on his FAI credit card. It discovered he had spent €499,127 on the card from 2015 up to April 2019. It flagged a significant number of 'transactions of concern', including 279 cash withdrawals and the purchase of flights for Emma English. There was spending on jewellers, hotels and limousines on overseas trips. Purchases in shops, bars, restaurants and online shopping sites were also of 'concern'. The value of personal expenditure on the card between 2015 and 2018 was calculated by the FAI to be €125,057, with €49,639 withdrawn in cash up to early 2019. Despite a new FAI credit-card policy, effective August 2018, that prohibited cash withdrawals, KOSI noted that €5,528 in cash was withdrawn on Delaney's card after that point. All Delaney's cash withdrawals were presumed by the FAI to be 'non-business related'.

The FAI's liberal credit-card culture was not limited to Delaney. There were sixty-eight different cards in use by the organization's staff between 2015 and 2018. Out of the FAI's average total €48 million expenditure in each of those years, an average of just over €2 million of it went through the credit cards. Two cards had spending of between €200,000 and €299,999 for three of those years and in 2015 one card had spending of between €300,000 and €399,999.

KOSI reviewed Eamon Breen's card for March 2018, a month when Ireland played a friendly in Turkey. It found there were five spa treatments at a hotel resort charged on the Finance Director's card for Delaney at a cost of €1,003.24. There was a supporting receipt on file. On this same trip, 1,000 Turkish lira (€209.92) was withdrawn in cash from Breen's card.

*

KOSI analysed the FAI's cash positions through the four years from 2015 to 2018. The analysis showed the association was repeatedly on the brink of insolvency during that period. To assist it through one of these moments in 2015, when it had a €3 million overdraft facility in place, the FAI 'borrowed' €115,000 from its dedicated Education Training Board accounts, which are to be used exclusively for joint projects with local authorities. On another occasion that year, the FAI took a €50,000 loan from the Leinster Football Association and repaid it three months later.

In 2016, for April and almost all of May, the FAI did not have enough funds in its accounts to pay all cheques it had issued. In June, its overdraft facility was halved, to €1.5 million.

From February through to June of 2017, KOSI found, the FAI again did not have enough cash to honour all its issued cheques. In the week in April 2017 that Delaney made his bridging loan, the FAI had available funds of €169,000 through its overdraft but had issued cheques totalling €593,000; a deficit of €424,000.

KOSI said the analysis 'paints a picture of the FAI's precarious and at times perilous financial position from 2015 to 2018'. There was a practice of drawing down on funds from future years to meet 'immediate cash requirements'.

The KOSI investigation shed new light on the bridging loan. On top of the €100,000 cheque, Delaney made out two smaller cheques of €5,000 each to the FAI that month. KOSI also found that, in 2017 and 2018, Delaney made a total of seventeen lodgements amounting to €228,000 into the FAI. One €50,000 payment covered some of Delaney's fiftieth birthday party costs, and another €50,000 payment in June 2018 was believed to be Delaney donating a portion of his €160,000 UEFA ExCo payment to the association. A third €50,000 payment in December 2018 was described as Delaney 'investing in the FAI', according to a signed Delaney letter dated 11 December that year.

It was, presumably, these payments that Delaney had in mind when he told the FAI board on 26 March 2019 that he was 'broadly €100,000 in credit with contributions to the FAI'. KOSI found that, according to the evidence it had seen, 'this was not the case'.

It undertook an analysis of the various ways in which the FAI 'absorbed' Delaney's personal expenditures – on his fiftieth birthday party, credit-card use, on legal expenses, and on rent and travel, amongst other things – and found that the FAI's total personal expenditure on Delaney was €952,495.76.

Even after subtracting the €227,866.34 that Delaney had paid into the FAI, Delaney came out ahead to the tune of €724,629.42. This figure did not include various other things, such as the money he had received in settlements arising from FAI-funded legal actions, the discount granted on his Vantage Club tickets, the payments to the name of Susan Keegan, the value of personal phone costs covered by the FAI or the tax charges related to Delaney's personal expenditure, also covered by the FAI.

The one positive for the FAI was that KOSI found no public monies had been misspent. However, given the litany of systems failures, KOSI recommended that no public funding should be given to the association until it brought in a series of new control measures, including that no payments greater than €50,000 could be authorized without board approval.

18. The Accounting

On 6 December 2019 the FAI finally released its 2018 annual accounts and restated accounts covering 2017 and 2016. As foretold by Paul Cooke, who took on the 'executive lead' position when Mooney returned to UEFA in November, the results were shocking.

Relations had sharply cooled between the auditors Deloitte and the FAI leadership. Despite the FAI's accounts being due for completion in July, it was only in August that Deloitte agreed to carry out its field work in Abbotstown. Unhappy at the delay, the association asked Deloitte to consider resigning as auditors over fears the FAI could be struck off by the Companies Registration Office for failing to file books of account on time.

On 1 August Deloitte wrote to the new board and said it considered the request to resign as 'inappropriate'. It said it declined to step down, given what had emerged about the FAI's finances after it paused the audit in late March. In response, on 9 August Rea Walshe wrote that she understood that Deloitte had been asked to resign because it had not progressed the audit nor even told the FAI when it would start. Following a meeting with the new board in August, Deloitte agreed to complete an audit for 2018 and restate the financial results for 2016 and 2017.

In a presentation to the board, Richard Howard, the long-time Deloitte partner in charge of the FAI audit, wrote that it had determined that it was 'not possible to rely on internal controls within the association due to the pervasive risk of management override of controls'.

On the morning of the presentation to the media on 6 December, there was a final row over the wording used by Deloitte in the accounts. The signed-off accounts had to be scrapped and reprinted that Friday morning. Frantic discussions took place in the FAI boardroom between the directors and Howard while journalists milled around the reception area swapping the latest rumours with staff. As the FAI's board walked into the press conference, thirty minutes late, the ink was still wet on the printed accounts they carried with them.

'It's a very dark day,' said Cooke, who could have been excused a hint of smugness, given that he had raised a red flag about the FAI's finances back in 2009.

The FAI's net liabilities up to the end of 2018 were €55 million. This included almost €30 million of the Bank of Ireland Aviva Stadium debt. Because the FAI was in breach of its banking covenants, the bank could call in the loan at any time, hence the mortgage had to be booked as a current liability. Deloitte had refused to sign off on the FAI as a going concern because of the spiralling debt and a concern that the FAI had not disclosed all the necessary financial records during its audit.

The 2016 results had been restated from a €2.344 million profit to a revised surplus of €66,000. For 2017, instead of the reported profit of €2.75 million, the FAI accounts now showed a loss of €2.85 million.

'The 2018 figures don't get much better, with a loss of €9 million,' said Cooke, speaking from a podium to the room of shocked journalists.

The 2018 losses included €2.14 million booked on Delaney's previously unknown €3 million golden handcuffs deals – which was being detailed in the FAI's accounts for the first time. There was €1.67 million related to the Sports Direct 'sponsorship' that had been booked as income but now had to be written off. All the professional fees to cover investigations into the FAI's finances brought a bill of €3.6 million.

The FAI had made Revenue a settlement offer of €2.71 million to cover unpaid taxes, including the non-payment of benefit-in-kind tax on personal expenses incurred by Delaney. All told, the FAI underpaid taxes on €6.8 million worth of expenditure over the last four years of Delaney's time as Chief Executive.

Asked about Delaney's legacy at the FAI at the press conference, Cooke said: 'The figures today speak for themselves.'

In the lead-up to the publication of the accounts, the FAI had been hit by a double blow. First, John Foley, a former Chief Executive of Athletics Ireland and Waterford Crystal, pulled out of becoming the new interim Chief Executive the night before he was due to meet staff, forcing Cooke to step into the breach. Foley walked away after he was effectively vetoed by Shane Ross, who had learned of his occasional involvement with the FAI under Delaney.

Ross had instituted an unofficial boycott of the FAI and asked that no ministers accept the traditional offers of match-day tickets and hospitality from the association for home games. He hoped that this gesture, along with the refusal to restore state funding, would pressure the association into bringing in the four promised independent directors. There were angry words exchanged between Ross and Michael Ring, the Minister for Rural and Community Development, when Ross learned that Ring had ignored the 'cold shoulder' policy and had brought Pat Breen, a junior minister, with him to a match.

A further blow for the FAI came in the unexpected announcement that Three, the Ireland team's sponsors, would end its commercial relationship with the association. The announcement was made two days before the FAI's accounts were published.

The publication of the FAI's accounts meant the FAI could reconvene its 2019 AGM, and a date of 29 December was set. The FAI was in serious danger of going bust before then, however. Cash-flow forecasts prepared by Grant Thornton cast doubt on the FAI's ability to meet a payroll run of €625,000 for a large sub-set of its 200 staff in the week before Christmas. The wage bill would help put it in a negative cash position of €1.96 million with only a €1.5 million bank overdraft available.

Ross, angered at the FAI's failure to appoint any independent directors since its July AGM, refused to meet the new board. However, after a furious round of direct and indirect lobbying of TDs and government ministers, he agreed to meet the new directors, minus Donal Conway. The FAI President stayed in Buswells hotel as his fellow board members walked across to meet Ross in Leinster House. John Earley, the director representing schoolboys, had already resigned after a stormy question-and-answer session between the board and staff over the new accounts, admitting that he 'naively believed and was reassured' that the FAI's professional staff had ensured the asso-ciation's finances were run in an orderly manner. Earley insisted he was not trying to absolve himself of blame. 'As a board member for the last four years, I take ownership of my part in the collective responsibility for what has transpired,' he said. Uniquely even for the FAI, Earley had now resigned from the board twice in six months.

The FAI representatives outlined to Ross and his officials the cata-clysmic fate facing the association. It was shortly going to become insolvent. The Grant Thornton forecast showed the FAI running up possible losses of €16.3 million by the end of 2020.

The business plan presented by the FAI showed the association returning to profitability in 2023, if it could receive short-term fund-ing of €18 million and make a series of job cuts. The plan envisioned the FAI reducing its €10.4 million annual payroll bill down to €8.1 million in 2021 by reducing its net headcount by twenty-one.

The FAI had negotiated a six-year, €54 million TV deal with UEFA running from 2022 to 2028. Its plan was that it would use €6.5 million of this each year for running costs. The remaining €2.5 million a year would go straight to Bank of Ireland to repay a new €18 million loan it needed immediately for its survival. Both the bank and UEFA required the state to act as a guarantor for the FAI on the new loan.

Ross and the civil servants were adamant that the state would not ride to the rescue. The minister told the waiting press outside Leinster House that there would be no state bailout of the FAI 'in any circumstance'.

When Ross divulged at an Oireachtas Sport Committee hearing the following day that the FAI was seeking €18 million and that the futures of the Aviva Stadium, Irish international matches and the League of Ireland were all at risk due to the FAI's possible insolvency, it prompted a furious statement from the association. It complained that the minister's breach of confidence had made it harder for it to secure funding.

The FAI wrote directly to the Taoiseach, complaining that Ross had breached the confidentiality of the meeting by divulging com-mercially sensitive information. It claimed this had put the FAI's negotiations to obtain a refinancing package in jeopardy and that Ross's 'derogatory comments' had stymied its reform efforts. The letter warned that if the FAI went into liquidation 'the consequences for football and indeed for the country cannot be underestimated'.

The letter asked Leo Varadkar to meet the FAI board. Instead, the Taoiseach talked to Ross, who agreed to meet the FAI again. This time there was no public grandstanding from the sports minister. The FAI's bankers felt there was now enough prospect of state support for it to assist the FAI in meeting its Christmas payroll run.

The most tumultuous year in the FAI's history ended with it tee-tering on the brink of insolvency. Fifteen years after he had first taken Deloitte to task, Brendan Dillon rose to his feet at the reconvened AGM in Citywest hotel on 29 December to again challenge the audi-tors. There was a strong feeling of anger amongst delegates over Deloitte's failure to answer questions about its work, for which it had been paid €500,000 over the previous two years. This was not lessened when the company announced it was quitting the role it had held for twenty-three years. Prior to the AGM, Fergus O'Dowd, the chair-man of the Oireachtas Sport Committee, asked for Deloitte's work on the FAI to be investigated by the accountancy regulatory bodies.

Richard Howard, reading from a script at the AGM, had earlier insisted that Deloitte had been 'misled' by the FAI. When Dillon demanded to know if Howard and Deloitte had tested samples of the FAI's credit-card expenditure to see if there was spending on per-sonal items, Howard declined to comment. As Dillon cross-examined Howard on Deloitte's years of signing off on the FAI's books without any red flags, Howard looked like he would welcome a hole opening up under his chair.

There was frustration, despair, but also an air of self-reflection amongst the FAI's delegates.

Speaking outside the meeting, John McCarthy, from University College Cork, said his club had to compete for players against both rugby and GAA. 'It was bad when they were laughing at us, but it's worse now because they're saying they actually feel sorry for us,' he said.

Denis Bradley, a representative from Derry City, told the meeting that when he had asked a question at a council meeting under Delaney everyone had looked at him like he was 'Oliver [Twist] looking for food'. Bradley, a former priest, suggested that the FAI apologize to the Irish public for the mess it found itself in.

Conway, whose presence on the FAI board was increasingly seen as an obstacle to getting government support, had already agreed to bring forward his departure from the summer to the end of January. Speaking at the release of the FAI's accounts three weeks earlier, he had said he didn't believe that public apologies served any purpose. However, following Bradley's suggestion, he agreed: the FAI would publicly say 'sorry'.

That evening, the FAI board issued a short statement of apology addressed to the hundreds of thousands of people involved in football, the Irish public and its staff for 'the mistakes of the past'. The apology was welcomed by Shane Ross, who also said in a statement that evening that the government would not countenance the FAI going bust. At last, the FAI had a backstop of assurance from the state. With a general election coming in early 2020, no government TD wanted to be going to the polls against the background of the FAI being put into liquidation.

For Ross, the key to unlocking government support was the FAI appointing independent directors. This issue had dragged on for months with no clear explanation as to why a process run by executive search consultants Amrop had not delivered the four directors. FAI sources suggested prospective candidates feared being held liable for reckless trading if no bailout was on hand.

With the prospect of government financial support on the horizon, Roy Barrett – the Goodbody Stockbrokers' Chief Executive and Visionary Group member – emerged as the FAI's new chairman on 8 January 2020. Two other independent directors, Catherine Guy, a solicitor and businesswoman, and Liz Joyce, Director of HR at the Central Bank, joined Barrett on the FAI board. A fourth prospective director was said to need time before he could take up the last position.

Soon after Barrett came in, he recruited Gary Owens to be the new FAI interim Chief Executive, taking over from Cooke, who remained in his role as a director and FAI Vice-President. Owens, in turn, brought Niall Quinn into the position of interim Deputy CEO. The three men who had sat around a table in the K Club talking about the woes of Irish football at the Euro '88 reunion just over a year previously were now running the FAI.

The day after Barrett was appointed, Shane Ross had a private meeting with Packie Bonner, John Byrne and Brendan Menton, three senior ex-FAI employees who had all fallen foul of Delaney a decade or more previously. The three persuaded Ross that he was now in a position of power, with the FAI desperate for a state bailout. He had to use this opportunity to force change in the FAI's internal structures.

The meeting came as it emerged that John Earley and Denis Cruise, a Delaney loyalist, were amongst a number of 'old-FAI' members seeking positions on the FAI's internal committees as they remained on the FAI Council. Ross recalls, 'They really stiffened our resolve: "This is your one chance. Get the council. Reform the council. Do it."'

Asked about his previous warm words about Delaney, Ross says he wasn't aware of the 'other side' of the FAI Chief Executive until the stories about the FAI's finances broke. He points out that he did bring in term limits for board members in the face of strong objections from the FAI. 'Delaney was basically telling us to "bugger off",' says Ross. 'And there wasn't an enormous amount we could have done because we were only giving them €2.5 million to €2.9 million. And they were kind of getting there by 2021, but maybe we should have been a bit more pushy. But we had raised it and we were told to "lay off" as we were "interfering", and that had other connotations. It is easy to say "you should have seen it", but as far as I'm aware nobody did. Nobody saw the appalling vista that we now have.' Ross says it was only after the first *Sunday Times* article on the €100,000 payment in March 2019 that people like Brian Kerr, Brendan Menton and others made contact with him to offer advice on dealing with the FAI.

The deal to save the FAI from insolvency involved a troika of the Irish government, UEFA and Bank of Ireland. UEFA was highly suspicious of Ross when its high-powered delegation came to Dublin on 14 January. The UEFA group was led by Theodore Theodoridis, its General Secretary, who had previously warned Ross that Ireland risked being banned from international football if he interfered.

'Once they saw that we were serious and we were prepared to move, I've never seen such relief on people's faces,' says Ross. 'The UEFA guys were expecting confrontation as we had been confrontational before. There was a bit of an advantage in people thinking we were a bit mad. They thought they had a real maverick here that was prepared to go a bit mad. So, when they sat down there was a bit of apprehension. The body language wasn't good . . . I made a very conciliatory presentation saying we were prepared to do a fair amount, but it's conditional on you guys and the banks helping.' Once UEFA knew the government was willing to put money on the table, they were 'all smiles'.

A deal was forged that involved UEFA agreeing to act as guarantor on a new €24 million Bank of Ireland loan, increased from the €18 million sought in December partly due to an FAI commitment not to make low- or middle-income staff redundant for at least eighteen months. The bank would agree to extend the remaining €28.5 million mortgage on the Aviva Stadium from a 2021 final payment out to 2040. The FAI would now owe Bank of Ireland €52.5 million. The bank agreed to return as a sponsor of the FAI as part of the deal.

The state's rescue package involved paying the FAI an extra €19.2 million in funding over four years. This included €7.6 million in interest-free loans to cover the FAI's Aviva Stadium running costs for three years. The annual Sport Ireland grant was doubled to €5.8 million for four years.

In return, Roy Barrett signed a memorandum of understanding that obliged the FAI to carry out extensive reforms and to subject itself to close oversight by the Department of Sport and by Sport Ireland. The FAI would have to change its internal rules so that six of its twelve board members would be independent directors, with the independent chairperson getting the casting vote in a deadlock, while at least 40 per cent of the board, council and committees would be female from the end of 2023. Barrett agreed to 'retire' all members of the FAI Council who had served over ten years. Former board members would be barred from sub-committees.

There were many in Irish football who welcomed Barrett, Owens and Quinn coming into the FAI with no obvious agendas or allegiances. But there were also many who said it was bad corporate governance for three friends from the same group to be effectively handed the reins of the FAI. Neither of the interim positions taken by Owens and Quinn was advertised.

Ross, however, rejects these criticisms. 'At some stage in this you have to trust somebody,' he says. 'You have to say "look, go and do the job" and don't interfere. Don't get into the nitty-gritty and say "you can do it but you can't employ him". We took an early decision that we trusted Barrett completely. It was such a relief to have somebody there that just had the interests of football [at heart] and there was no reward or pay. OK, he was obviously very interested in bringing along Quinn, who is trusted by the public, by us and by Barrett. That is so important. It's important that he is trusted by the public more than anyone else. Quinn's got a huge responsibility here. He's that figurehead. He's that guy.'

Ross argues that 'it would have been absolute madness [to reject] someone of that calibre and whose good faith you couldn't begin to question – and he is prepared to do it. There's a lot of people who wouldn't touch the FAI with a barge pole and they'd just walk away from it. So, no, I don't have a problem there but that's because there is a lot of trust now in there. In a year we've come a long way, thanks to the stories that came out.'

While Quinn effectively became the FAI's public face and the point-man on football matters, Owens was charged with getting under the FAI's bonnet to sort out its finances. When he arrived, he found that the FAI's financial reporting system was a mess.

'Procurement was a big black hole,' says Owens. 'If you take the big things – travel, security, food. They are all things where I'd say, typically, we didn't know what was going on. What was happening in the FAI was that people were responsible for doing things, but they weren't responsible for managing costs or managing budgets. So therefore, there was never any accountability for the numbers or financial expenditure.'

In the absence of clarity on how much various cost centres were making or losing, Owens doesn't know how the previous FAI regime could possibly have made informed decisions. 'You can't make sensible decisions until you know how each of these cost centres are performing,' he says.

Owens's three immediate priorities upon getting into Abbotstown were implementing 'simple accounting practices', having 'a proper procurement policy' and introducing a 'fair and open ticketing policy'. 'I keep saying to the guys, let's become brilliant at the basics,' he says. 'Getting that financial information gives you accountability and transparency. It gives you all the data that you need to be able to run the organization the way you want so you can share information with people.'

Owens says he cannot understand how basic management accounts and controls were not in place in a high-profile organization with a turnover in excess of €40 million. 'I would challenge the [previous] board, I would challenge the auditors, all the key stakeholders: "How did you miss this?" Nobody could actually understand the management accounts. If you're on the board and responsible for actually governing what was going on, how can you ever sign something that you couldn't understand?

'I'm used to having audit and risk committees, I'm used to having oversights. I'm used to having very good financial templates, Key Performance Indicators on how we performed. They need to be very transparent because if we don't do that you'd be fired. As a CEO, you'd be fired. I came from a business world that had all of these things and they were just basic and I came into a world without them. I just went "wow".'

After fixing the FAI internal financial management processes, which Owens says is 'a relatively simple task', his focus will shift to the League of Ireland. 'Where the League of Ireland has ended up, it's embarrassing,' he says. 'It's our national league where we have our professional players. But as an association we have to take responsibility for driving that improvement.'

Owens believes Delaney was too focused on maintaining his power with the grassroots and growing his influence in UEFA to bring Irish football onto the next level. 'John actually worked up [to UEFA] to the benefit of himself,' he says. 'What we need to do is work up to UEFA for the benefit of everybody. There's loads of intelligence and expertise over there we can really use. When I sit down to talk to the team, I say, "OK, in your part of the business, how do you deal with UEFA?" They don't. He was the only connection.'

In amateur football, Owens believes standards need to be improved, and that means consolidating leagues and clubs. 'I think John liked having loads of clubs and loads of leagues. He never wanted a big consolidation that would potentially undermine his power base.'

Owens, a former chairman of the Athletics Ireland board, believes that Delaney learned this strategy from his former mentor Pat Hickey in the old Olympic Council of Ireland. 'They thought the same, they acted the same,' he says. 'John took him as a role model. Never get them strong. Keep them weak. If people are divided, then no one will ever be able to work out what you're up to.'

Asked about one of Delaney's last deals, giving Mick McCarthy a 'termination fee' of €1.13 million, Owens smiles. 'I'd say he got John on a good day,' he says.

★

In late March 2020, when the Covid-19 pandemic caused the shutdown of football, Owens announced pay deferrals for FAI staff. Staff earning over €25,000 had wages deferred on a sliding scale of up to 50 per cent for the highest earners until 'the national economic situation improves'. When UEFA announced that each of its fifty-five associations would receive an advance of €4.3 million in grants to help ride out the lockdown, it became apparent that this was of no benefit to the FAI, as it had already drawn down that money.

The postponement of the Euro 2020 tournament for a year led to questions over the future of Mick McCarthy, who was to step down after the tournament, and of Stephen Kenny, who was to replace him. Would the FAI have to allow McCarthy to stay on for another year until the tournament was played? When it became clear that Ireland's playoff qualifier would be delayed past 1 August, the start date of Kenny's contract, Owens and the FAI moved decisively. In early April 2020 Kenny was installed as Ireland manager and McCarthy was removed earlier than envisioned. It was another Delaney legacy that came with a hefty cost in the form of McCarthy's contractual exit payment of €1.13 million, but at least it was one headache the FAI was able to resolve reasonably quickly.

Robbie Keane's contract proved more troublesome. His conversation with McCarthy at Niall Quinn's K-Club soirée had borne fruit. With McCarthy happy to have him on board, Keane was given a four-year contract, rising to €250,000 a year, as an Ireland assistant coach, even though McCarthy would be in the job less than two years.

It was another crazy Delaney deal that would have its day of reckoning, and that day duly arrived when Kenny took over from McCarthy and announced that his assistant coaches would be Keith Andrews and Damien Duff. Kenny didn't want Keane, and his contract clearly stated that he could choose his own backroom staff. Ireland's leading goal-scorer and all-time caps holder had been spectacularly snubbed, and he couldn't turn to Delaney. Nor was he going to just walk away. Instead Keane verbally lashed his old friend and teammate Quinn over the telephone and put the matter in the hands of his agent, Ciarán Medlar. Settling the standoff, which was still ongoing at the time of writing, is likely to prove costly for the FAI.

On 12 June 2020, 447 days after Delaney stepped aside from the position in Gibraltar, the FAI finally advertised for his replacement as permanent Chief Executive. The job advert, which was placed by the executive recruitment firm Odgers Berndtson, stated that the FAI was seeking someone who was 'analytical, numerate, a disciplined thinker, a steadfast and resilient individual with a high level of personal integrity'.

The ad appeared at a time when there were grumblings from some within the football community about the leadership of the K-Club trio as they tried to plot the game's return from its Covid-enforced hiatus. Owens, for his part, had expressed interest in the position. Whoever is hired as Delaney's permanent replacement will have to grapple with all the internal politics that come with the job, even while trying to steer Irish football off the rocks.

*

Shortly before this book went to press, the authors saw parts of the draft Mazars report, which contained some intriguing new findings as well as adding fresh detail to what was already known about the FAI's finances and spending.

One transaction that Mazars looked at was a €100,000 payment made by the FAI on 7 February 2019 to Paddy Goodwin, a solicitor who worked for the association and for Delaney. The bank details supplied by Goodwin referenced a 'client account'. Mazars could find no invoice related to this payment. The FAI finance official who processed the payment told the investigators that it was 'not unusual' to receive an instruction from Delaney or Eamon Breen to make a payment without an invoice having first been received. Breen told Mazars that Delaney instructed him to authorize the payment. When Breen asked Delaney about the purpose of the payment, Delaney said it was related to a family law case.

Mazars concluded that the €100,000 payment to the Paddy Goodwin client account in February 2019 did not relate to FAI business. Delaney refused to be interviewed by Mazars, so could not be asked to clarify what the payment was about.

In its draft report, Mazars calculated that the FAI made a total of €300,000 in rental payments for its CEO from 2005 to 2016. Only about half of that amount was properly declared for tax, according to the report. Mazars found evidence of a 'series of errors' by FAI finance staff which 'indicate relatively poor knowledge of the operation of payroll taxes by the association'.

In 2016 Breen emailed Delaney to say that a 'random selection of expenses/payments' queried by Deloitte's audit included a €39,000 FAI payment on Delaney's rented house in Kilmacanogue. Delaney responded by saying, 'why are they even raising such a small matter . . . ?'

In relation to Delaney's fiftieth birthday party, Mazars put the total FAI spend in the neighbourhood of €82,000 – a higher figure than that calculated by KOSI, because it included Delaney's accommodation costs, €1,117 in cash withdrawals and food on Delaney's credit card, €7,595 on chauffeurs and a cash payment of between

€4,000 and €5,000 to the High Kings. Taking account of Delaney's €50,000 payment to the FAI, the net cost to the association was around €32,000. The draft report noted that there was no record of board approval for any FAI expenditure on the event. It also stated that the 'absence of evidence of any formal arrangement or communication by the former chief executive to obtain formal approval from the board to use association funds and suppliers for a birthday party was highly unusual when considering good corporate governance and [was] potentially inconsistent with [his] duties as a director'.

In relation to the €100,000 bridging loan, the draft Mazars report pointed out that, although Delaney had claimed at the Oireachtas committee hearing that he had been 'surprised' to learn how close the FAI was to breaching its overdraft when he attended a meeting with the FAI finance team in April 2017, records showed he was regularly informed of the FAI's precarious financial position in the preceding weeks. Karen Campion, the FAI's Financial Controller, emailed Delaney and Breen on 21 March, saying that 'we are under pressure from suppliers and managing as best we can with credit card payments'. That week the FAI had to pay a 'final demand' of €246,000 from Revenue and make a €560,000 payment on the stadium loan. Another €400,000 in cheques had been issued for payments to Irish internationals but had yet to be cashed. FAI cheques, Campion warned on 22 March, were in danger of 'bouncing' if there was any delay to expected incoming payments.

The investigators found that Eamon Breen did not investigate the disclosure requirements for the €100,000 transaction or seek advice from Deloitte on the matter until March 2019, when the *Sunday Times* reported on the payment.

Breen told Mazars: 'It was confusing to me at the time because it was now fully paid. There was no balance left at year end. I wasn't fully, hundred per cent aware of company law requirements, accounting requirements, so I said I'll come back to [Delaney] on it. I never went back to him.' Asked why he didn't, Breen said: 'To be honest, I forget [sic] about it at the time . . . it should have come up.'

Regarding both Delaney's and Breen's roles as senior executives in the FAI, Mazars said their failure to disclose the payment prior to March 2019 was 'highly unusual, in particular, when considering their day-to-day executive level roles and responsibilities and, we understand, their capacity as professionally qualified accountants'.

★

As the FAI looks to install a permanent new leadership team to grapple with the legacies of Delaney's time in charge, it is worth asking a question Delaney himself often posed: how did he do over the full ninety minutes of his time as Chief Executive?

The financial crisis that the FAI was plunged into in 2019 was undoubtedly the result of woeful mismanagement of the business side of the association. Delaney's greed and obsession with control and secrecy ultimately caught up with him.

On the football side, the figures are nearly as stark. In the 2004/2005 season, when Delaney became Chief Executive of the FAI, the Irish domestic league was ranked thirty-eighth out of fifty-one leagues across Europe in the UEFA coefficient table based on results. Fifteen years on, in the 2019/2020 season, the League of Ireland was forty-second out of fifty-five national leagues across Europe.

When Delaney took over the job of interim Chief Executive of the FAI in November 2004 Ireland were fourteenth in the FIFA world rankings, close to an all-time high. In October 2019, the month after Delaney resigned, Ireland had slipped to thirty-sixth. The FAI had thrown big money at four Ireland managers during Delaney's time as CEO – much of it provided by Denis O'Brien – when a huge emphasis was put on qualification for major tournaments. Had Ireland qualified for a World Cup during that period, the approach could have been deemed a success, but a haul of two European Championship qualifications in that fourteen-year period was a modest return.

John Giles's assessment is that 'Delaney started well' but that 'like a lot of dictators, he got carried away in the end'.

Patrick Nelson, the Chief Executive of the Irish Football Association, which runs football in Northern Ireland, came to the same conclusion as KOSI about Delaney's dominance of the FAI. 'I just got the feeling that everything had to be run through John,' says Nelson. 'It was almost like even if you wanted a toilet break you needed a ticket from John to do that. There was never a feeling that the cadre below him were sufficiently exposed to anything in terms of thinking, seniority and politics. Little did we know that there was probably a reason he kept everything to himself.'

Amongst Delaney's former directors, there is an acceptance that they allowed Delaney to become too powerful. He not only kept a close grasp on the FAI's finances and decision-making levers but also hogged ceremonial duties to ensure he could tend to the grassroots support that the FAI structure is built on.

Donal Conway, the FAI President from 2018 until January 2020, says, 'We have to put our hands up, as we allowed John to become the FAI, almost. And we allowed a CEO to become so powerful. That's not the way a good federation should work. That's not the way a good board should work. I'm wiser about it all now than I was at the time.'

Kieran Mulvey, the chairman of Sport Ireland, says that whatever good Delaney achieved in his fifteen years at the top of Irish football is now 'lost' because of the financial mess left behind. 'We are relying on an international organization to fund our national game, apart from what has just been put in by the Irish government and renewed by the Bank of Ireland,' he says. 'That legacy will be there for another five or ten years.'

Brendan Dillon, a long-time critic of Delaney's leadership, says, 'Apart from the shock, I have a huge overwhelming sense of sadness and despair. I coached my young fella, so see all the teams and coaches who do all that stuff like line the pitch and put up the nets. All these decent people turning up on a Thursday night and selling tickets for this draw and that draw and giving up their time, and every single one of these people has been betrayed by these people. It is just the complete lack of any sense of care or obligation to the wider interests of football. They just had this agenda to keep John Delaney in power at any cost, and unfortunately the cost looks like it is now between €60 million and €65 million. How can any organization pay that back? It's just bonkers, so depressing.'

What will hurt Delaney as much as anything else is that he has become the punchline for jokes on financial incompetence. This was displayed in stark terms during the televised Irish general election debate between the leaders of the three biggest parties on 4 February 2020. In what many political commentators said was his best line of the night, Taoiseach Leo Varadkar said bringing Fianna Fáil back into power after that party presided over Ireland's economic collapse up to 2011 would be like bringing John Delaney back in to run the FAI in nine years' time.

Fianna Fáil supporters were quick to remind Varadkar that as Minister for Transport, Tourism and Sport for three years from March 2011 to July 2014, Delaney's power grew substantially under his watch. He was at best ambivalent when the issue of FAI's governance and financial issues flared up during that period. When it comes to the prominent politicians who turned a blind eye to what was going on, he was towards the front of a lengthy queue.

*

After his resignation from the FAI in September 2019, Delaney would go on to secure work in London, returning to Ireland on weekends. Sources close to him said he was relieved to get the settlement, while maintaining he had done nothing wrong. He also established a presence on social media. His LinkedIn account described Delaney as 'a highly commercial CEO with a powerful track record at the highest level'. Delaney's stint on the UEFA ExCo, where he had been effectively suspended from April 2019, ended with his resignation in January 2020, just before the government bailout of the FAI was agreed.

John Delaney did not respond to invitations to be interviewed for this book.

A number of the people who have agreed to be interviewed for this book, both on and off the record, have given formal statements to the gardaí involved in the ODCE's ongoing investigation. In February 2020 Delaney was joined as a notice party to a High Court application that the ODCE made seeking a ruling on whether documents it had seized during a search of Abbotstown were legally privileged. The judge hearing the case suggested Delaney needed to be represented, as the documents may raise private issues for him. Delaney had earlier made a complaint to the Data Protection Commissioner about the FAI after it failed to respond in the prescribed time to a request he made for copies of files containing his personal data going back fifteen years.

At the time of writing, the Mazars report on the FAI's finances had just been referred to the gardaí and the ODCE by the association's board.

Susan Keegan, Delaney's ex-girlfriend, agreed to be interviewed by Mazars' chief investigator, Justin Moran. Keegan, who now manages a gym in the Murcia region of Spain, told Mazars that she had never worked for the FAI in any capacity. Keegan said that she accepted some money from Delaney when they were in a relationship, which she had used to buy dresses for her daughter's wedding and to purchase a car, but was unaware of most of the payments said to have been made to her. Keegan has admitted to being 'embarrassed' and 'ashamed' that she was in a relationship with Delaney. Keegan's former husband, Gary Keegan, a sports consultant who was largely credited with transforming another crisis-hit Irish sport, boxing, has been touted by some in the media as a future CEO of the FAI.

Delaney and Michael Cody refused to be interviewed by Mazars, even though the former Chief Executive had gone on voluntary gardening leave with full pay on the condition that he co-operate with the investigators. Cody's solicitor, Cahir O'Higgins, said Mazars was overlapping with the work of the ODCE, and he sought to protect his elderly client from over-exertion.

In April 2020, Delaney reimbursed the *Sunday Times*'s legal costs from his failed High Court injunction case. The bill of €20,265 was paid after the newspaper had initiated proceedings with the Office of the Legal Costs Adjudicator.

*

Sitting at home watching the horse racing from Wolverhampton on his TV, a seventy-nine-year-old Joe Delaney took a phone call from

Paul Rowan in January 2020. He said he was happy to be quoted, voicing his contempt for 'yellow-press' journalism. 'You are scumbags, that's all you are,' he said. 'Here's a quote if you like: Power without responsibility. Scumbags. OK?'

Of his son, he said: 'John is employed and earning plenty of money. Everything is grand.'

Authors' Note

This book is based on interviews with more than 120 people, including many current and former FAI staff, directors, council members, players and supporters. Quotes that are attributed using present-tense verbs like 'recalls' or 'says' are comments made directly to us. Quotes attributed to John Delaney and other directors at FAI board meetings are sourced from FAI board minutes that we obtained and, in some cases, the recollections of directors or staff who attended those meetings.

Some sources spoke to us on condition of anonymity, whether wishing to protect their privacy or because they did not want their comments to have a bearing on the ongoing investigation by the Office of the Director of Corporate Enforcement. Many former FAI staff were conscious that they had signed non-disclosure agreements in their exit deals, but some decided to speak out despite signing such agreements. Any quotes from emails, reports, affidavits or other documents are verbatim and based on documents seen by us or reported contemporaneously in the media.

We thank all the sources that came forward or took our calls, some taking personal risks to assist, and the many journalists from other publications or broadcasters who offered support and advice.

We thank all our colleagues in the *Sunday Times* for their support, especially Frank Fitzgibbon, John Burns, Colin Coyle, Nick Greenslade, Michael Foley and Les Snowdon. Solicitor Hugh Hannigan's expert legal advice was key in ensuring the newspaper was able to bring a number of FAI stories to light in 2019.

We thank Michael McLoughlin and Brendan Barrington in Penguin, thought-provoking and stimulating editors.

Mark thanks his wife Cara and his children for all of their love and patience, and the lucky blue hoodie. Thanks also to his parents Mary and Liam, and his brothers Stephen and Simon, for their support. A special thank-you to Philomena Greene for all the emergency babysitting.

Paul acknowledges the work of his predecessors in the *Sunday Times*, Dave Hannigan and John O'Brien, plus the support of Paul Hyland and others on the football beat, working in what were sometimes difficult circumstances. The ongoing support in lockdown of Kathleen Rowan is also greatly appreciated.

Index

JD indicates John Delaney.